T0367955

# Against the Tide

LESTER FISHER

authorHOUSE

*AuthorHouse™*
*1663 Liberty Drive*
*Bloomington, IN 47403*
*www.authorhouse.com*
*Phone: 833-262-8899*

*Published by AuthorHouse 11/10/2021*

*ISBN: 978-1-6655-4360-6 (sc)*
*ISBN: 978-1-6655-4359-0 (hc)*
*ISBN: 978-1-6655-4358-3 (e)*

*Library of Congress Control Number: 2021922827*

# Contents

# Dedication

I dedicate this memoir to my grandfather, Meritt Ambrose Seeley and my Stepfather James George Klungness.

# Preface

As I wrote this memoir, I had to reveal some painful episodes in my life; hence, the pristine Mt. St. Helens on the front cover and its exploded crater on the back. Beginning with Happenstance, the first book in the trilogy, I covered my life from childhood to my tour in the Peace Corps. This book describes the troubled times trying to establish my education and career, while bringing a Kenyan family to the United States. There were joys, and there were sorrows, successes and failures, and the inexorable influences of fate, happenstance, and the consequences thereof.

My return from Kenya was a government decision, not mine. I had wished to extend my tour in Kenya, but the draft and Richard Nixon sealed my fate. What I did thereafter were my own decisions, some foolish, some wise. Since Kenya, agriculture, both farming and research, have been important elements of my career. . I began my Master's Degree program at the University of California Davis. I managed a berry farm, and an apiary, and succeeded in buying a 4 acre homestead, while doing forestry research for Weyerhaeuser Company. This book ends when I return to Davis to finish my degree in International Agricultural Development.

During those seven years so much happened! I brought the family from Kenya. My own son was born! I climbed the research corporate ladder, and then quit. I failed at contracting my skill as a microscopist. Nevertheless, the family survived those seven years with no government assistance. I can acknowledge that we had assistance from many friends and relatives, for which we were all grateful.

Unfortunately, there were chinks in the armor, and for all my efforts to steel us from dissolution, the end of this bold experiment came. Was it fate, or finances, or failure to communicate?

"Again I saw that under the sun the race is not to the swift, nor the battle to the strong, nor bread to the wise, nor riches to the intelligent, nor favor to those with knowledge, but time and chance happen to them all." Ecclesiastes 9:11 English Standard Version

# Acknowledgements

Again I want to thank my dear wife, Gretchen, who has been so patient and supportive through this whole process, and Jana Huffhines (1915-2000), her mother, for documenting our life together. I thank my daughter, Colleen Malia, for not saying: "Are you crazy, Dad?" They have both assisted me with editing and moral support. I also would like to acknowledge Rev. Christian Mondor OFM (1925-2018) for the inspiration he provided to so people many for so many years.

# Chapter 1

# The Fates Conspire?

So they shall fear the name of the LORD from the west,
and his glory from the rising of the sun; for he will come
like a rushing stream, which the wind of the LORD drives.
**English Standard Version (2001) Isaiah 59:19**

Where we left off, I had just arrived in Chicago's O'Hara Airport, after my
tour of duty in Kenya with the Peace Corps, and my visit to University of Guelf
to visit Dr. Gordon Townsend, Chairman of the Bee Biology Department
at the Univ. of Guelf, Canada. I was surprised to hear "Amazing Grace"
being played over the Musak as I walked down the causeway. As I said in the
conclusion of the 1st volume of my memoir, it gave me a glimmer of hope that
the country was on the right track. However, hopes do have a way of being
dashed. Personally, I believed that I would be returning to Kenya, and to my
adopted family of nearly two years. The purpose of the detour to Canada
was to talk about the CIDA[1] Kenya Honeybee Development Project. I was
making arrangements to assist their project while working for the Peace Corps
at the Mtwapa Tropical Tree Crop Nursery which was in the process of being
established by the Ministry of Agriculture.

---

[1] **CIDA** (Canadian International Development Agency) was formed in 1968 by the Canadian
government. CIDA administers foreign aid programs in developing countries, and operates
in partnership with other Canadian organizations in the public and private sectors as well
as other international organizations. It reports to the Parliament of Canada through the
minister for International Cooperation. Its mandate is to "support sustainable development in
developing countries in order to reduce poverty and contribute to a more secure, equitable, and
prosperous world." http://en.wikipedia.org/wiki/Canadian_International_Development_Agency

One wee little glitch, I had received my "invitation" to take my induction physical for the military. The youngsters among you will not remember the time when any able-bodied young American could be called up for canon-fodder at any time. We were under the lottery selection system but having been deferred by my first two years of Peace Corps service, I was now eligible for immediate enlistment.

Still, hope springs eternal in the human heart, and I was sure the good Lord would make it possible for me to return to my work and "my family" in Kenya. I had purchased my *Handbook for the Conscientious Objector*, but I was not too sure I was going to be able to mount a defense in the event of my being drafted. After all, I had been trained in a seminary of the Catholic Church, a religion that has long supported the "moral foundation of war".

Of more immediate concern, and the reason I came to the US to take the physical, was that my mother was having further health issues, which involved her heart. Instead of opting to take my physical in Italy (as the military offered), I chose the alternative to take the induction physical in Oakland, California. I decided to take my home leave (also an option for extending Peace Corps volunteers at that time) and visit her in California. The least a dutiful son could do. My first stop-over in the US would be Seattle, where all my Christian friends from the Honeycomb Fellowship and the Catholic Charismatic movement were located. Then I would visit my Father and his new wife in Longview down in Southwest Washington, and then on to California, where my mother lived in the Central Valley town of Galt. She had lived with the parish priest under the guise of housekeeper ever since my father and mother separated.

The Honeycomb fellowship had given me a big send-off when I left for Peace Corps, and true to form, several of the group came to welcome me home. I cannot remember who was present, but I think I spent the nights at either Tom Griffith's or Roy Gillette's house or both. I think Emily and her new husband came to see me. I had brought back carved wooden figures from Kenya and gave several of them to people from the Fellowship. I had intended to sell some, so I left them on consignment at the Christian bookstore on University Ave. in the University of Washington district. I don't remember if they were ever sold. The bookstore was owned by a man named Clyde; I can't remember the name of his family or his wife. I do remember going to visit him after they sold the bookstore and moved to Lynden, Washington. They had first tried to homestead in British Columbia, but the mosquitos drove them out the first summer. The farm they acquired in Lynden was a pleasant commune with a big old barn and a Clydesdale draft horse (it might have been a Percheron, but it seemed more appropriate that Clyde would own a Clydesdale). I don't remember who went with me to visit them in Lynden, but I remember being impressed with the communal life they had established. Later I heard that this venture also did not work out for them. Even Christian communes are made up of people.

It was interesting to see the culture of the Christians after the eye opening experience of Kenya. I realized that a large part of the culture of a religious community is just that, culture. The religious component is almost like trimming on an otherwise ancient bond of friendship and mutual support that probably pre-dates all organized religions. People of like mind and like interests come together under the banner of a common belief. In some ways, it really doesn't matter what the belief is, as long as they hold it in common. The problem is that holding that common set of beliefs and interests is a hard thing for human nature.

Even the Honeycomb Fellowship was showing signs of splintering. Tom Griffith, a counselor at Chief Sealth High School, was one of the original Fellowship founders with his wife Jean. But Tom was intent on following his calling to the missions. He eventually did take his wife and 5 children to Europe. His oldest daughter went to school in Italy, and there may have been other arrangements for others in the family. But some of the Griffith clan ended up in Iran... or was it Lebanon. This was before the overthrow of the Shah of Iran, which eventually drove Tom and clan out of Iran (or Lebanon). You never know where a mission will take you, but traditionally it tends not to be towards tranquility.

I think, at this point in time (1971) the Griffiths were still in Seattle and hosting the fellowship at their large old University neighborhood house. I believe I slept on their floor that night, my first day back in the good old USA. Jean was such a sweet and generous person; she was the glue that held the immediate and extended family together. There were always people like me dropping in for dinner or a place on the floor. Roy and Ruth Gillette were also founding members of the Fellowship. Roy had been very kind to rent his basement to me when I was in transition to the Peace Corps. In addition, he agreed to hold my possessions, including my bass, until I returned from my Africa tour. He enjoyed playing the bass for the Fellowship. I was not ready to take my possessions at that point in time, because I had no car and was traveling by public transportation. Roy said I could leave everything with him.

Martha Patton was no longer with the Honeycomb when I returned from

Africa. Like me, she had been swept away by the charismatic movement, and had eventually ended up in a Christian commune associated with an African American church in the Central District of Seattle. I went to visit her there, and I met the man that she eventually married. I do not know what happened to them after that, and I was not able to attend their wedding. I was a bit suspicious of the pastor of the Black church; he was expensively dressed and drove a high-end automobile, while the members of the commune looked like they had to ration their finances carefully. They were obviously living a lot closer to the gospel example than the pastor who guided them!

By then, Emily Du, who had originally brought me to the Honeycomb Fellowship, had, or was about to marry another member of the Fellowship, John Mattson. She was working at the University of Washington Hospital in an immunology research lab, where I visited her the day after I arrived. She had obviously become a crackerjack immunology technician but was not happy with the pay scale. So she was intending to or had already started taking classes (I can't remember which). She was intent on getting a degree in computer programming, which is what John did for a living. Eventually they both were programmers for the same Seattle Bank, and to the best of my knowledge became quite financially secure. Given the financial upheavals of the late 2000s[2], I hope they are still doing well. I have tried to find them on the internet, but without success. It would not be the last time I would see

---

[2] The largest bankruptcy in history was of the US investment bank Lehman Brothers Holdings Inc., which listed $639 billion in assets as of its Chapter 11 filing in 2008. 5

| Company | Filing date | Total Assets pre-filing | Total assets pre-filing at today's value | Filing court district |
|---|---|---|---|---|
| Lehman Brothers Holdings Inc. | 2008-09-15 | $639,063,000,800 | $646 billion | NY-S |
| Washington Mutual | 2008-09-26 | $327,913,000,000 | $332 billion | DE |
| General Motors Corporation | 2009-06-01 | $82,300,000,000 | $83.5 billion | NY-S |
| CIT Group | 2009-11-01 | $71,019,200,000 | $72.1 billion | NY-S |
| Chrysler LLC | 2009-04-30 | $39,300,000,000 | $39.9 billion | NY-S |

http://en.wikipedia.org/wiki/Chapter_11,_Title_11,_United_States_Code#Largest_bankruptcies

Emily and John, but the circumstances would be entirely different the next time we met.

Having made contact and reacquainted myself with the Fellowship, I proceeded to Southwest Washington and a stay with my dad and his new wife, Elizabeth. They must have picked me up at the train station in Kelso. I remember it was a dark and dreary Washington winter's night. The welcoming was cordial, and I was immediately impressed with the intensity of Dad's new wife. She was very engaging and had obviously done her homework regarding me. There were a number of personal possessions and writings that I had left with my dad, and she had taken the time to read them. She was an Internal Revenue Agent, but she was the daughter of a newspaper editor, and an aspiring writer herself. She has since published several books. Dad really didn't have many questions to ask, because Elizabeth held the conversation the whole trip home. She asked a lot of questions and listened intently to my answers. Most often I have found people to be only marginally interested in my "adventures" in Africa, but Elizabeth was all ears. I assume that Dad was interested too, but conversation was not an easy thing between us. I think he was glad that Elizabeth had assumed the responsibility.

It was sweet to arrive back on the Toutle River and be greeted by Tippy. I think my mother had taken the little girl, offspring of my favorite dog Sox (deceased), when she moved to Galt, CA. However, the roar of the trains and the strange circumstances had made the normally timid dog become borderline terrified most of the time. My mother realized that her decision to spend her life with the priest was not the best decision for Tippy, so she gave her back to my Dad. Nor did my mother have another pet, until after Fr. Carl died of cancer. Fr. Carl had once had a beautiful German Shepherd, but when that dog was killed, I think the priest could not feel right about having another dog (like my grandfather and his only dog, Buck). After the priest died of cancer, when my mother was living by herself, she went overboard with dogs, cats, horses and hummingbirds.

Elizabeth liked animals, and she, my Dad and Tippy seemed well adjusted on the Toutle River with the gentle roar of the winter flood waters, and the howling of the wind through the trees. Tippy was the spitting image of her sire but was only one quarter the size of him. She was so named because of the white tip on her tail. Otherwise she had a multicolored coat with white leggings and long soft fur with a large bushy tail. Her mother was Fox Terrier, but Sox was a Boxer/Australian Shepherd mix. Perhaps part of the reason Tippy was so timid was that we had been forced to put Sox down because of a buck-inflicted injury that refused to heal. Up to that time, Tippy always had her sire to protect her; after he died, she would run under furniture at the sign of strangers and stayed close to Elizabeth or my Dad's lap. The stay in Galt had made her even more skittery.

I don't know if Tippy actually recognize me after two years, but it was not long before she was in my lap. I missed the affection of a good dog, because in Kenya dogs are treated like riff raff. Kenyans keep dogs to eat trash and scare away critters, but they don't show affection to them. Consequently the dogs are unkempt and usually sporting swollen ticks all over their bodies. We acquired a puppy for the kids when I was in Kenya, but it died eating table scraps. It tried to swallow a floret of broccoli, but the dog had nearly expired when the kids finally called me to try to save it. So for the duration of my stay in Kenya, we did not have pets. We had many rabbits and chickens, but they were all destined for slaughter; you don't want to get too attached to the animals you intend to eat or sell. So it was nice to be back with a cute little lap dog that would lick your face and sleep on your bed.

My Dad had always had a pet since our first dog, Boy, adopted us, and he kept Tippy until she died of old age. Elizabeth and Dad also had cats, I believe, but in later years they did not have pets. When my Dad was getting kind of senile and expressed the need for a pet. Elizabeth bought him an electromechanical pet called a Furby[3]. It was actually unnerving to me to see my Dad interact with the robotic fluff ball. It was so unlike the masterful way he had trained Sox to fetch the newspaper and Tippy to perform her repertoire of tricks.

Waking in the morning on the enclosed porch with a flannel lined

---

[3] A **Furby** (plural Furbys or Furbies) was a popular electronic robotic toy resembling a hamster/owl-like creature which went through a period of being a "must-have" toy following its launch in the holiday season of 1998, with continual sales until 2000. Furbies sold 1.8 million units in 1998, 14 million units in 1999, and altogether in its three years of original production, Furbies sold over 40 million units. Its speaking capabilities were translated into 24 languages.

Furbies were the first successful attempt to produce and sell a domestically-aimed robot. A newly purchased Furby starts out speaking entirely Furbish, the unique language that all Furbies use, but are programmed to speak less Furbish as they gradually start using English. English is learned automatically, and no matter what culture they are nurtured in, they learn English. In 2005, new Furbies were released, with voice-recognition and more complex facial movements, and many other changes and improvements. The Emoto-Tronic Furbies (Furby, Furby Baby, and Funky Furby) continued to be sold until late 2007, when these toys became extremely rare. http://en.wikipedia.org/wiki/Furby

sleeping bag to keep me warm, I just laid there for a long while soaking in the clean, damp, winter air and listening to the low rumbling sounds of the swollen Toutle River which was less than 100 feet away across the road. Soon the smell of breakfast wafted in from the little kitchen with the birds-eye pine cupboards. Elizabeth was not one to skimp on breakfast, and she has prepared some good vittles.

I think it might have been that very next day that Elizabeth insisted on taking me to Portland to buy a whole new wardrobe. I didn't understand why. My boots, purchased when I started work at the pulp mill when I was 18, were now held together with leather hand-sewn patches (they do that in Kenya). My Logan, also several years old, was tattered and torn in several places (very monkish in appearance with its hood and rope ties). Elizabeth was determined to remove the emblems of my adventure from off my very back. The intention was so sincere that I could not refuse.

I think Dad had to work that day, because Elizabeth and I went to Portland without him. I don't remember where we went, but it was some kind of clothing warehouse. I think we were able to get pants, shirts, boots, and a coat, all at the same store. We debated about the boots, but she eventually insisted that I take sturdy high-top logging boots. They were of good quality and lasted a long time. However, they were not a good choice for me. I have a foot problem in that I walk over the edge of my right shoe, maybe a little on the left too. Eventually the boots, which had a fairly tall heel, were run over so badly that I should have stopped using them. Of course, being frugal, I kept using those boots for years. I wore them though beekeeping, doing tree inventories in the Cascades, farming in Tenino, and all points in between. The old Penny's brand $25 boots would have been a better replacement for the boots that got me through Kenya, but one does not want to look a gift horse in the mouth[4].

Boots are important to a young man. They sort of define who you are and what you can do. A good fitting pair of boot will let you go farther, do more and show your stamina. More importantly, the boots you wear in your heavy-work years may save you from problems in your later years. I have never been

---

[4] **Look a gift horse in the mouth:** to criticize or refuse to take something that has been offered to you. Example: "I know the car's not in great condition, but you shouldn't look a gift horse in the mouth."

Usage notes: usually follows never or not, as in the example.

Etymology: based on the idea that you can discover a lot about a horse's condition by looking at its teeth http://idioms.thefreedictionary.com/look+a+gift+horse+in+the+mouth

very coordinated and having a pair of tall-heeled boots which were wearing unevenly, added to my ungainliness. Sometime my ankle would give way and twist my foot over on its side. That was always painful. To this day, my shoes wear out on the inside and my heels turn out. To a young man, these issues are hardly considered worthy of concern. I am glad my son learned early in his fire-fighting career, that good boots are essential for survival. It probably saved his life on at least one occasion; he was almost trapped by a fire that jumped the controlled burn zone. The fire got his all-terrain vehicle, but his all-terrain boots got him out! He later told me that the rubber foot peddle had melted to his boot, but his protective gear had saved him from burns. He did, however, have to run 40 yards without breathing to keep from inhaling the lung-searing hot air.

I can't remember exactly how long I stayed with my Dad and Elizabeth, but I assume it was not too long. I know I did visit Gretchen at the law office of Walstead Mertsching, where she had worked since her return from San Francisco. She was surprised to see me but pleased. She was already engaged to marry a man with whom she had attended Lower Columbia College in Longview, WA. I explained to her my situation with Charity and the family in Kenya. Had I stayed in Longview longer, I probably would have visited Gretchen's parents, but both Gretchen and I think that I did not visit them. Sadly, I left a potted flowering plant for Jana when Gretchen's father died of Parkinson's and cancer. I meant to visit her but she was not home. I did call her later, and she appreciated the condolences. In fact, she told Gretchen I would have made a good priest because I had a sincere manner. Unfortunately, I did not actually see her again until Gretchen and I were considering marriage years later. Most assuredly my loss; she was a good woman, who had been kind to me over the years.

I was, of course, all wrapped up in my life and what I was going to do. I still had to get to California, to take my induction physical in Oakland CA. I think I must have taken the bus to Galt, because I remember being picked up by Fr. Carl and my mother in the center of town. Of course I was lugging my 90 lb. duffle bag with various and sundry artifacts from Kenya, and my personal possession, which were few. My mother was, of course, most enthusiastic to see me. Fr. Carl was circumspect, but welcomed me, nevertheless. The parish house had a guest room for visiting priests, and I was offered temporary lodging in Galt while deciding what my next turn in life would be.

It felt a bit awkward to be back in a Catholic Parish, with my mother parading me around to all of her friends in the parish. There were a couple of very lovely daughters of the Portuguese dairy farmers, and I suspect my mother had intentions of "lining me up" with a good Catholic girl, so I would forget all this foolishness about my African family. This, in spite of the fact that she had already become quite vicariously involved with my little Taita tribe, sending gift etc. and waiting longingly for the next installments of my tape recordings from Africa. Still, I guess she had to try, because it certainly did not seem the sensible thing for me to commit my youth to a family of seven.

I think the date of the induction physical came soon after I arrived. I may have taken the bus to Oakland for the medical exam. I was one of several hundred. We were lined up and told to strip down to our shorts, and then the examining physician proceeded down the line. He was doing a cursory examination of eyes, ears, nose, and throat so to speak, and then he would put his hand up the groin of each inductee to check for herniation. This was probably the first step in the examination, because I don't remember taking any other tests. As we were being dismissed from that exam, the physician called me and told me to wait in a room down the hall. This was peculiar because no one else was so instructed. In fact, I sat in that room for a number of minutes. During this time I was able to read the list of Un-American Activities which were grounds for being disqualified for military service. Organizations like the Communist Party were on the list, but also a number of other organizations that I would have considered benign at best, inconsequential at worst. It made me realize how much our country, and especially our military, were still reactionary and paranoid, thanks to the efforts of Joe McCarthy.[5] It made me wonder what I had done; why was I

---

[5] **McCarthyism**

U.S. anti-Communist propaganda of the 1950s, specifically addressing the entertainment industry

McCarthyism is the practice of making accusations of subversion or treason without proper regard for evidence. The term refers to U.S. Senator Joseph McCarthy and has its origins in the period in the United States known as the Second Red Scare, lasting from the late 1940s through the 1950s and characterized by heightened political repression as well as an alleged campaign spreading fear of Communist influence on American institutions and of espionage by Soviet agents.

What would become known as the McCarthy era began before McCarthy's term in 1953. Following the First Red Scare, President Truman signed in 1947 an executive order to screen federal employees for association with organizations deemed "Totalitarian, Fascist, Communist or subversive" or advocating "to alter the form of Government of the United

selected out? Was I involved with any organization on the list of un-American Activities?

Finally the Physician came back to the room and invited me into his office. He asked me to remove my pants again and proceeded with a more thorough examination of my genitals. These days I would have been suspicious, but then the whole process was so commonplace that I was not even surprised. I was still concerned about what the devil was going on? Then the physician said "Sorry, we can't take ya." I was stunned at first. What was wrong with me? Why, was I unfit? Funny things run through the mind of a young man that is trying to figure out how to get out of the draft, only to be told that he wouldn't be eligible. "You have a pre-hernia condition, and I can't approve you for basic training." The physician said. Sometimes it is hard to imagine how fateful a decision like that can be. I might not be writing this now if that doctor had been a little less thorough. To this day it boggles my mind that I was the only one picked out of the line that day. How many of those young men that passed the physical that day are alive to tell the story? At times I have thought of it as karmic or divine intervention. At other times I think what a

---

States by unconstitutional means." In 1949 a high level State Department official was convicted of perjury in a case of espionage and the Soviet Union tested an atomic bomb, while the Korea War started the next year, raising tensions in the United States. In a speech in May 1951, McCarthy presented a list of members of the Communist Party working in the State Department, which attracted the press' attention, and the term appeared for the first time in a political cartoon by Herblock in the Washington Post that same year. The term has taken on a broader meaning, describing the excesses of similar efforts. The term is also now used more generally to describe reckless, unsubstantiated accusations, as well as demagogic attacks on the character or patriotism of political adversaries.

During the McCarthy era, hundreds of Americans were accused of being communists or communist sympathizers and became the subject of aggressive investigations and questioning before government or private industry panels, committees and agencies. The primary targets of such suspicions were government employees, those in the entertainment industry, educators and labor union activists. Suspicions were often given credence despite inconclusive or questionable evidence, and the level of threat posed by a person's real or supposed leftist associations or beliefs was sometimes exaggerated. Many people suffered loss of employment or destruction of their careers; some even suffered imprisonment. Most of these punishments came about through trial verdicts later overturned, laws that were later declared unconstitutional, dismissals for reasons later declared illegal or actionable, or extra-legal procedures that would come into general disrepute.

The most notable examples of McCarthyism include the investigations made by Senator McCarthy himself, and the hearings conducted by the House Un-American Activities Committee (HUAC). https://en.wikipedia.org/wiki/McCarthyism

fluke it was. I have never had trouble with that "hernia" and the next thing I did was take a job lifting 100 lb. beehives.

For a moment, I need to step back. Very soon after I arrived in Galt, my Aunt Mary and Uncle Vernon visited us in Galt. I was impressed that they would do that, since their son, Ralph, was still in Vietnam. He expected to have home leave sometime in the near future, but I was grateful that my aunt and uncle thought enough of me to make the trip up to visit. They also invited me to visit them in Hayward, and I told them I would do so when I went down to take my induction physical.

So when I walked out of the Induction Center in Oakland as a free man, I called my uncle to pick me up. There are several ironic details about that fateful day about which I must comment. First, it is so ironic that one of the largest induction centers on the west coast of the United States is in one of the largest population of African American on the same coast. Second, I had just returned from an all-black community in a post-colonial African country, and I would be allowed to remain, whereas so many blacks were being shipped off to Vietnam to fight a senseless war for a post-colonial country in Southeast Asia. I guess the biggest irony is that I didn't even want to be in this country, and as fate would have it, I never left.

Mary and Vern were very hospitable, but both were working so we did most of our getting reacquainted in the evening. Ralph was not back yet, but I can't remember if Cousin Vern was living in the area at the time with his first wife and daughter. I don't remember seeing much of him. However, their cousin on their father's brother, Eldon's side of the family, was visiting Mary and Vernon. I remember taking her in Uncle Vernon's 1959 Chevy pickup to the Zellerbach Hall for a concert or a dance performance. He would probably not be happy to know that I was driving on a suspended license; but I didn't know it then myself. Karen probably had not been to a concert like that; I really could not tell if she enjoyed it. I do remember that Vernon was very concerned because we were late getting home. I don't think he was worried about the two of us, but more about my driving. I had not driven in the big city since before Kenya. Nevertheless we made it back in good condition. I think that was the last time I ever saw Ralph's cousin Karen. Vern sends me pictures of her family periodically, so I know she is happily married in Ashland, OR.

The other humorous event of that visit, from my standpoint, was when I asked my uncle to drop me at a movie theater to see "The Pawnbroker." I had read reviews of the movie which gave glowing praise to Rod Steiger for his

11

performance.[6] The humor in the request was where the movie was playing; it was at the Castro Theater in the middle of the Castro District. Of course I was totally unaware that this was the heart of the gay community, but my uncle certainly knew. He queried me, "Are you sure you want to go THERE?", but he did not explain why he was concerned. So he took me there, but he dropped me at the street corner, and didn't wait around. To this day I have to laugh about how naïve I was, but I just watched the superb movie and then called my uncle, and he came to pick me up. I don't think he even asked me anything about the movie. My mother told stories about my uncle when he was young, but I am not going to repeat any of them, because there is no way of knowing if any of them are true. Even if they were, telling the stories would be to what purpose now? Vernon was married to Mary until he died at age 80. He had two sons and a parcel of grandchildren. After the Navy, he worked hard all of his life as a steelworker and later as an ironwork inspector. If he was a victim of anything, it was the tobacco industry since emphysema plagued him in his later years.

When I returned to Galt, I was stoked about the prospect of returning to Africa, and I wrote a letter to the PC Director in Nairobi as soon as I returned. But in the meantime I would have to find something to do with myself. I was loaned an electric bass and asked to help out with the Folk music Mass on Sunday, but aside from a Thursday night practice and 11 o'clock Mass on Sunday, which was not much to keep me busy. I don't even remember if they let me mow the lawn. Of course, my mother and I had long conversations about the family, and what I was going to do with my life. Fr. Carl must have thought we were totally nuts, because sometimes we would talk until three AM. She had to get up and cook breakfast for father after the 7 AM Mass.

I decided I needed to find out more about beekeeping, so I visited Ward Stanger, the Extension Apiculturist, at Univ. of California Davis. He

---

[6] **The Pawnbroker** is a 1965 drama film, starring Rod Steiger, Geraldine Fitzgerald, Brock Peters and Jaime Sánchez and directed by Sidney Lumet. It was adapted by Morton S. Fine and David Friedkin from the novel of the same name by Ed Lewis Wallant.

The film was the first American movie to deal with the Holocaust from the viewpoint of a survivor. It earned international acclaim for Steiger, launching his career as an A-list actor, and was among the first American movies to feature nudity during the Production Code and was the first film featuring bare breasts to receive Production Code approval.

In 2008, The Pawnbroker was selected for preservation in the United States National Film Registry by the Library of Congress as being "culturally, historically, or aesthetically significant". http://en.wikipedia.org/wiki/The_Pawnbroker_(film)

arranged for me to attend a couple of beekeepers meetings. The hot topic at the time was the Africanized bee that was working its way up the South American continent. Several of the scientists were heavily involved with the US Department of Agriculture's attempt to determine how that sub-species could be stopped from entering the United States. I remember Professor Norman Gary was a particularly vocal part of the investigative team. At one of these meeting he addressed the Beekeepers' meeting by saying that he did not believe that the African honeybee would be that difficult to manage. Ward mentioned that I had just come from Africa, and the beekeepers were interested to hear what I thought of the pure African honeybees. I said that they were very aggressive, even in their native state.

I did not mention that I myself had been attacked by a recently caught swarm, and they fanned out into the neighborhood around the Wundanyi Farmers Training Center and killed a goat and stung members of a family within fifty yards. I only escaped because another Peace Corps volunteer drove up as I came under attack for the second time. I was walking back along the road around the training center and the bees picked up my scent again (buggers don't forget!). He backed the truck up to me, and I dove into the back as we drove off. Later we came back to assess the damages. We ended up taking an elderly man and two children to the Wesu hospital for bee sting treatments. I believe I paid the man for the dead goat.

Norm Gary was disdainful of my report, and the beekeepers agreed that they should send a team to Brazil to find out first-hand what the European African cross was really like. A few years later I watched a documentary that was made on that exploratory trip. I had to laugh! Dr. Gary and the other scientist were equipped with full bee suits, while Norm was sporting a black leather patch on his chest. They entered the hives without smoke and proceeded to examine the frames. Almost immediately they were under attack. Norm was stunned at how aggressive they were. He could hardly maintain his observational dialogue into the microphone. Soon they all began to leave, and the video ended abruptly as the cameramen began to flee. I guess maybe Norm had underestimated the hybrid? Dr. Gary later appeared in several movies such as *The Swarm*[7]. The reason he was hired for these

---

[7] **The Swarm** is a 1978 American disaster film about a killer bee invasion of Texas. It was adapted from a novel of the same name by Arthur Herzog.

The director was Irwin Allen, and the cast included Michael Caine, Katharine Ross, Richard Widmark, Richard Chamberlain, Olivia de Havilland, Ben Johnson, Lee Grant, Patty

projects was because he made a practice of demonstrating covering a person with honeybees by spraying queen pheromone on the person. The willing staff or students who participated in those demonstrations were usually not severely stung. Although it is inevitable when you are covered with 40 lbs. of bees, that one or the other bee will get caught in your clothes and deliver a sting. To his credit, Norm sometimes played the farmer or bystander under attack by the bees. I guess you could call him the honeybee stunt man. Of course, in the movie, they always used the docile European honeybee, not their mulatto sisters.

On the subject of the Africanized bee, there is one other person I must mention. Dr. Harry Laidlaw was a much older, wiser, and knowledgeable professor of Apiculture at University of California, Davis. He was the first bee geneticists to maintain pure selected strains of bees using artificial insemination. In fact, the Honeybee Laboratory at UC Davis is now called the Harry H. Laidlaw Jr. Honeybee Research Facility. His argument about the Africanized honeybee was that they would eventually be able to breed out the aggressive characteristics just as they had done with the original European strains of bees that were first brought to the Americas. In Hawaii we call them the 'Nasty Germans'. Although the Africanized honeybee did spread all over South and Central American and into the southern regions of the United States, Harry Laidlaw's prediction is now being realized in countries where the beekeepers have adapted to the hybrid; unlike the United States where we are still trying to eradicate them.

Beekeepers in Guatemala and other Latin countries report that the domesticated Africanized bees are not only gentler and manageable, but they are also resistant to parasitic mites that threaten to decimate honeybees all over the world. It is this resistant African gene pool that may, in the end, save the honeybee from total annihilation by the ubiquitous *Varroa destructor*. Ironically, the later was originally a parasite of only *Apis cerana*, the Asian honeybee. Naturally, *V. destructor* did adapt to *Apis mellifera*, the western honeybee, in the last quarter of the 19th century.

Ward Stanger also invited me to attend the meeting of the California

---

Duke, Slim Pickens, Bradford Dillman, Fred MacMurray (in his final movie appearance), and Henry Fonda. Despite negative reviews and being a box office failure, the film was nominated for an Academy Award for Best Costume Design and retained a cult following for Jerry Goldsmith's score to the film, its all-star cast, as well as being part of the horror film genre. http://en.wikipedia.org/wiki/The_Swarm_(film)

State Beekeepers Association at the later part of October, at which he would introduce me to beekeepers for whom I might be interested to intern. By the time I attended that meeting I had still not heard back from the Peace Corps. I wanted to know whether I would be returned to Kenya to assume the assignment to which I had previously been posted at the Mtwapa Tropical Fruit Tree Nursery in the Coast Province. But I attended the meeting thinking it would be useful to meet the beekeepers.

One in particular impressed me. His name was Oliver Hill; he was an officer in the Association, and he was very interested in my experience and seemed the very image of the thoughtful, scholarly beekeeper that I had in my mind's eye. I interviewed with other larger Apiarists, but their operations were massive, and the prospects of moving all over the country was not appealing to me. Oliver left me with contact information and told me to contact him if I wanted to participate in the spring packaged-bee business. The California apiaries derived a large portion of their annual earnings by producing queens and packaged bees. This happens during the massive colony build up in February and March, when all the flowers in California bloom profusely. Harry and Ward had assured me that Oliver was one of the best of these queen breeders, and that I would learn a great deal from him. I said I would definitely keep his invitation in mind.

The news from Peace Corps was a shocking blow. It did not come from the Director, Ed White. Rather, he left the difficult task to Dave Redgrave who was the Agriculture Program Director and my direct supervisor in Kenya. The argument was that the Nixon Administration had slashed the Peace Corps budget, and that volunteers that were already on home leave between tours of duty would not be returned to country. I was of course devastated because my whole future, and that of my adopted family, was all tied up in this fateful decision. Of course, I was suspicious that there were deeper implications and that Ed White had decided that it was not right for me to have an African family. I said so in a letter to Dave, but in his reply he assured me that there was not ulterior motive. Rather, it was a simple but tragic matter of the Nixon Administration defunding the Peace Corps. They were probably lucky he didn't axe the whole program, lock stock and barrel. I don't know how many other volunteers were in my position, but what a wasteful decision it was. Here you had volunteers with two years of on-the-ground experience, who knew the local language, and who were willing to offer two more years of service, surreptitiously cut from the program.

I was desperate; I did not know what I would do. I felt like a pawn in an international chess game being played by despots who had no empathy for the plight of ordinary men. Still, I had to do something. About that time, Dr. Townsend had sent me a letter informing me that he would be in Davis and asking if I could meet him. Of course, I jumped at the chance, and he was on close terms with Dr. Laidlaw, so it was a chance for me to be introduced to the Bee Biology Program at Davis. I was, of course, hoping that Dr. Townsend could put some pressure on the Peace Corps to take me back. In Dr. Townsend's case, he was, in fact, prejudicial against my plans to marry a Kenyan. He strongly suggested that I forget the family relationship and concentrate on getting more education or experience in beekeeping. I found out later that he had been in communication with Mr. Moon, who had also recommended that I not be encouraged to continue my relationship with Charity. It was Mr. Moon who introduced me to beekeeping in Kenya, where he was a Near East Foundation Advisor. Of course, I felt very strongly that the forces were arrayed against me, and I was not pleased. I did not say anything to Dr. Townsend or Dr. Laidlaw, but I decided to go to work for Oliver Hill and see if I could make enough money to fund a new strategy.

# Chapter 2

# The Trials

In the morning sow your seed, and at evening withhold not your hand, for you do not know which will prosper, this or that, or whether both alike will be good. **English Standard Version (2001) Ecclesiastes 11:17**

Here I sit sipping my coffee at the Hilo Coffee Mill (HCM, which is actually in Mountain View, Hawaii). I think what a long and circuitous route I took from failing my induction physical to here. Forty years of a life filled with hardship, friendship, despondency, euphoria, struggling and coasting... in other words, just an ordinary life. This is one of those coasting times, but I am having trouble adjusting. Life has been such an uphill battle until now that I cannot accept that everything seems to be working out. I just received notification that I have been approved for disability retirement by the State of Hawaii. When I stop earning too much to qualify for Federal Disability Social Security, the State decision might help me obtain the federal dispensation as well. So for once in my life, I don't have to worry from whence will come my next paycheck. Still, Gretchen and I have trouble just sitting still, much as we dream of relaxing on the beach. Even the beach is a 50 mile round trip and gas is $3.47/gal., using our discounted Aloha Gas card I assume that readers of this book in future will say, "Imagine that they only had to pay $3.50 for gas back then". Of course, we remember when gas was $0.35/gal. Such is life in the American fast lane.

So I occupy my mornings writing and sipping the local brew at this lovely little Shangri-La that Jeanette, Kathy and Juanette have created from an old sugar cane field on the slopes of Mauna Loa. Beautifully landscaped with tropical plants and even some of the original native Ohia Lehua trees, the visitor's center and coffee processing plant is a very progressive addition to the aging community of Mountain View. Juanette makes a killer cranberry scone (and I mean that in the best way), and the coffee exceeds the standard for this coffee producing state. It is particularly pleasant to drive up to the facilities when they are roasting coffee. The stimulating smoke from the chimney is enough to wake up every sensory organ in your body. Not to mention that the free-range chickens at the HCM produce the fine, plump, multicolored eggs that we purchase every week. No need worry about *Pseudomonas* in these eggs.

When I think about how relaxed our life is now compared to 1970, it boggles my mind to realize how much a young person is capable of enduring, as opposed to an elderly man comfortable in his conveniences, doting on his pasts. Because I had some hard lessons to learn after Dr. Gordon Townsend Delivered his verdict on what I should do with my life. When I got back to Galt, my mother and I had more long discussions, with her trying to calm me down, and me trying to convince her how certain I was that I was destined to marry Charity and adopt her family -- of which there were 5 children that I knew of. At that point I did not know that Gertrude had already conceived Teddy, and she was not married. Teddy Mshoi Thurman now serves the USA in combat in Iraq. I think I wore my mother down, and finally she accepted that I was determined to be reunited with the family. I am sure she got more sleep after I left to take a job with Oliver Hill Apiaries in Willows, California.

Let me first give my impression of Oliver. He was a tall (better than 6 ft.) slender man with snow white hair and spectacles. Be not deceived by his slightness of build, I watched this wiry man off-load 400 2-story beehives stacked three tiers high from a tractor-trailer that his brother-in-law had brought to the Pacific Northwest. The man was a strong as the hive-loaders that he built using all of is engineering training. He had been in an engineering firm when his father died, but he decided to take over his father's apiary because he really did not enjoy the life of a corporate engineer. This ended his marriage to his first wife, but by the time I met him he was married to a woman who was his equal in the hard life of a beekeeper. He made one concession to Nora after she took on the life of a beekeeper's wife. She loved to walk barefoot through the cow pies, so he bought her some land, I helped roof a barn, and she raised a small herd of cattle on the north end of Willows. Well, bees don't provide beef for the winter larder. Every spring Nora was in the packing house supervising the transfer of queen cells to the nuclei (small hives to which a cup of bees are added before they are taken to the nun[8] yards). There the queens are able to fly and mate with the drones. Nora managed the whole queen rearing process.

During that season, Oliver averaged 16 hours per day on the go. Whenever there was a break, Oliver preferred to catnap at the table while the crew gabbed and swilled their coffee. I had the irritating habit of asking Oliver questions during those sessions, which I am sure he would have preferred not to answer but did in his slow deliberate pattern of speech. On one occasion, in an effort to divert my incessant string of questions, Nora asked Oliver to talk to Sam. Now Sam was a huge male Siamese tom cat who always followed Oliver around whenever he was in the home yard Oliver began the conversation with a mournful complaint about the prices of honey falling while the price of supplies rose. I did not know the meaning of caterwauler until I heard this cat's response. He sounded like an old man moaning at the top of his lungs. I got the point that the conversation with the cat was far more entertaining than my lame efforts to keep Oliver awake.

I started working at the Hill Apiaries in November of 1971, so the workload was light. This gave me a chance to adjust. One of our first trips was to the Lassen National Park, where Oliver took his bees in the late summer to catch the aphid honeydew. That's right; cedar trees come under attack from aphids in the late summer. Aphids feed on the sap of the tree, and because they take in more liquid than they can hold, they exude a syrupy liquid through the end of their abdomen. This is collected by both ants and honeybees. When it is the latter, the product is called honeydew. Cedar honeydew has a distinctly nutty flavor and a rich dark color. It is quite tasty because it is not aphid poop, but the exudate of the cornicles (siphunculi). The purpose of our trip was to bring back the hives to the valley and harvest the honeydew. By November it is cold enough that the honeybees are "hibernating" for the winter. It really isn't hibernation by the literal definition. The bees simply cluster around the queen and the honeycomb and maintain their colony temperature by feeding on the honey. Honeybees cannot move if their body temperature drops below 50 °F (10 °C), so there is not much activity outside of the hive, even when you are

---

[8] Nuc (nūk) is short for nucleus, which consists of a small cluster of bees on three small combs where the queen cells are positioned, so they can be taken to the field to emerge and then mate, after which the queens are collected and packaged for shipment.

loading them to move. They know to stay close to the cluster. I am sure the 3 hour journey added a little stress to the bees, with cold wind blowing in the hive entrances, but the bees survived nicely. After all, a well-stocked beehive can survive at 50 below 0 °F in a 50 mile per hour wind. It is not by accident that humans have taken them every place on earth except the arctic poles.

When we arrived back in Willows, my job for the next few weeks was extracting honey. I would occasionally go with Oliver to feed beehives. The Hill sons were also involved in the winter maintenance activity. I would have been more useful if I had possessed a valid driver's license. Unfortunately, I learned that there was a hold on my license because I had not cleared up a payment to the owner of the Thunderbird I had rear ended before I went to Africa. The problem was that I could not find the man to pay him his $100. Ergo, I could not drive for Oliver. That left me doing work around the home yard most of the time. I painted hives, repaired old redwood hives that had belonged to Oliver's father. I rendered out old comb in the furnace that Oliver had built for the purpose, and I extracted and bottled honey.

The wages were low ($3.45 per hour), but Oliver provided housing. Over the years the Hills had bought several of the small houses in their neighborhood, because they knew there was always the threat of problems with the neighbors. The home yard was the original home and warehouses of Oliver's father, who was probably the only one in the neighborhood when he built the home. As is so often the case, development kept pushing the farmers and beekeepers out of business or out of the land. The Hills were not going to let that happen. As far as I know, they are still located on the same block in Willows[9]. The house that I was given to occupy was what they used to call a shotgun house. If you stood in the front door you could shoot buckshot

---

[9] An article in the "Willows Review" in 1910 predicted that **Harry K. Hill's** new business venture would be a great success. More than a century later, those making the prediction were correct. The alfalfa farmer had a 14-acre tract of land in Willows on which he decided to establish 20 stands of bees. Honey and beeswax were in great demand at the time, and the Willows area had no such enterprise.

The business grew to become Hill & Ward Apiaries Inc. who became one of city's leading honey, beeswax and queen bee producers. **Oliver Hill**, the son of the founder, is sharing the company's history at the Willows Museum. Except for the lives bees, the exhibit, which opened on May 8, will be on display just inside the museum through the month of May. Visitors can learn about the life of the queen bee, egg laying, drones and other information related to honeybees production. The museum, at Walnut and North Plumas streets, is open from 1 p.m.-4 p.m. Thursday, Saturday and Sunday. By Susan Meeker/Glenn County Transcript May 19, 2015

through the back door without hitting anything. It had two bedrooms and one bath, a small kitchen and front room. It was more than I needed.

I had begun to experiment with different designs of the Greek top-bar hive in my spare time, so I kind of took over the living room with various incarnations of hive designs. In other words I messed it up; you would have thought it was a poorly maintained cabinet shop. About the first part of January, the Canadians started to arrive. The first was George Semaneau, and he was assigned to the house I occupied. I did not see much of him off the job, because he was a hard-living fellow and spent every evening at the local watering hole.[10] But he was up and working every morning; I didn't understand how he could do it. Years of practice, I presume.

At first our interactions were more of neophyte and warhorse. I placed George on a pedestal that he felt obligated to maintain. Oliver started sending me out with George, probably so he would not have to deal with my incessant questions. I was duly intimidated by the Frenchman's cowboy attire, Canuck accent, and sheer endurance. However, that was to change. We were replacing feed on some bee yards one freezing sunny day. George would crack the lids to see what hives needed feed, and I would place the cans of syrup on the ones he marked. I was fully suited with coveralls and vale, but George didn't bother with bee gear. I was impressed that he seemed not to be stung. But then he decided he needed to piss, so he walked over to the fence and whipped it out within 5 foot of the beehives. The next moment I heard a horrific yell followed by a string of French expletives-deleted. Sure enough, one stealthy bee found her way to the family jewels. That broke the ice between George and I, and I laughed uncontrollably for several minutes. George himself could see the humor in it, despite the pain. The thaw was permanent and we got along well after that incident.

The next Canadian to arrive was Charles Ducham. He and George both owned apiaries in the Peace River region of Canada. I should explain why the Canadians were working for Oliver. They lived in an area where the flow of clover and rape honey could bring in 400 lbs. of honey per hive per season. But if the bees had to be kept over the winter, they would lose half or more of the honey. So, since California produced an excess of bees in a spring, the Canadians had long ago started to kill their bees in the fall and buy packages

---

[10] **Watering hole** is a bar, nightclub, restaurant with popular bar or other social gathering place where alcoholic drinks are sold. (Urban Dictionary)

(2 lbs. of bees and a queen) in the spring.[11] They would pay for part of the cost by working for Oliver in his busiest season, almond pollination. This is when all the colonies would build up rapidly, and management of the colonies lead to the production of packaged bees.

Oliver used his winter evenings to develop equipment for his operation. When I arrived he was working on a high-tech hive loader for his new International Harvester (IH). Old Blewy, a vintage International Harvester was the only truck with a hive loader, and it was a simple armature (boom) that could only swing out to the side and over the bed of the truck. Oliver's new loader was going to be an engineering marvel. The controls were made from a fighter jet control stick. The boom was attached to a motorized rotating cylinder which allowed the boom to be raised and lowered. At this same connecting point the boom was on a motorized wheel that allowed the loader to be rotated around the entire circumference of the flatbed truck. The boom was longer than the length of the flat bed (probably 25 ft.) so Oliver had to do extensive test to insure that the metal could stand the torque. But it was not a solid boom; it was jointed in the middle and could be moved like a human elbow. That totals to four different vectors that could be controlled from the fighter jet stick. It was a wonder, but only Oliver understood it well enough to operate it.

George prided himself on his skills as an operator. He was adept with the forklift and had probably had heavy equipment operator experience. So he took to the new hive loader with gusto. One night we went out together to collect a load of bees from an almond orchard. The beehives were not on the edge of the orchard but inside it. The hives had been unloaded by hand from the low flatbed Ford But that truck had been stuck in mud up to its floorboard on a subsequent rainy excursion. Almond trees have low-hanging wide-spreading canopies. It was going to be a trick getting this large truck into the orchard to pick up the 100 hives.

George negotiated the orchard pretty well, and the extra joints and motion of the new loader made it possible to work around the canopies to pick up the hives. The problem came when we tried to leave the orchard. Each

---

[11] This whole economic system of **replacing the bees in Canada** with California bees came to an end when the Vorroa mite caused the Canadian Government to shut the boarders in 1987. At attempt was made in 2009 to open the boarders again to US reared honeybees but the issue has not been resolved. Now many of the bee breeders are kept busy trying to replace domestic queens and colonies that have died from Colony Collapse Disorder.

tier of hives are stacked two or three high (usually two supers to one hive), and then tied down with a rope, over the tier, synched down with a "truckers hitch" knot[12]. As we started to leave George noticed, just in the nick of time, that the last two tiers of hives had gotten caught by the branches and were leaning precariously over the back of the flatbed. When we went back to look, bees were boiling out the separate hive bodies, and the whole stack could have collapsed at any time. George and I got stung quite a few times before we got the hives up righted and synched down with extra ropes. Luckily, we made it out of the orchard, unloaded the hives at another location, and marveled at our accomplishment all the way home.

Charles had asked Oliver to build a hive loader on his truck which he had driven down from Canada. This meant that Charles took over a lot of Oliver's hauling duties and freed him up for engineering. The design was simple, but Oliver would not do anything sloppily. He did as much testing on Charles' loader as he had done on his much more complex creation.

Charles was not a drinker, and so he was not out carousing to the wee hours. Charles was bunking with us in the small house. Consequently, he and I had more time to talk in the evenings. I found out that Charles had a growing apiary, but he was a much more driven man than George. So much so, he took great offence at the bears destroying his hives. Not one to wait for the Canadian Wildlife Service to deliver bear traps, he took it upon himself to carry strychnine to bait beef for poisoning troublesome bears. He should have followed the law, because he was carrying his son with him in the truck one day and left him alone in the truck for a short time. The boy found the strychnine in the glove compartment and ate it. Charles said that they could have saved him, but the Emergency Room staff waited too long to get him on the stomach pump and he died. That is a heavy price to pay for putting success ahead of caution.

By the time the colonies were approaching full strength, the package bee operation began, and would proceed without a break until the end of the season. Every day all available hands would be out in the field shaking bees.

---

[12] How to tie the **Trucker's Hitch Knot.** Use the Trucker's Hitch to cinch down a load. This combination of knots allows a line to be pulled very tight. Probably the most useful hitch there is, the Trucker's Hitch, allows a line to be pulled tight as a guitar string and secured. It is used by truckers to secure heavy loads in place and works equally well tying canoes and other objects to the tops of cars. Once the line is pull to the desired tension using the pulley effect of the loop in the middle of the line, the knot is secured with a couple half hitches around one or both lines. https://www.netknots.com/rope_knots/truckers-hitch

This involved knocking bees out of the hives into a screen box, and then using the box to pour out two pound clusters of bees into the packages. A bank of caged queens[13] is carried in the shaker truck, and one is added to every package. These are usually shipped the day they are collected.

I was included on the shaking crew for a week or two, but then I was transferred to the queen processing crew. That involved rising at 4:30 AM, in order to load the nucs onto a truck and deliver them to mating yards in the Coastal Range foothills. I was startled the first time I heard the queens, in the nucs, piping. Literally, the queens make a loud piping sound before they emerge from their cell. This elicits a response from the other queens, and the first queen out of her cell will track down the other queens and kill them. Of course, in each nuc there is only one queen, so no regicide occurs. The entrances to the nucs were not opened until we arrived at the mating yards.[14] Subsequently, the queens will take their maiden flight, and encounter drones that come from colonies placed in the area. Once mated, they start to lay eggs in the small 3-frame nucs. Later, a crew will come around and catch the queens inside the nucs and put them in a queen cage. The queen cages are then transferred to a queen bank, where the bee population is kept very strong because the many queens are very demanding of food and attention.

On these Foothill trips, we always had breakfast in an old orchard on a farm in the hills. It was a beautiful spot with all the wildflowers and fruit trees in bloom. It was well worth the early rising and compensated for the remainder of the day, during which I was the bee scooper. That means that for the rest of a long workday, I would dump packages of bees into a large cardboard box, and then scoop up bees one cup at a time, to place in the nuclei. Meanwhile Nora and her daughter would cut queen cells to install in the nucs. It was literally an assembly line, but the products were tiny colonies of bees.

---

[13] A **queen bank** is a hive that does not have its own queen but is filled with frame upon frame of caged queens. In order to maintain these queens it takes a large number of worker bees, so queen banks are constantly restocked with worker bees shaken from other hives. This does not lead to fighting between the bees, because they are overwhelmed with all the queen pheromone being passed around in the queen bank.

[14] A mating yard is a term for an apiary which consists primarily of queen mating nucs and hives which raise drones. A queen bee must mate in order to lay fertilized eggs, which develop into workers and other queens, which are both female. Queens can lay eggs parthenogenetically, but these will always develop into drones (males). https://en.wikipedia.org/wiki/Mating_yard

Before the packaged-bee season had hit full stride, I had made a visit to U. C. Davis and applied to enter the graduate program. I first talked to Dr. Laidlaw, but he advised me that it would be a lot of work for a Bachelor in botany major to do a graduate degree in Entomology. I would basically have had to take the whole undergraduate series of entomology courses. I don't know who suggested the International Agriculture Development major, but it was a godsend. I use that word advisedly because what are the chances? The IAD program advisor was Dr. William Flocker[15], who had just returned from a sabbatical in Uganda. He had been at the Makerere University in Kampala when Idi Amin took over the government. He described to me the very dangerous situation for intellectuals in that country. What was written in

---

[15] **William J. Flocker**, Vegetable Crops Professor: Davis 1917-1980

Bill Flocker will be longest remembered for his humanitarian efforts, particularly with students. Any student with a problem found a sensitive ear if he or she approached Bill with a problem. Bill would move heaven and earth and sometimes even the administration to solve a student's problem. If the problem was financial, Bill would try every avenue of aid. If no money was obtainable from loan or grant sources, he would often loan the student money out of his own pocket.

Bill's interest in students is best demonstrated by his creation of the course, Plant Science 2, in 1965. It was designed to orient students in plant science and to develop in them awareness and an appreciation of agriculture. He soon recognized both the need and the potential for new approaches to teaching agriculture. His pioneer work in audio-tutorial teaching techniques created Plant Science 2 as an outstanding example of these innovative techniques. Much of Bill's success as a teacher was due to his dedication to advising both undergraduate and graduate students, especially his ability to relate with each student.

The practical experience in farming that Bill acquired before coming to the University of California enabled him to appreciate the importance basic research has for actual farming practices. He was an authority in soil physics, soil physical properties, and soil-water movement. His interests included procedures for maintaining and improving soil structure for maximum crop production. He showed the importance of the soil compaction problem in commercial tomato and potato production. With the increase in interest in environmental quality, Bill did research on incorporating solid wastes, particularly cannery wastes, into soil to improve marginal land. For this research he was given an environmental quality award from the American Society for Horticultural Science.

Bill had a varied career. He was born and raised on a farm in Clinton, Indiana. After graduating from the University of Illinois in 1936, he joined the U.S. Air Corps and served as a fighter pilot and squadron commander in World War II. After the war he returned to farming in Illinois and in Arizona. However, his practical and academic desires led him to return to school. He obtained his Ph.D. in Agricultural Chemistry and Soils at the University of Arizona in 1955. Shortly thereafter he joined the Vegetable Crops Department at UCD. Excerpter from http://content.cdlib.org/xtf/view?docId=hb1j49n6pv&doc.view=frames&chunk.id=div00034&toc.depth=1&toc.id=

the footnotes about Dr. Flocker's regarding his dedication to helping students was very true. I really didn't have a high enough GPA to get into Davis, but, because I had been in Peace Corps in East Africa, Dr. Flocker enrolled me on probation. I did not fail him, maintaining a higher than 3.5 GPA throughout my graduate program. The irony here is that I had gone to the Northwest in the summer of 1972 to work to earn enough money to bring the family from Africa. I did not return to UC Davis until 1979, the year before Dr. Flocker died. He was 63, the same age I am as I write this memoir. How much more would he have accomplished if he were given a few more years on this earth. I certainly appreciate what he did for me.

IAD is an Interdepartmental Group. That means that there were core course requirements for the program, but the graduate student was free to develop a program in conjunction with other departments in the School of Agriculture. I talked to one of the new professors in Entomology on my visit, but it was not until later that the details were arranged. I didn't know immediately whether I had been accepted, and it was not until weeks later that I received word from the IAD Department that I could start my graduate program in Spring Quarter. I had presented a proposal for estimation of honeybee pollination to Robbin Thorp, who was the professor of pollination ecology in the entomology department. He thought my proposal was too expansive, but it put me on his radar for future study and work.

Back at the Hill Apiary, I did not want to let them know that I was thinking about leaving at the end of March. I felt guilty about this; because I had told Oliver that I would be available for the season. I tried to make myself as useful as possible so that they would not be thinking of me as the young "whipper snapper". I didn't want to leave and burn my bridges behind me. So I threw myself into the nuc building business, where endurance was what was needed. Rising at 4 o'clock every morning, I was always ready to load the nucs and leave for the foothills. When we arrived we would place the new nucs in the breeding yards, have breakfast in the orchard, and head back to Willows. Then we would pack nucs until the daily quota was met. I can't even remember if we ate lunch. I also don't remember if we did anything after the nuc-building. All I remember is being tired and ready for bed early. I don't even remember cooking dinners. The existence bordered on monastic. But then, even monks eat.

I will say that one excruciating pleasure of working with honeybees is not the multiple stings, but the aftermath. When the venom and the swelling are wearing off, stepping into a hot shower is amazing. It is kind of like poison oak without the oozing warts. Quite honestly the intense itch is not unlike the sensation of sex. It doesn't substitute, but it definitely reminds you that you are alive.

Sundays were interesting. In spite of the demands of the season, Oliver was always up early to listen to the Mormon Tabernacle Choir on the radio. Sometimes he would take out his trumpet (might have been a cornet) and play. I had found a little church a couple of blocks down the street. It was a black church; basically it was a black family. There were only the occasional other church attendee, but the regular congregation was the family of the pastor. He was a white haired man of limited education but of patriarchal authority within his family. His interpretations of the King James Version were glaringly contrary to the literal meaning of the archaic language, but he was convincingly certain of his revelation. Sometimes I wondered if it was the preaching or the community meal that brought the family together. Literally, lunch was in the oven, and served to all in attendance after the sermon concluded.

I also attended the Catholic Church, but I think the black church fulfilled some need I had to maintain some connection to Africa, however many generations removed. I was spending a lot of time trying to divine from random selections of biblical text whether I should pursue my efforts to bring my Taita family together in America. Although I had been able to rationalize some revelation from this method in earlier years, now the passages that would appear seemed more and more random. Did this indicate that I was on the wrong track or did they not indicate anything? Watching the pastor misinterpret King James' English made me realize how subjective the whole process of divination could be.

Although living like a monk, I certainly was not feeling close to God. Everything that I had hoped and prayed for was not happening, and what was happening seemed more circumstantial than providential. It reminded me of my effort in major seminary to decide whether to follow St. Francis in every detail or take the more pragmatic route of leaving the seminary to court my first love, Gretchen. Will I always wonder if that was a right decision? But at least it was a decision, and it is a lot more concrete to try to follow a plan than wait for the "grand plan" to be revealed.

The letter from UC Davis finally came, inviting me to the IAD graduate program. It was a relief to know that I was still in the running for higher education. Being the only one in my family to have aspired to that level made it a little unnerving. My grandfather had been the Woods Manager for the whole logging operation of McCloud River Lumber Co., but he only had an eighth grade education. My mother had attended one year of undergraduate college and later tried for an associate of art (I don't think she ever finished). Nevertheless the Army trained her to the point where she became an X-ray technician. My stepfather came right out of World War II and right into the post office where he worked for 33 years. I think my half-sister was in college at the same time as I was but I think I graduated before her. Nor were any of my cousins headed for higher education. In short, I was a pioneer in the family. My grandfather once asked, "Are you still in school?" But I was the primary contributor to my undergraduate education at the University of Washington, and I was determined to make it in graduate school on my own.

Broaching the subject of education with the Hills was also nerve wracking. It probably would have been better to be straightforward with them from the start. Whereas now I had to worry what they would think of me springing the news on them. It wasn't as if they were shorthanded or had turned anyone away because they had hired me. In fact, in addition to the Canadians, Nora's daughter had come with her boyfriend to work, and Oliver's two sons were also working with the family. Nora's sister had also moved to Willows with her beau, and they were both working in the package-bee operation. In some ways, I was probably superficial. Nevertheless, I think they were beginning to appreciate my willingness rise at 4 AM, and to bend over a cardboard box full of bees in a darkened room for hours on end; it was not a job that any of the crew wanted. Still, when I finally told Oliver and Nora that I would be leaving for spring quarter at Davis, I think they understood. Nora was a little miffed at me because I was on her crew. Oliver not so much; in fact he was probably a little relieved that I had gone over to Nora's crew earlier in the season. I think he thought I talked a little too much, and I called the smoker fuel "rags" instead of "burlap". That was offensive to Oliver. I also think Oliver was a believer in the Bee Biology program at Davis, and thought it was a good opportunity for me.

It is a different sensation being a short timer. People treat you differently. You are all excited about what you are going to be doing, but you can't tell anyone, because they are all still in the thick of it. The Canadians liked to talk about their plans, but they were going back to the Peace River to be their own bosses. On the other hand, the bulk of the crew could only foresee the long hours in the scorching sun, being stung, on the rotation from bee yard to bee yard, listening to "Bye Bye Miss American Pie"[16] on the radio, and falling into bed exhausted. This only furthered my withdrawal from the break-time banter.

There was no going away celebration; there was too much work to do. Oliver and Nora wished me well as I departed with Fr. Carl and my mother. They had come to help me move my accumulated possessions (including experimental hive). I don't remember how or exactly when I left the Hill Apiary but it was just at the start of the spring quarter. The one day I had in Davis, before the quarter began, was occupied looking for a place to stay. I found an apartment where a Guatemalan, a Chilean, and an acting student from the States were looking for a fourth roommate to reduce their rent. Divided four ways, the two bedroom apartment was the same price ($36) that I had paid for the little one bedroom studio at the University of Washington three years before. It was one of the few costs that had not succumbed to inflation. Books were certainly higher, but tuition was about 6 and 1/2 times higher than at University of Washington, but I can't remember if that included out-of-state tuition. I had managed to save enough working for Oliver to pay the school fees.

I also needed a job to feed myself, and that came from Ward Stanger in the Bee Biology facility. He needed someone to collect together information on the history of beekeeping in California. This was very interesting because the U. C. Davis Library has one of the largest collections of apiculture publications in the United States. There were periodicals of the California Bee Association that dated back to its foundation in Gold Rush California. If there had been the computer resources that I have now, I could have written a large tome. As it was, I had to resort to writing up index cards referencing the articles that I was finding. I still have the cards written in a precise tiny print that I could not write now. I don't know if Ward ever used the material to write a history.[17] I might include a little of what I can remember here. Ward also had me work on other information gathering assignments that he was

---

[16] "American Pie" is a song by American singer and songwriter Don McLean. Recorded and released on the American Pie album in 1971, the single was the number-one US hit for four weeks in 1972 and also topped the charts in Australia, Canada, and New Zealand. In the UK, the single reached number 2, where it stayed for 3 weeks, on its original 1972 release. https://en.wikipedia.org/wiki/American_Pie_(song)

[17] **Ward Stanger** did publish Fundamentals of California Beekeeping. Manual 42 which is out of print, but is available from Division of Agriculture and Natural Resources (ANR) of the University of California at http://anrcatalog.ucdavis.edu/

asked to do from time to time. I remember one was a request from Max Factor Inc. They had heard that doctors were using honey in surgery in Vietnam, and they wanted to know what information was available about the medicinal properties of honeybee honey, wax, and propolis. Apparently I was coauthor on another publication from 1972, although, I was not aware of it for years. I finally found it in the archives of *Gleanings in Bee Culture*[18].

This income paid for a bike and the food energy to get me the 2 miles from the apartment to campus and from there to the Bee Biology facility, which was also about 3 miles from campus. Davis is Bicycle City. From an early stage, when it was an Agriculture Research Station for University of California, Berkeley, the campus has been bicycle oriented. The City of Davis also saw the advantage of accommodating the bicycle on this flat real estate where the weather is fair more often than not. At one point the City had a policy of providing free bikes anyone could take and then deposit in a city bike rack at his or her destination. By the time I arrived, bike theft had become so rampant that whole racks of bikes were being stolen. Consequently, the City had stopped subsidizing this most cost-effective transportation and student were obligated to purchase Kryptonite bike locks to protect their wheels.

I have to comment on the symphonic precision of a bicycle roundabout on the campus at UCD. The motion is like the flow of a river. The traffic merges effortlessly into the turn and exits on another fork with elegant fluidity. At first I did not understand the physics. I would hesitate to cross the flow of traffic on foot, but I would be left waiting for the whole period between classes. When I did venture into the stream hesitantly, it would cause mass confusion and near collision. Finally, by process of observation, I learned to walk right into the roundabout without even looking at the oncoming wall of bikes. Amazingly, the riders flow around the pedestrian as if he were a rock in the stream. As long as I moved at a predictable pace, the bike riders could adjust their speed and direction to let me pass. If I stopped unexpectedly, it could cause a major mangle of man and machine.

The Bee Biology Facility, more recently named for Harry Laidlaw, was of great interest to me. The main classroom contained for observation hives where you could lose yourself watching the bees work, dance, rest, and nurse.

---

[18] Nazer, I.K., **Klungness, L.M.,** Renkow, P. and Wynholds, P. 1972. Agricultural teaching and research at the University of California, Davis. Gleanings Bee Cult 100:8 229-231

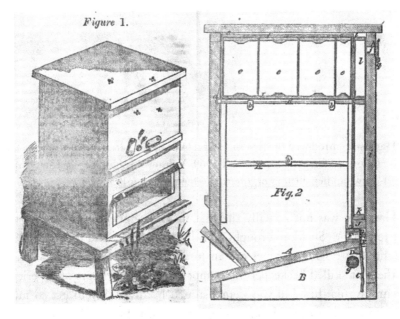

The hive design of J. S. Harbison developed in the mid-nineteenth century. (*San Diego Historical Society Quarterly*, Fall 1969, Volume 15, Number 4, Rita Larkin, Editor)

There were also some interesting memorabilia stored away in the mezzanines. Among these there was one redwood hive of John Harbison. He called it "the California hive"; the design of which he patented in 1859.[19] Harbison had read about the gold rush in California in 1848, but he had also been informed that there were no honeybees (*Apis mellifera*) west of the Rocky Mountains. Although that may seem hard to believe, it is true that man has basically carried the honeybee to every corner of the earth, and John was determined to be the one that would bring them to California. He could see dollars in his head and prepared very well for the enterprise. He prepared hives that could be shipped around the Isthmus of Panama; that is a long time to confine a swarm of bees through tropical conditions. Five of his hives died in transit, but he managed to get 62 off loaded at the docks in San Francisco Bay from the steamer "Sonora" on November 30th, 1857. This was strategic on Harbison's part, because this was the center of trade for the incoming hoard of would-be prospectors.

---

[19] Harbison, J. S. California Adjustable Comb Hive. 1860. The Lawrence Journal, New Castle Pennsylvania. 32 pp.

**J. S. Harbison** introduced the first successful honeybee apiaries into California. (*San Diego Historical Society Quarterly*, Fall 1969, Volume 15, Number 4, Rita Larkin, Editor) www.sandiegohistory.org/journal/69fall/images/p19.jpg

Harbison was not actually the first to bring honeybees to California: Christopher A. Sheldon brought one hive in 1853, and William Buck brought 18 surviving colonies to San Jose in 1855. Nevertheless, Harbison was the first skilled beekeeper to attempt it. Having 15 years of experience in Pennsylvania, his skill was demonstrated by his ability to get so many colonies to California.[20] His apiary in Pennsylvania had suffered 50% losses because of drought in 1854, which had forced him to come to California via Nicaragua to try panning for gold. He quickly abandoned that pursuit to take employment with the Sutter Ville sawmill of T. F. Gould & Co. After a year, he leased some land and started a nursery, shipping fruit tree seedlings from Pennsylvania, which became some of the first temperate fruits grown in northern California. At this time he was also planning how to ship bees from Pennsylvania; for this he designed a small hive with a screen porch where the bees could expand to cool the cluster.

After they arrived, he went to work immediately, first shipping the colonies up the Sacramento River by the riverboat "New World", arriving on December 2nd in Sutter Ville. This was the town where gold was first discovered[21]. After consolidation of the weak hives he was able to set up 50 colonies, which prospered in the spring bloom, to the point that he sold his first 16 hives for $100 in gold each. By the end of that season he had 100 colonies of which he sold all but six at the going rate of $100 each. He went

---

[20] Lee H. Watkins 1969. John S. Harbison: California's First Modern Beekeeper. *Agricultural History.* 43: 2 239-248. Available at http://www.jstor.org/pss/4617662.

[21] Lee H. Watkins. 1969. **John S. Harbison**: Pioneer San Diego Beekeeper in Rita Larkin, Editor. *The Journal of San Diego History* SAN DIEGO HISTORICAL SOCIETY QUARTERLY Fall 1969, Volume 15, Number 4. Available on http://www.sandiegohistory.org/journal/69fall/harbison.htm

on to be the leading apiarist in California, eventually moving his operation to San Diego. Harbison pioneered the shipment of comb honey by rail to the east. In 1876 he shipped 25 freight carloads. The history of California beekeeping would have been very different if John Harbison had not shown the Californians how to do it right.

# Chapter 3

# In the Brigg

My son, eat honey, for it is good, and the drippings of the honeycomb are sweet to your taste. Know that wisdom is such to your soul; if you find it, there will be a future, and your hope will not be cut off.
**English Standard Version (2001) Proverbs 24:13-14**

The first quarter at UC Davis was the best! Not necessarily the most fun, but the best for accomplishments. It was daunting at first, but in a different way than the elegant old halls of the University of Washington. By comparison, Davis was a young campus. The oldest building on campus was a shake-covered complex of two wooden buildings that were part of the original dairy outpost of the University of California in Berkeley[22]. Those two buildings

---

[22] In 1905, Gov. George Pardee signed into law an act to establish a university farm school for the University of California. The new law also created a commission to pick the site and appropriated $150,000 to buy the land, setting into motion a furious competition among more than 70 communities around the state vying for the University Farm. It would be more than a year before that commission, after crisscrossing the state, selected a tiny town then known as Davisville. In 1908-09, the first students arrived. Nine days after the bill was signed into law, the Sacramento Union newspaper endorsed the Davisville site as "absolutely the nearest point to Berkeley which possesses all the requisites."

A newly organized Davisville Chamber of Commerce — led by two UC-educated neighbor farmers George Pierce Jr. and Jacob "Gene" LaRue — began promoting the site with a pamphlet titled "An Ideal Spot for a University Farm." Besides fertile soil, the pamphlet lauded the area for its temperate climate, plentiful water, low taxes, good roads, train service, proximity to Berkeley and Sacramento, "13 incoming and 13 outgoing mails each day," two telephone systems and two telegraph offices.

By Kathleen Holder, Associate Editor of U. C. Davis Magazine, available at http://www.ucdavis.edu/spotlight/0305/centennial.html

were called North Hall[23]. It held Student Services and Financial Aid, which I made a point of frequenting. It was an inviting building with its wood stairs, wide porch, and old cork trees. I frankly can't say the same for many of the buildings of the post WWII period. All boxy, stone, brick or concrete buildings with lots of aluminum framed window glass. The most grotesque of these was Briggs Hall, the biological sciences building which included Entomology.

Architecturally, Briggs may have been a fairly efficient design. The concrete awnings that covered every set of windows helped protect the building from the scorching Central Valley sun, but it gave a cold and ominous appearance to this concrete castle of gray parapets. So proud of this architectural "wonder" are the U. C. Chancellors that I could not find one picture of Briggs Hall on Google Image. The only photo I could find was sequestered on the website of AE[3] Architectural Firm (Oakland, San Francisco, and Phoenix), one of which three partners was commissioned to refurbish Briggs Hall in 2005. I had to laugh. When I was working in Washington, after my first quarter at U. C. Davis, I went to a drive-in theater to see a movie called "Phase IV". In this science fiction movie, the protagonists were entomologists trying to defeat a plague of intelligent ants. The scientist resorted to building a fortified pod from which they could study ways to attack the ant colony. Instead, the ants surrounded the pod with grey towers of clay, the tops of which were flattened reflective mirrors aiming concentrated sunlight at the pod.[24] I don't know why, but the structures built by the ants, although not resembling Briggs Hall, reminded me thoroughly of that stone edifice. I guess the resemblance was symbolic.

---

[23] **North Hall** was one of the three original dormitories (with South Hall and West Hall) on the UC Davis campus, and was finished on September 6, 1908. It was the second building built on the University Farm, a year after the dairy barn was erected. http://daviswiki.org/North_Hall

[24] **Phase IV** is an American science fiction film, made in 1974. It is the only feature-length film directed by the noted title designer Saul Bass. It starred Michael Murphy, Nigel Davenport and Lynne Frederick.

The film was a box office flop and as a result this was the only feature film directed by Bass. It has since gained a cult following due to TV airings beginning in 1975 and also when the film was shown on "Mystery Science Theater 3000".

The film bears some similarity to an earlier film, The Hellstrom Chronicle. Both feature extensive use of close-up photography of actual insects. Despite the lurid tone of its poster art based on one of the shocking images from the film, Phase IV approaches its subject matter naturalistically, with relatively little melodrama. The film contains relatively little dialogue, mainly relaying the storyline visually. http://en.wikipedia.org/wiki/Phase_IV

My only two reasons to go to Briggs Hall were to "report in" with Ward Stanger, who kept his office in that building, and a Group Study course in Pollination Ecology that was taught jointly by Robin Thorp and Grady Webster. This was an extremely interesting course about all the interactions of insects and plants purely for the purpose of propagating. Fascinating stuff like the African milkweed plant that presents its pollen in little saddle bags.[25] It tricks the pollinating insect to catch its foot in a fissure in the flower head, and when the insect frees itself from the plant, the saddle bags are attached to its legs. When it flies to the next flower and gets its leg caught again, the saddle bag is deposited and fertilization occurs. Or how about the many species of orchid whose stigma looks like or smells like the female of a species of wasp? One even vibrates in the wind like a female wasp feeding on the nectar. When the male tries to copulate with the stigma, the pollen attached to his body fertilizes the flower. The hammer orchids[26] of Australia have really

---

[25] **Milkweeds** have a unique and fascinating pollination mechanism in which the plant relies on butterflies, moths, bees, ants, and wasps for pollination. Hundreds of pollen grains are packaged into two connected sacs, which is collectively referred to as the pollinarium. When a foraging insect lands on a flower, the pollinarium can easily attach itself to its leg. Once removed from the flower, the pollinia actually re-orient as the translator arms bend as they dry. Upon landing on another flower, the properly oriented pollinarium is deposited into a receptive stigmatic groove where the pollinia breaks down and the pollen germinates, growing pollen tubes through the stigma to the ovules in the ovary. http://hannibalsanimals.blogspot.com/2009/07/saddle-bags-full-of-pollen.html

[26] Drakaea is an endangered genus of orchid that is native to Australia. Orchids in this genus are commonly called "**Hammer Orchids**". The common name refers to the shape of the orchid, and the way it moves, resembling a hammer. The genus was named after Miss Drake, a botanical artist who drew orchids and other plants to assist taxonomists in England in the 19th century. Members of the Drakaea genus are characterized by an insectival labellum that is attached to a narrow, hinged stem, which holds it aloft. The stem can only hinge backwards, where the broadly winged column carries the pollen and stigma.

Hammer orchids have specified their method of pollination by only being pollinated by the Thynnid wasp. The female wasps being flightless wait on top of stems for the males, to fly in and carry them off. Then they will mate in mid-flight. Hammer orchids being deceitful mimic the female wasps, their labellum being similar in color and in structure to the female wasp's abdomen. The orchids also produce pheromones very similar to those that the female wasp produces. The female wasp produces the pheromones to attract the male. When the male becomes attracted by the pheromones released by the orchid and its shape, it tries to fly away with the labellum, which makes the stem holding it move backwards. Which in turn brings the male wasp's thorax in contact with the sticky pollen packet. The male wasp will become tired of trying and fly off. In order for the Hammer orchid to be successfully pollinated, the male wasp must be fooled by another individual orchid, where it goes through the same procedure. But this time the pollen is deposited in the stigma, and so that plant has been pollinated. This form of symbiosis is not mutualistic, the wasp getting nothing in return for having pollinated the hammer orchid. http://en.wikipedia.org/wiki/Drakaea

outsmarted the Thynnid wasps that pollinate them. The wasp does all the work and gets nothing in return.

Objectively, I had assumed I would be attaching myself to the Entomology Department as my major emphasis, but I had not found a major professor, and I was also taking courses in the Botany Department. I took a plant physiology seminar and a synecology course. The plant physiology was team taught, and I was amazed at how much they had learned since I was at University of Washington. Not only had they described the entire photosynthetic pathway, but they had discovered three of them, and suspected there were probably more. A far cry from the days of Our Friend the Sun, and the little cartoon chef who went behind the curtain to "bake up" some sugars (i.e. photosynthesis).

Synecology is one of two broad subdivisions of ecology and means the study of groups of organisms associated as a unit (essentially a biological community), as opposed to autecology which studies the individual organism or species. My professor was Jack Majors, and until I read his memorial[27] I did not realize how influential he had been in the field of Ecology. He was an impressive man, tall

---

[27] **Jack Majors** was born 15 March 1917 in Salt Lake City, UT and completed high school there in 1935. He went on to Utah State Agricultural College (now Utah State University) and received a B.S. in range management in 1942. For the next several years he served in the Army's 10th Mountain Division, the justifiably famous unit of 1000 skiers and alpinists who trained hard in the mountain west before participating in the Italian campaign of World War II. Afterwards, a number of men from the 10th went on to become conservationists, ecologists, and leaders in the promotion of recreational skiing. Between 1946 and 1953, Jack attended the University of California, Berkeley, obtaining a Ph.D. in soil science under the direction of Professor Hans Jenny. During this time he also met and married Mary Cecil, thanks to an introduction from brother Teed who had met Mary by chance on a rock climbing expedition in the Grand Tetons. She, too, had a love for the mountains.

Jack was then hired into a young weed science group in the Department of Botany. His strong interest in the ecology of undisturbed mountain vegetation, however, conflicted with the group's focus on plants in agronomic, low-elevation settings. He gradually moved away from weed science, and a 1964 Fulbright Fellowship to Innsbruck, Austria was to cement a lifetime's focus on vegetation science.

One measure of Professor Major's vision and impact is that several of his earliest papers are still cited today, in some cases more often than when they were first published. Four articles published between 1951 and 1966 – on topics that ranged from the theoretical to the descriptive – have collectively been cited 620 times in the past 25 years and continue to be described in textbooks published a half-century later.

His forte in teaching was with small groups because his low-key manner was not well suited to large lecture sections or busloads of field-trip students. His method of teaching was Socratic, inviting questions and asking questions back, usually including his stock phrase, "Is this alright?" He was mentor to more than 20 graduate students of his own and to many more

and sinewy as a result of his extensive field trips, which began in WWII in the Ski Corps. Traveling to a mesa in northern California, one became very aware of Jack's comprehensive assessment of the natural world. One time he had the class discuss a paper that was very seminal in my mind and to my future career. The author had put his students to work making an inventory of every plant on an acre of land. Then they subjected the plot to all the known methods of quantitatively estimating the populations of plant species. The most accurate technique, as they discovered was the Wandering Quadrant technique[28], but it required up to 600 measurements to obtain 80% accuracy, and all that for only one species. Lyons gleefully pointed out, in the discussion section, that the author had asked experienced field ecologists make an educated guess at the species densities and found them to be more accurate than most techniques, and with far less effort. Jack was one of those kinds of ecologist; he just understood the dynamics of a growing, evolving community of plants. Not unlike the people of the Modoc-Lassen tribe, he knew the land so well that he could tell you where the wild onions would grow. He was also a very interesting teacher, and I managed to get an A in his class.

I also enrolled in Dr. Laidlaw's class, Advanced Apiculture 219. I would say that the title was appropriate because I think we were given as contemporary information as was available in any honeybee research program in the world. First, we were learning Dr. Laidlaw's seminal insemination technique for which "He is recognized by his peers worldwide as the 'father of honeybee genetics', and perhaps is best known for developing artificial insemination technology for honeybees. His work enabled selective breeding of honeybees and the fundamental study of insect genetics."[29] Second, we were learning the latest approaches to disease management with particular emphasis on American Foul Brood. Third, we were gaining a fundamental understanding of the intricacies of bee biology and the importance of managing bees with their fundamental behavior in mind. Harry took us to visit Oliver Hill's

---

via correspondence or by way of serving as a member on their thesis/ dissertation committees. Excerpted from http://www.universityofcalifornia.edu/senate/inmemoriam/JackMajor.htm

[28] **Lyon** (1968) found that the wandering quarter method gave an accurate estimate of density in a shrub community in which all individuals had been enumerated. To achieve a reasonably precise estimate of density, however, actual counts were quicker than sampling with points and distance measures.

Lyons, J. L. 1968. Any evaluation of density sampling methods in a shrub community. *Journal of Range Management* 21: 16-21.

[29] http://www.universityofcalifornia.edu/senate/inmemoriam/HarryHydeLaidlawJr.htm

Apiary and the Apiary of a friend of Oliver's father who was still alive and managing bees in the very careful way of the true beekeeper. Harry also took us to the biggest commercial apiary in Glen County and pointed out the inconsistency of trying to maximize production by mechanization. Dr. Laidlaw was of the opinion that the failure to pay attention to the basic biology of the bees would eventually lead to problems, and, as anyone who listens to the news these days knows, it did! I learned a lot from Harry H. Laidlaw, and he gave me an A for the course.

Pollination ecology was particularly fascinating (although I only got a B in the course) because Grady Webster was one of the most expert taxonomists of Euphorbia in the world and Robbin Thorp was rapidly becoming one of the top authorities on pollinating insects. Grady died in 2001 but Robbin[30] was still going strong, still publishing, and, although emeritus, very much involved in expanding the reputation of the H.H. Laidlaw Bee Biology Center. According to a recent correspondence with him, UC Davis has hired a Sustainable Pollination Biologist and is in the process of restoring the faculty position of Apiculture Scientist, which they have been without for several years. I would venture to say that the graduates of that course knew as much about pollination ecology as any in the United States. Of course, there are scientists all over the world that specialize in unique pollination systems, but this course had a most comprehensive approach to the subject.

This is what I meant when I said that the first quarter at U. C. Davis was the best. In one short quarter, I learned as much about pollination, apiculture, and ecology as I would need throughout my career. I left Davis at the end of that quarter to work in the Environmental Research Unit of Weyerhaeuser Company. Although it was supposed to be a summer job, it led to a permanent job in the Wood Morphology Group, where, besides learning all forms of microscopy, I obtained funding for a study of pollination in Douglas fir, *Pseudotsuga mensiesii*. That, in turn, led to my being hired to head the Pollination Project at the Weyerhaeuser Forestry Research Lab under Dr. Jess Daniels, the geneticist. Basically, I owe these jobs more to my experience in the first quarter at U. C. Davis than to the whole undergraduate program in Botany. Not that the latter was unhelpful, and that knowledge has been with me throughout, but it was the U.C. Davis first quarter experience that gave me the direction to pursue.

---

[30] **Robbin Thorp** died in 2019 at age 85 https://ucanr.edu/blogs/blogcore/postdetail. cfm?postnum=30463

Although it had been a busy quarter, and I had not had much time for socializing, we did have some interesting times in the apartment. Our arrangement was to have community dinners, where the cooking would rotate between three of us. Raul was on a very tight budget, so he opted to cook on his own. His weekly fare was one roasted chicken, one pot of rice, and ketchup, which he managed to stretch over the week. Of course, if we ever invited him to join us in the community meal, he very eagerly accepted! I remember Fernando's meals to be quite interesting because it was like Mexican food with flair. His food was not so spicy but it would have things like beets julienne on a tostada -- it was similar to Southwestern Cuisine before we knew there was such a thing. Fernando had a very sweet girlfriend from Sacramento who would join us for dinner from time to time. He eventually married her and took her to Guatemala. However, political conditions brought them back to the USA, and Fernando, now Dr. Juan F. Medrano, is a faculty member in the Animal Science Department at U. C. Davis.

Raul was a very sociable guy, and I liked him as much as any of the roommates. We also had the International Agriculture Development program in common. I think Raul could probably have gone on to get his doctorate but was so excited about the coming of Salvador Allende to the Presidency of Chile that he finished his master's degree program and hurried home to serve in the new socialistic government. I have no idea what happened to Raul when Pinochet overthrew the legally elected government of Chile with considerable help from the United States.[31] I can only hope that Raul somehow learned to lay low or emigrated from Chile to Argentina.

---

[31] Augusto José Ramón **Pinochet** Ugarte (25 November 1915 – 10 December 2006) was a Chilean army general and president who assumed power in a coup d'état on 11 September 1973. Among his titles, he was the Commander-in-Chief of the Chilean army from 1973 to 1998, president of the Government Junta of Chile from 1973 to 1974 and President of the Republic from 1974 until transferring power to a democratically elected president in 1990. Pinochet is alleged to be responsible for various human rights abuses during his reign including murder and torture of political opponents. According to a government commission report that included testimony from more than 30,000 people, Pinochet's government killed at least 3,197 people and tortured about 29,000. Two-thirds of the cases listed in the report happened in 1973.

The U.S. provided material support to the military regime after the coup, although criticizing it in public. A document released by the U.S. Central Intelligence Agency (CIA) in 2000, titled "CIA Activities in Chile", revealed that the CIA actively supported the military junta after the overthrow of Allende and that it made many of Pinochet's officers into paid contacts of the CIA or U.S. military, even though some were known to be involved in human rights abuses.

However, while the US certainly supported the Pinochet regime after the 1973 coup, there is no evidence that the US assisted or backed this coup. The Church Report concluded

Lance and I shared a room, but our schedules were very different. Being a drama major, he was often out to the wee hours of the morning, while I was usually up and gone hours before he arose. He was available for dinner more often than not, so I really don't remember what his schedule was. From his conversation it was clear that the arts are <u>far</u> less rigid than the sciences. I was a bit shocked when he would talk about the nude gatherings that were necessary to accustom the students to being comfortable in their skin. I can't remember if we were ever invited to any performances in which he acted. I cannot Google him to see what happened to him because I don't remember his last name. I will admit that, although I was still in monastic mode in that first quarter at Davis, when I returned seven years later, my lifestyle changed considerably as did my moral certitude.

Third annual Whole Earth Festival poster.(Was available CC BY-SA 4.0 from the Whole Earth Festival archive at Shields Library, Univ. California Davis) http://wef. ucdavis.edu/old/wefhistory/Posters/index.htm

---

that while the US had not supported the 1973 coup, it had supported an attempted coup in 1970, and had directed money to anti-Allende elements during the period 1970-1973, including possibly terrorist groups. http://en.wikipedia.org/wiki/Augusto_Pinochet

I don't even think I attended the Whole Earth Festival that quarter. This hang over from the Sixties was held in the spring when the weather brought out the wild side of the pressured students. Hippies from all over the West Coast were in abundance. I don't know if Wavy Gravy[32] was there that year, but he was still attending the festival in 1979 to 1983. The music went on all day and well into the night. Most of it I missed because I did the bulk of my studying in the Library or far off in the Bee Biology Facility.

U. C. Davis had a premier lecture series, but I don't remember attending any. I did hear Ed Teller[33] pontificate in his growly voice while pounding his cane on the wooden stage. I had recently seen "Dr. Strangelove"[34]; the resemblance was uncanny. This probably was in 1972, because, by the time I returned to Davis in 1979, Teller was advocating for President Reagan's Star War Initiative. I don't think the subject was discussed at Teller's lecture. I do remember noticing how similar Teller's voice was to that of Henry Kissinger. Henry the Hard was already suspected of being involved in the sinister actions in Chile. I remember thinking, "Is this the voice of the devil?" Probably the reason I attended the lecture was because the lecture committee could not charge the usual admission for fear no one would attend.

I didn't even use the athletic facility that quarter. I am not sure that the Recreation Activities Center (ARC) had been built yet in 1972, but the Recreation Pool and the Hickey Gym pool were both available. I guess I got most of my exercise riding the 2 miles back and forth from campus to the apartment and the additional 6 miles round trip to the Bee Biology Facility

---

[32] **Wavy Gravy** (born Hugh Nanton Romney 15 May 1936) is an American entertainer and activist for peace, best known for his hippie appearance, personality and beliefs. His moniker (which is the name he uses on a day to day basis) was given to him by B.B. King at the Texas International Pop Festival in 1969. "It's worked pretty well through my life," he says, "except with telephone operators – I have to say 'Gravy, first initial W."

Romney's clown persona resulted from his political activism. Frequently being arrested at demonstrations, he decided he would be less likely to be arrested if he dressed as a clown. "Clowns are safe," he said. He does, however, enjoy traditional clown activities such as jokes, magic tricks and entertaining children.

[33] **Ed Teller** (Hungarian: Teller Ede, January 15, 1908 – September 9, 2003) was an Austro-Hungarian-born American theoretical physicist, known colloquially as "the father of the hydrogen bomb," even though he did not care for the title.

[34] **Dr. Strangelove** or: How I Learned to Stop Worrying and Love the Bomb (commonly known as Dr. Strangelove) is a 1964 black comedy film which satirized the nuclear scare. It was directed, produced, and co-written by Stanley Kubrick, starring Peter Sellers and George C. Scott, and featuring Sterling Hayden, Keenan Wynn, Slim Pickens, and Tracy Reed. Loosely based on Peter George's Cold War thriller novel Red Alert, a.k.a. Two Hours to Doom.

often against a strong coastal wind that blew up the Sacramento River. On the whole, it was a very intense academic quarter and yielded the highest GPA I ever had, 3.7. Needless to say it got me off academic probation, but there were no girls, no beer blast, no drugs, and no typical college student behavior. I was there to learn and I did.

# Chapter 4

# Forced Labor

Your people are scattered on the mountains
    with none to gather them.
There is no easing your hurt;
    your wound is grievous.
All who hear the news about you
    clap their hands over you.
**English Standard Version (2001) Nahum 3:18-19**

What is success? Is it for what you decide to strive, or is it for what society tells you to strive? Are you bettered by conforming to the needs and dictates of society or are you more likely to better society by stepping beyond its boundaries. It is a risky decision either way; the horns of a dilemma as old as man. If you let society decide your fate, are you then responsible for the consequences? But if you collar your own fate, you have no one to blame but yourself. Or do you even have a choice? Are we all just pawns in a game of chance, where the best laid strategies are subjected to the vagaries of existence? Probably?

As the end of the quarter approached, it was clear that I did not have the money to continue without finding substantial employment. And while there were summer jobs on campus, these tended to go to the students of the professors, or the research associates or the work-study recipients, whose tab was paid in significant part by the government. I was not yet in any of those categories, so I was contemplating returning to Hill Apiaries. But the pay rate at Willows was not attractive, and I saw a job posting on the departmental board. It was at my old stomping grounds in Longview, WA.

It was being offered by the company that got me through my undergraduate degree, Weyerhaeuser. What's more, I did not know that it was being offered in the company's Environmental Services Group, the Director of which was a member of my parish and the father of a classmate in my elementary school, St. Rose. Maybe it is not who you know, but who knows you.

What goes into the decisions of a young man, who has just successfully completed his first quarter of graduate school, and hopes to continue? Find out how I can make the most possible money in one summer, that's what! In that, I shared objectives with every graduate student that ever went to college. The problem is that money was not my only objective. I was still trying to figure out how I could possibly get back together with my adopted family in Africa. At that time, I think I realized that it would take the additional education to ever be able to return to international service. But I also realized that the education was not going to happen if I couldn't figure out how to pay for it.

I had left the family in Africa thinking I would return. I had left them with everything I had acquired over my tour of duty in Peace Corps, and I had purchased a house and ~4 acres of land for them. Although it was not my intention to leave them, I thought they would probably survive by using their subsistence farming skills. I did not realize that the property's greatest benefit was, at the same time, its greatest hazard, proximity to a lowland swamp. While they had moisture to grow their crops, they also had to deal with abundant mosquitos and the ubiquitous malaria. The oldest daughter was a nurse in Tana River, far from Taita. She was sufficiently well paid to have helped her mother out in a pinch (until she became an unwed mother also). The oldest son was in high school, and capable of helping with the farm chores. The youngest daughter was able to help with the younger boys, and free Charity for the task of running the farm. I don't remember how much actual money I was able to send them to subsidize their income, but a US dollar went a long way in Kenya in 1972. And of course, there was always the extended family, which, in most cases will come together to help a family member in need. That is if they have the resources to do so. In some ways, Charity and the family were more secure in their situation than I was in mine.

Not knowing whether I might or might not be considered for the job at Weyerhaeuser, I nevertheless applied. At least I would not have to find a place to live, because I knew that my father and Elizabeth would be willing to let me stay with them in the little cabin on the Toutle, which by then had been nearly doubled in size by the addition of a master bedroom and bath. The tent platform was still in the woods behind the house, and I would have only to erect the tent to have private quarters. In addition, they were offering me a little sixties-vintage Toyota Corolla to solve my problem of transportation to and from work.

I had not visited my Mother at the parish in Galt often, if at all, during the spring quarter, so I made an effort to get back to visit them just after I heard that I was to be hired by Rudy Thut at Weyerhaeuser that summer. I think Fr. Carl had brought my mother over to Davis a couple of times during the quarter on his Thursday *diem liberate*. We would have dinner at one of the local restaurants, and Mom would usually be hauling along a "CARE" package, not unlike the ones she used to bring to St. Francis Seminary on visiting days when I was in high school. Actually it is more likely that Fr. Carl came with my mother to pick me up from Davis when I was leaving the apartment. I generally traveled light, but I am sure there was more paraphernalia than I could have carried on the bus back to Galt.

What I don't remember is how I managed to work out the deal with Oliver Hill to take 50 hives to the Pacific Northwest with me. I can only think that Oliver's brother-in-law, who was himself from the Tenino area in Washington, brought the bees to the Toutle River in Oliver's flat-bed Ford I vaguely remember off-loading the bees with him in a couple of yards I had arranged along the Tower Road on Toutle River. I am not sure whether this happened after I had already started work at Weyerhaeuser, or whether I actually travelled to Washington with the brother-in-law (which is the more likely scenario). I remember bringing the hives back to California, but not how they got to Washington. Oliver had even thoughtfully included a hand-cranked extractor, so I could extract honey if the supers filled up before I could return the beehives to California in the fall. The arrangement was exploratory. Oliver had little honey flow in the mid to late summer, and usually had to feed his bees to keep up there population through the winter. We were hoping the Northwest would provide an alternative honey flow to tide the honeybee colonies over the winter.

More important to the decision to take beehives to Washington was whether my parents would approve. I am sure my Dad was skeptical, but Elizabeth was, I guess, impressed that I was intent on trying to subsidize my income with business. Once we got the bees to the northwest, Elizabeth, who was an Internal Revenue agent, helped me understand how to keep books and control business costs. I don't think they knew what they were getting into. Nor did I!

When I started work at Weyerhaeuser Environmental Research, I met Dr. Gene Haydu, the Director, briefly before Mr. Rudolf Thut took me over to meet the staff. Rudy was the Forest ecologist, I believe, and Bob Herrmann was the limnologist. Or was it the other way around? I am not sure. I went to work for Bob initially because there were ongoing surveys at the Gray's Harbor Pulp mills effluent area. The oyster farmers on Gray's Harbors were claiming that the pulp mill effluents were killing their spat. Spat are the baby Oysters, and they are sensitive to water salinity. Grays Harbor has been an oyster growing area for many years.

So, once a week, we would load up a truck, and three of the staff including myself would go to Grays Harbor the day before we were to boat out to take the samples. I guess we needed to be early so that samples could be transported back to the lab and analyzed that same day. I am sure the overnight at a local hotel with topless bar had nothing to do with the scheduling. One of the staff was a Nez Perce Native American, who had relatives in Grays Harbor. I enjoyed the visits to his relative's house, although the conversation was hard to follow. Native Americans have a cryptic sense of humor, which impresses the outsider as a kind of slapstick, but I am sure has much deeper meaning that only the tribe understands. I had a bit harder time following the movements of the topless dancers… or should I say the difficulty was following the staff's conversations when distracted by the writhing half-naked bodies. I generally would excuse myself after about one beer.

Very early the next morning, we would meet the resident staff person, who piloted the Weyerhaeuser boat. He would take us to a series of pilings along the waterfront, and we would take turbidity readings with the white disk, lowered into the water on a graduated chain. Then we would pull up the water sampler and collect and replace the vials. These would be analyzed for nitrogen, dissolved oxygen, precise acidity, and acid for mineral content. The results of the long months of testing had indicated that the clarifying ponds[35] did a good job of removing effluent before it reached the river. I think we also brought back jugs of river water that were used in a live bio-toxicity test. Fingerling trout (I think that was the species) in flowing water tanks were subjected to the effluent from Greys

---

[35] PAUL Hodges Aug. 14, 1945 (files Jan. 19, 1942) U. S. Patent Number 2,382,010 "PROCESS FOR THE TREATMENT OF PAPER MILL EFFLUENT" http://www. freepatentsonline.com/2382010.pdf

Harbor, to see if they would survive. These were conducted by a couple of ex-Vietnam helicopter pilots.

Bob took the fact that these tests all came back negative to mean that something else was affecting the spat, so he took it upon himself to collect runoff data from the flow monitors on the Chehalis River which feeds the bay. This data he assigned to me to calculate the regression over the 30 years from World War II to the present. We had the latest and greatest technology. It was a Wang Calculator[36]. To my knowledge, it could not be connected to anything else, and it could be programmed to perform calculations. It was probably the earliest and simplest model. It took me almost a month to calculate the regression, which required that I manually compute all the squares and sums of squares, and then perform the calculations of the regression equation. I remember it was so peculiar to watch the little number displays, each of which had separate filaments shaped into the numerals 0 to 9 inside of each vacuum tube. When a given tube needed to read 0, that filament would glow. Ah the marching progress of technology. The first computers were also built of vacuum tubes.

**Wang calculator** with vacuum-tube lighted display. (CC BY SA 4.0)

---

[36] **The Wang** LOCI-2 (an earlier LOCI-1 was not a real product) was introduced in 1965 and was probably the first desktop calculator capable of computing logarithms, quite an achievement for a machine without any integrated circuits. The electronics included 1275 discrete transistors. It actually performed multiplication by adding logarithms, and roundoff in the display conversion was noticeable: 2 times 2 yielded 3.999999999.

From 1965 to about 1971, Wang was a well-regarded calculator company. Wang calculators cost in the mid-four-figures, used Nixie tube readouts, performed transcendental functions, had varying degrees of programmability, and exploited magnetic core memory in ingenious ways. One model had a central processing unit (the size of a small suitcase) connected by cables leading to four individual desktop display/keyboard units. Competition included HP, which introduced the HP 9100A in 1968, and old-line calculator companies such as Monroe and Marchant. One little documented "feature" of these calculators was that you could predictably lock-up the calculator display heads, getting the Nixie tube display to endlessly "roll" numbers, by entering the sequence 30311142.59 [Enter] 99 [Enter] 9 [Enter].

The Wang Calculator.
In 1969, electronic calculators had arrived in the department. This is a picture of the Wang "shared logic" calculators being used in Chemistry. A central electronics package (5" x 8" x 24") was connected to up to 8 user stations by a multiple conductor cable. These stations were distributed throughout the building. The Wangs were still in use in 1972. http://www2.chemistry.msu.edu/History/CPUHist5.shtml

The net effect of the calculations was that they showed a gradual linear increase in watershed runoff, but you could clearly see from the plot of the readings that post WWII and mid-sixties runoff was higher than normal. These were, of course, periods of population growth when a lot of new homes were being built all over the country. I think Bob was ordered to tone down that part of his report when he submitted the data on Grays Harbor Pollution. The pollution was not coming from the pulp mills. It was, in fact, too much fresh water that was coming from destruction of watershed and was reducing the salinity of the harbor. Oyster spat don't survive in pure salt water or pure rainwater; they have a very specific requirement for brackish water.

The calculators were not the only computing technology that Weyerhaeuser had at the time. As I calculated away on the Wang, I sat next to a keyboard console that converted typed data into rolls of punched tape. This was then fed into what was, I assume, a DEC mini-computer that was about as big as a small closet. So, although I was not shown how to use any of this "higher technology" I was being absorbed into 'cyber space' by proximity alone.

On one occasion I was assigned to accompany one of the technicians on a highly prestigious assignment. I didn't really realize what it was about until we arrived at the new Weyerhaeuser Corporate Headquarters building in Federal Way, Washington. It seems the corporate executives had wanted a small lake in front of the building so they could look out their office windows onto the pristine waters. Of course it was not pristine, because it had been dredged out of the woods when the building was constructed. I will say that Weyerhaeuser did leave a nice stand of second growth Douglas fir around the headquarters campus, but the lake was not a natural formation by any stretch of the imagination. Consequently, the "lake" began to develop its own biota, which frankly resembled that of a slough more than a lake. This was a matter of much concern to the corporate magnates, so Environmental Research was tasked with the "proper" evolution of this aquatic creation.

The staff had previously stocked the lake with trout, so our first duty upon launching our dinghy on the lake was to fish. Of course, these were not fish to take home and eat. We measured the fish and threw them back in the brown water. Then we measured the turbidity with the white disc, which disappeared almost immediately as it sank in the water... not too impressive. Then we took dissolved oxygen samples etc. It was such a productive day, with all of that high priority work, we decided to stop for steak and lobster on our way back to Longview. This was at George Weyerhaeuser's expense, of course!

All of these samples that were being brought back were analyzed by two chemists. The older of the two was from North Carolina. I kick myself for not remembering his name, because he was a character in the true southern sense of the word. He loved to hunt and talked about hunting and fishing all the time. He would eventually be following my bees (*i.e.* Oliver's) to the mountains to hunt "Bar".

One week, we went as a group to the high Cascades for some sampling expedition, the purpose of which I cannot recall. I was in a truck driven by one of the Vietnam pilots. Now that was a hair-raising experience! I had the distinct sensation of being bounced around in a Huey gunship, presumably under enemy fire. It was a beautiful day, and we saw some really elegant herds of elk with the males calling their harems. It would have been so much more enjoyable if I had not spent all the driving time worrying about whether we would run into a 50 ton, loaded, logging truck around the next curve.

The other regular task was to sample the experimental stream that the Environmental Group had constructed on the Kalama River. It consisted of 3 identical stream beds that were built to allow different amounts of chemicals to be feed into the streams and then observe what impact that had on trout in the streams. There was one big problem, A Great Blue Heron had discerned the plan, and was intent on foiling the experiment. The Environmental Research staff did everything they could to try to discourage the bird from eating the trout in the test streams. Even the sound of the sonic blaster was too regular and predictable to outsmart the wily heron. In the end, the only effective control method was to send a hunter after it. This fell to the Nez Perce, who would take a shotgun, and spend the night at the mountain research lab/lodging and stalk the great bird. My impression was that the intention was not to kill the magnificent bird, but just shooting at it unexpectedly. This was a more effective deterrent than all the automated control methods.

My last assignment that summer was from Rudy Thut. There was an old growth stand of forest that had never been logged next to the mountain laboratory on the Kalama River. That patch of forest was scheduled to be clear cut that fall, so Rudy wanted to get an inventory of the plant species before that habitat was destroyed. It was along a stream, which I believe was called Cold Creek. Since I had taken Plant Taxonomy and Synecology, Rudy assigned this task to me. I will describe that activity later.

Meantime I am trying to get squared away with the honeybees on my weekends. It was certainly enough to keep me out of trouble, and probably Elizabeth's adopted son Jerry as well. Jerry was prone to juvenile delinquency when he was in high school, but he seemed interested in learning about the honeybees. So I took him with me for bee inspections. Oliver had provided me with a couple of bee veils, and I think I had a pair of gloves, which, by that time, I no longer used to work bees. But I did not have an extra set of coveralls, which is what I always wore to work bees. So Jerry would follow me into the bee yards with his veil and gloves but wearing jeans and a shirt. Now, Oliver's bees were well bred and not aggressive, but you couldn't help getting stung once in a while. I was trying to bring the best methods of beekeeping that I had learned from Harry Laidlaw to this small apiary, so I showed Jerry how to inspect a hive, frame by frame, and record the important details. These included the presence of a queen, which you knew to be the case if you could see eggs younger than 3 days old. We were also looking for any signs of foul brood or Nosema diseases, treating with Terramycin as needed. We also counted frames of brood and capped honey. He took to the challenge, but I would occasionally hear some expletives when a bee would find her way into his shirt or under his veil. By the way, Jerry went on to worked on a dredge in the Columbia and joined the Navy Seals (I don't remember in which order).

Soon it became necessary to move supers (boxes of honeycomb frames) around from one bee yard to next. I could fit a couple of supers in the trunk of the little Toyota, but it was becoming clear that I needed a more substantial vehicle for this work. And the Toyota was not running well. It would die when idling at a stop light and it was getting harder to restart. Meanwhile I was eying a grand old 1949 GMC one-ton that the neighbor down the road owned. He was a mechanic and had restored the truck to good condition, with an aqua marine paint job and a 4 ft., white, wooden rack around the 10 ft. flat bed. Finally I got the nerve to come out and ask him if he wanted to sell it. He was reluctant but asked what I was offering. I said I would trade a late model Toyota. He said, "I'll take a look".

So we drove the Toyota up the Tower Road until he was satisfied that he knew what was causing the problem with the ignition. He said, "Give me 50 bucks and the Toyota, and you can have the truck". I was ecstatic, but I was not too sure the folks would be. However, after some discussion of the consequences, they agreed to sign the title over to the neighbor, and I took possession of my second General Motors truck. Only this was a real truck! Dualies on the rear axle, one-ton load capacity, straight six block with low gear ratio. Perfect for keeping bees, with the one exception; it had the big old split-rim tires wheels, so the bed hit me about at my solar plexus. Try lifting fifty 100+ lbs. beehives to chest height.

We were not far into the summer when I determined that we were not getting much honey flow on the Tower Road sights that I had chosen. In the summer, there is a lot of evergreen, but flowering trees and bushes have pretty much finished blooming in June. There are later blooms of fireweed and tansy ragweed on the Weyerhaeuser clear cuts, but the woods along the Toutle River consists mostly of fir and alder and hemlock, some sugar maple. Salal, blackberry and grass are the most common ground cover, but they bloom early also. The only solution for the bees was to move to higher elevation, where flowers were still blooming.

I greatly appreciated Jerry's willingness to help with the move, because it would have been a lot harder to load the bees by myself. I had not yet seen Oliver perform the gargantuan feat of un-stacking 400 beehives off a semi (tractor) trailer. As night set in, we drove into the pasture at dusk and collected the hives. Then we proceeded up the Toutle River highway, and off on a Weyerhaeuser road that led to a ridge, along which we deposited the bees. I had previously scouted the area and obtained permission from Weyerhaeuser. It was on one of those many ridges surrounding Mount St. Helens, and there was an impressive view of the mountain from the ridge. The fireweed was just beginning to bloom, and I was assuming that there would be a good flow of nectar from the open valley below where the hives were placed. I was not entirely wrong about that, but I was forgetting about black bears. They like open berry-laden valleys when they are trying to build up their fat reserve for winter. If I were more of an outdoorsman, I would have known that the beehives were placed right along a bear trail. But we left the hives thinking all was well and anticipating clear white fireweed honey.

I enjoyed being back on the Toutle again, being wakened by the chattering chipmunks in the trees above my tent. Of course, this time I did not disturb their expeditions during the daytime, because I was out the door at 7 AM to get to Weyerhaeuser by 8 AM. Not quite banker's hours but close enough for one who had worked shift work all through college. I suppose I did some swimming in the Toutle but I think I must have been too busy to do that often. In that regard, the Spartan life was continuing.

There were a couple of summer interns who were women, but I did not work with them often. They were doing streambed samplings for Rudy Thut (who was, in fact the limnologist). After they collected samples they would spend the rest of the week counting copepods and other aquatic life forms under the stereoscope. I would have found that tedious, but they seemed to be very happy to do it. Of course, they could both talk and count. Maybe that is a fundamental difference between the sexes? One of those women eventually ended up at Weyerhaeuser Forestry Research in Centralia as did I. I would not be surprised if she might still be working for "Mother Weyerhaeuser." I hear that the other woman went to work as a biologist at the Trojan Nuclear Power Plant[37].

Unfortunately, that only gave that biologist temporary job security, because the nuclear plant had to be shut down and demolished after only 16 years. That was one of the misguided brainchildren of Dixie Lee Ray[38]. What

---

[37] **Trojan Nuclear Power Plant** was a pressurized water reactor nuclear power plant in Rainier, Oregon, United States, and the only commercial nuclear power plant to be built in Oregon. After sixteen years of service it was closed by its operator, Portland General Electric (PGE), almost twenty years before the end of its design lifetime. Decommissioning and demolition of the plant began in 1993 and was completed in 2006, except for the spent fuel pool containing highly radioactive waste such as the spent fuel rods still stored at the Trojan site.

The Trojan steam generators were designed to last the life of the plant, but it was only four years before premature cracking of the steam tubes was observed.

In 1992, PGE spent $4.5 million to defeat ballot measures seeking to close Trojan. It was the most expensive ballot measure campaign in Oregon history until the tobacco industry spent $12 million in 2007 to defeat Measure 50. A week later the Trojan plant suffered another steam generator tube leak of radioactive water, and was shut down. It was announced that replacement of the steam generators would be necessary. In December 1992, documents were leaked from the U.S. Nuclear Regulatory Commission showing that staff scientists believed that Trojan might be unsafe to operate. In January 1993, chief plant engineer David Fancher, acting as spokesman for PGE, announced the company would not try to restart Trojan. http://en.wikipedia.org/wiki/Trojan_Nuclear_Power_Plant

[38] **Dixy Lee Ray** (September 3, 1914–January 2, 1994) was the 17th Governor of the U.S. State of Washington. She was Washington's first female governor. Ray was a marine biologist and taught at the University of Washington from 1947 until 1972. In 1952 she received a prestigious John Simon Guggenheim Memorial Foundation fellowship grant for Biology. From 1963 until 1972, Dr. Ray became the director of Seattle's Pacific Science Center, guiding its future after the founding as part of the 1962 World's Fair. An advocate of nuclear power,

they don't tell about her on Wikipedia is that she had plans to authorize the construction of 20 nuclear plants in the Pacific Northwest, an area that has one of the greatest resources for hydroelectric power in the United States. Instead she wanted to convert the state to nuclear energy? The poor performance of the Trojan plant helped the environmentalist defeat her potentially cataclysmic plan. Every time I hear talk of reviving nuclear energy in the United States, I think about the Trojan. In case you thought it was history, the following sad commentary demonstrates that we still do <u>not</u> know what to do with the nuclear waste.

> In 2005, the reactor vessel and other radioactive equipment were removed from the Trojan plant, encased in concrete foam, shrink-wrapped, and transported intact by barge along the Columbia River to Hanford Nuclear Reservation in Washington, where it was buried in a 45-foot-deep (14 m) pit and covered with 6 inches (150 mm) of gravel, which made it the first commercial reactor to be moved and buried whole. The spent fuel is stored onsite in 34 dry casks, awaiting transport to the Yucca Mountain Repository. The iconic 499-foot-tall (152 m) cooling tower, visible from Interstate 5 in Washington, was demolished via dynamite implosion at 7:00 a.m. on May 21, 2006. This event marked the first implosion of a cooling tower at a nuclear plant in the United States. Additional demolition work on the remaining structures was to continue through 2008. The central office building, and the reactor building were demolished by Northwest Demolition and Dismantling in 2008. Remaining are five buildings: two warehouses, a small building on the river side, a guard shack, and offices outside the secured facility. There is also extensive underground infrastructure still to be demolished. http://en.wikipedia. org/wiki/Trojan_Nuclear_Power_Plant

---

she was appointed by Richard Nixon to chair the U.S. Atomic Energy Commission in 1973 and was the only woman to serve as chair of the AEC. In 1975, Dr. Ray was appointed and served as the first Assistant Secretary of State for Oceans and International Environmental and Scientific Affairs. http://en.wikipedia.org/wiki/Dixy_Lee_Ray

Please excuse me for getting off on that tangent, but it is just another example of how the grandiose plans of men (and women) come unglued with predictable impact on the lives of ordinary people. The biologist probably expected to work at Trojan until she retired. If she was lucky, maybe the Tree Growing Company[39] decided to hire her back?

Where was I? Oh yes. Life on the peaceful Toutle River, and now I had a truck with which to roam the mountains. When I returned to check the honeybee colonies in the mountains, much to my surprise, two hives had been torn to shreds. I did not have time to go back immediately, and I figured the bear (s) would have been satisfied. Little did I know that honey is addictive to bears. On that Monday, returning to work I told my tale of woe to the chemist from South Carolina. I seem to recall that his name was Fred (at least that is what I will call him from here on). He was terribly excited to hear "there be bar in them thar woods". I did not realize that his interest was purely predatory. He wanted a bear hide in the worst way and was more than willing to accompany me to the mountain to see whether we could shoot the bear.

I thought it a little drastic to be so all-fired anxious to kill the bear just because it destroyed a couple of hives. However, when Fred and I arrived at the bee yard that night, there were 5 hives reduced to a pile of wax, wire, and splinters. I did not realize that the bears would be coming back every night until all the hives were destroyed. Fred and I did not see the bears that night, probably because we were whispering too loudly.

The next night I went up by myself with my Dad's 30 30 rifle. I parked a bit away from the hives but they were in plain view. Of course, that also means that I was in plain view to any bears that might be stalking the hives. I stayed in the truck with the window open (it was cold, and I was tired). I dozed off, only to dream of bears stalking me in the truck. Wide awake again, I could almost feel the eyes of the bears looking out from behind the vegetation. I imagined that they could probably circle around behind me. Needless to say, I was no great white hunter. Nor did I know what I would do if I saw one. But I was there defending the hives, and that night, it prevented the bears from doing more damage.

I was too tired to go by Wednesday, and I think that is exactly the way Fred wanted it. He knew it would be easier to stalk the bear by himself. That

---

[39] On Wednesday, January 28, 1998, a U.S. federal trademark registration was filed for **THE TREE GROWING COMPANY**. This trademark is owned by Weyerhaeuser Co. Federal Way, WA 98003. http://www.trademarkia.com/the-tree-growing-company-75425211.html

is what he did and shot the bear. Now remember, he is alone, he has to dress out the bear, to get the hide. I don't think he bothered trying to take the meat, but he did have to follow the bear into the valley where it died. Then he had to dress out this bear and haul the hide back to the road in a plastic bag. All of this was done in the dark, and he didn't get down from the mountain until the following morning. I can't exactly remember if he came to work that day, but I think he did, because he had to leave the pelt in the bag for the entire next day. This was a disaster as far as Fred was concerned! Because, when he took the pelt to the taxidermist to have the hide cured, the fur fell off the pelt the minute they put the hide in the tannings solution. All that effort he had expended for nothing except the satisfaction of knowing that he had saved the honeybees from total destruction. Of course, there is also the adventure factor. Whether fortunate or unfortunate, they left that gene out of me.

All of the preceding happened in the fall of 1972, because in October I left the Environmental Research Unit, and took the bees back to California in my 49' GMC. Loading the bees for the trip was a challenge which I met by myself. By then Jerry had moved on. There were fewer hives to load; the bears had paid for their inquisitiveness by the loss of one of their own. I removed the honey supers and loaded them separately at the front of the flat bed. This was so that I could drop the hives at their destination in Willows; then bring the honey supers into the honey house to extract.

There was honey on the hives and I had tried to extract some of the tansy rag weed honey before I took the colonies up the high mountains. That was a disaster of sorts. Tansy ragweed honey, besides having a pungent flavor, has a tendency to crystalize almost as soon as it is exposed to the air. It will even crystalize in the honeycomb if not removed fairly soon after it is collected. So I set up the extractor in the carport of Dad's house and began to process honey. Not too bright. The bees took a little while to find the source of free honey, but soon they were all over the extractor. I managed to keep the lid on while I was working, so not many got into the honey. The problem was that I had not planned to take as long as it did, so I was not able to finish the day that I started. So I left the honey in the extractor, thinking I would bottle it when I got home from work the next day. Well, not only did the bees find their way into the extractor, but they called all the bees for miles around. Elizabeth thought they were going to move into the house, so she kept the door closed all day. When I got home and saw what was happening, I started to try to drain off the remaining honey. Unfortunately it had already crystalized and would not flow. In the end I had to hose the whole thing out, dead bees and all. I don't know how much honey that wasted. I was beginning to realize that I did not know as much about this beekeeping business as I had thought.

The trick, traveling to California, was to get as far as possible at night. So I loaded the bees in the mountains before sunrise, then drove down to the house on the Toutle, had some breakfast and lots of coffee. I loaded a thermos and I think Elizabeth might have made me a lunch, and I took off. I was so proud of my ol' GMC and my load of honeybees. The truck, although slow, performed well, through the Willamette Valley. It was a sunny but cold fall day, so the honeybees roads well while the truck was moving. As I entered the Cascade Range, I realized that I was not going to make it to California before nightfall. So at Wolf Creek I pulled of onto a side road by a stream bed, and let the bees fly for the remainder of the day.

I can't remember if I ate at the little restaurant at Wolf Creek, but I do remember lying down by the side of the creek and sleeping. When I awoke, it was dark and the bees had all returned to their hives, so I headed up I5 again climbing through the Cascades. Somewhere along the way I picked up a family that was hitch hiking to California. They were obviously hippies, and they had one son. It was pleasant to have someone to talk to, not to mention help me stay awake. As we passed over the Siskiyou Pass and dropped down the long grade to the Dept. of Agriculture Inspection Station near Yreka, I realized that my brakes had glazed. I had been talking and not paying attention to proper downshifting. All I could do was shift into a lower gear, pump the breaks and hope to God that we would stop before we hit the Inspection Station. You can imagine what was flashing through my mind with a load of beehives and a family of hippies about to meet an untimely end.

By some miracle the truck came to a stop not 30 ft. from the Inspection Station. Oh, my God, did I breathe a sigh of relief! Once the brake casings cooled off, the breaks worked fine again, but that was a lesson to me. I was learning a lot of lessons that summer and fall. I had not had the bees inspected in Washington, but that year, the inspection certificate that Oliver had obtained on the bees before the left California was adequate to get me back into California. The rest of the trip was uneventful. I dropped the family in Yreka and headed on into the Central Valley. Because I knew where the hives were to be placed, it was a simple matter of continuing on down the Valley without stopping until I had deposited them at a bee yard in Willows.

I stayed at Oliver's for a day or two while I extracted out the honey from the hives into a 100 gallon vat that Oliver kept for such purposes. Then I took the GMC down to Hayward CA to buy jars to divide the honey and bottle my share. I think I stayed overnight with my cousins. They were probably surprised to see my drive up in a big old GMC. I was surprised that the brakes held on the incredibly steep street in front of their house. I got stopped by a cop on the freeway while heading to the Bay Area. He said I was driving too slowly, but he did not give me a ticket. He just advised me to get off the freeway as soon as I could conveniently do so. Not long after he stopped me, I witnessed another car spin out of control in front of me. I was so relieved that the traffic was light and I did not end up in one of those proverbial 50 car pile ups that happen from time to time in the Tully Fog on Hwy 80.

When I got back to Willows, the crew had sampled the Northwest Honey. Oliver exclaimed that it had a very distinct flavor. Nora dubbed it "out-house honey." It didn't matter to them, because they were blending it in there large storage tanks with their star thistle and safflower honey. My problem was that I had to take my half of this honey back to Washington and sell it. The question was who was being the more honest about the flavor of the honey, Oliver, or Nora? Well, the good news is that only one person who bought the honey had an honest to goodness allergic reaction to it, and he survived!

I bottled my honey anyway and loaded it up for the trip back to Washington. It was fun to be back and see everyone at the Hill Apiary. Oliver's brother-in-law was quite curious how everything had gone that summer, because he was conjuring a plan to buy 400 beehives (some from Oliver and the rest from other beekeepers in the valley) and take them up to Washington.

Before I returned to Oliver's with the honey jars, I think I drove down to Galt to visit my mother. The old truck got me around, but it probably had not had that many miles put on it in 10 years. After all is said and done, this was a 22 year old truck with a straight 6 cylinder block that was still working like a top. I was gaining a great deal of respect for that old work horse. The best thing about it was that it was uncomplicated. I guess my mother was duly impressed that I was showing so much initiative, not that I was making a lot of money at it. Albeit so, it is the effort that counts. I don't remember whether I took her for a spin in the GMC. She had certainly ridden many a mile in my original 1953 Chevy panel truck, reeking of pulp mill sulfide, when I was in high school and college. But now she had to follow my adventures from afar, and not unlike the time I was in Kenya, I really didn't have time to write that much or call on the phone. I think she would have preferred that I was continuing at UC Davis, both for my education, and so I would be closer. Nevertheless, she could not afford to help me, and my father was not in a position to pay for my schooling, so the plan took and entirely different course.

# Chapter 5

# Indentured Servitude

But we urge you, brothers, to do this more and more, and to aspire to live quietly, and to mind your own affairs, and to work with your hands, as we instructed you, so that you may walk properly before outsiders and be dependent on no one.**English Standard Version (2001) First Thessalonians 4:10-12**

I don't think I thought to try to find something to purchase to haul back to Washington in the old GMC that year. Of course, I was hauling my share of the honey I had managed to harvest off the colonies that I had just returned to Oliver. I don't actually remember the trip back to Washington, but it was certainly less eventful than the trip to California. The weather was cool but had not devolved into snow and heavy rains yet, even in the mountain pass. So the jars of honey in cardboard boxes were still intact when I arrived on the Toutle. In retrospect, I think I must have had a lucky star at that time. So many things could have gone disastrously wrong, but, by happenstance, they did not.

Now the job was to pack up for Seattle. During the summer I had seen an announcement for a job at the Weyerhaeuser Wood Products Lab on Harbor Island in Seattle. I think I had already made a trip up to meet Dr. Bill Nearn, who was the head of the Wood Morphology Group. The group was, basically, all the microscopy facilities for the Harbor Island Lab, but they also serviced that whole company. He had explained to me that the reason for the hire was that his electron microscopist had developed a technique for detecting Cherry brown stain in laminate beams. Cherry brown is a wood preservative, but what the company did not realize when they started making laminated beams was that when the stained beams were used for supermarkets, churches and other large structures, the Cherry brown stain prevented the glue from penetrating the wood that was being laminated. Consequently, some beams were starting to delaminate. It was Bill Nearn's electron microscopist that had identified the culprit using electron microscopy and EDX[40]. Once the Cherry brown was identified, Bill Nearn's lab developed a simple test for determining if a beam contained Cherry brown. Using a simple stereomicroscope to examine cores taken from the beams, one could spot the stain in the wood. This led to the hiring of a small army of men to travel around the country on full expense account to take beam core samples. These cores would be shipped or brought back to the Harbor Island lab. Guess who got assigned to examine all these cores? You guessed it, the very guy who had developed the technique in the first place. When he could no longer keep up with the job, Weyerhaeuser commandeered several other technicians to sit at the scopes all day cutting open beam cores.

It is not surprising that Bill's microscopist tired of this activity, even though he was only required to do it 4 hours per day. The remainder of his time was devoted to keeping the Wood Morphology Lab running. So he quit! The greater irony of this whole project was that when all had been done, and the last core examined, the manager of the project, who was married to a member of the Weyerhaeuser family, was given a big bonus. He, in turn, took the crew (who had done all the work for many months) out to lunch at Bart's Wharf (an upscale restaurant in West Seattle). Now, I don't feel too much sympathy for the field crew because they had been able to travel all over USA and Canada, with per diem and all expenses paid. But we lowly techs who had spent countless hours on the microscopes were miffed for not even receiving a little bonus check. And Bill's previous microscopist got diddly[41] for his discovery. Not even

---

[40] **Energy-dispersive X-ray spectroscopy** (EDS or EDX) is an analytical technique used for the elemental analysis or chemical characterization of a sample. It is one of the variants of X-ray fluorescence spectroscopy which relies on the investigation of a sample through interactions between electromagnetic radiation and matter, analyzing X-rays emitted by the matter in response to being hit with charged particles. Its characterization capabilities are due in large part to the fundamental principle that each element has a unique atomic structure allowing X-rays that are characteristic of an element's atomic structure to be identified uniquely from one another.

[41] **did·dly**-squat also did·dly·squat (delist)

  n. Slang

  A small or worthless amount.

  [Alteration of diddlyshit (influenced by doodly-squat) : diddly (probably from diddle) + shit, added as an intensive (from shit).]

Bill Nearn was acknowledged for solving what could have been a very serious problem for Weyerhaeuser. Such is the corporate culture, which I would find out after I took the job with the Wood Morphology Group.

During the interview with Bill Nearn, he had asked me if I had any electron microscopy experience. I told him that I had been exposed to the electron microscope. He probably should have asked more questions, because my "exposure" had been one day in Cytology lab at the University of Washington, when we were shown the microscope in action. Still, he offered me the job, and after returning the bees to California, he wanted me as quickly as I could move to Seattle.

Of course, I still knew people in the University District, so finding a place to live was not hard. Tom Griffith asked me if I would want to rent the large old house that he owned, right next to his house just off campus. I could sublet to other students, and that way keep my rent low, so I could pursue my efforts to get the family over from Kenya. I was making a whopping $800 per month, and it finally looked as if it might be possible to bring them to the USA. It did not look likely that I would be going back to Kenya. So Tom's offer looked like a pretty good opportunity. I knew that he and the Honeycomb Fellowship were supporting me in my efforts to reunite with my adopted family.

There was one co-ed renting the basement apartment, but initially the upper house was just me; and it was a big old house. It was kind of a strange feeling, after having lived with family for the previous 3 years, the old house was lonely and cold, and I could not afford to turn up the furnace. I got a little horny on those cold nights, and the young lady in the basement was quite attractive. She shared the kitchen so we would talk. We talked about her experiences at UW and my experiences in Kenya. I think I told her about my adopted family, although she probably already knew from Tom and the Fellowship. I began to have second thoughts about my commitment to Charity and the family. I would do stupid things like go to the head of the basement stairs and play my African drums as loudly as I could, thinking -- I guess -- that the young lady would be impressed. I think she was probably just irritated, but I think she knew that I was getting attracted to her. Finally, my conscience started bothering me, and I went to Tom to talk about my ambivalence. He was helpful. He didn't tell me whether I should or should not continue on this tack; he just asked me whether I knew what I wanted. Of course, I didn't, but not long after that, the young woman moved out of the basement.

Eventually, renters started to come in, which took the financial pressure off of me. I think we had 5 tenants at one point and I had a bedroom in the back of the house on the second floor. It was a strange position for me to be in, because I had never been "in charge" of a house full of tenants. Also, I really wasn't "in charge", and that made the situation a bit tense. We had a couple of house meetings to discuss the issues, and I guess we managed to keep the problems to a functional minimum.

I started the job at the Harbor Island lab in mid-October of 1972. At first I was cutting Cherry brown samples half of the day, and the rest of the time I was learning the ropes in the Wood Morphology lab. In fact, we dealt with many more issues than just wood. Paper products were a big one; usually testing some product failure or newly formulated product. Of course, I had used microscopes throughout my college classes, but I was not very familiar with the physics of a microscope. One day I was examining some wood samples for Bill with the Leitz compound microscope, when he came in to look at the sample. "Damn!" he said, "Don't you know how to use a microscope?" That was embarrassing, but he proceeded to show me how to align and adjust the condenser to produce the optimal image. Not long after that he sent me to Dale Quackenbush who had a microscopy lab in Longview Washington. Dale was a crackerjack wood products microscopist, and he was highly respected within his circle of professionals. He was published in trade and scientific journals for his very meticulous micrographs of paper coatings and laminated materials such as milk cartons. I learned a lot from Dale about embedding and microtomy (thin slicing) of samples. I also learned about interference-contrast microscopy, and photomicrography. Dale had a Zeiss Ultraphot microscope that was his pride and joy. The 4x5 inch camera made it possible to produce high resolution photomicrographs on a wide field of view. He used both transmission-light and incident-light micrography. That means he could either photograph with light shown through a thin sample or with light reflected off the surface of an opaque sample. I learned that different problems require very different techniques. Dale Quackenbush took me under his wing so to speak. He became my mentor and brought me into the circle of industrial microscopists. He also let me use his photo-developing lab and sharpen my microtome blades with his automatic blade sharpener.

In addition, Bill gave me other training opportunities. We did not have a lot of uses for the transmission electron microscope, because the technique is complicated and the applications are limited in the wood products field. Still, Bill wanted to have the capability in house, so he sent me to a lab in Vancouver, British Columbia to spend time with a very skilled electron microscopy technician at the University of British Columbia. The hardest skill to learn was making perfect fractured glass knives. Diamond knives could be purchased, but they are expensive. Glass knives work almost as well for making ultra-thin sections on an ultra-microtome. After spending long days and late nights perfecting my technique, I was able to do some decent electron micrography.

When I had saved some money, I contracted a priest in Taita, to ask if he could help Charity prepare to come to America. He was stationed at the High School in Mwatate, and that was convenient to where Charity was living at Mpizini. I don't remember how I came in contact with this priest, but I assume that it was probably Fr. Pat O'Connell that put me in touch with him. I had not previously met him and did not meet him in person until years later. His name was also O'Connell, but for the life of me, I could not remember his first name. I think I just started addressing him as Fr. O'Connell. I have since learned that his name was Sean, but I never heard him called Fr. Sean. He was very helpful, and, incredibly, before March of 1973, I was able to send him enough money to arrange for Charity's flight to America. I had sent an amount that I thought would be adequate to bring the three youngest children (how I saved that much I do not know). Nevertheless, that plan was not to be.

The first hurdle to jump was the Immigration office. I must have started this process much earlier because it seems to me that it was almost a year before I got past the man at the front desk. I may have mentioned it already, but I have observed that there are two kinds of government servants. There are those who really do consider themselves servants of the public and will go out of their way to help a citizen. In contrast, there are those who consider it their duty to protect the government and its coffers from the citizenry. The man I first approached at the immigration office in Seattle was one of the latter.

At first I thought he was being helpful, saying that I needed to file, and would probably have great difficulty getting permission to bring Charity into the country because we were not married. True, but there are provisions for obtaining a K visa to bring a prospective wife into the country, but it is a very long and complicated process. This line of reasoning went on for the first several visits over a 6-month period. At one point he actually suggested that I needed to contact the Canadian Embassy and get a travel visa for Charity to come into Vancouver, Canada. Then, he suggested that I should cross the border, bring her back with me, marry her, and then apply for a K visa. I actually did go to the Canadian Embassy and found that the clerk at the US Immigration Office was blowing some serious smoke. Not only was that approach not legal but would probably have precluded ever being able to get Charity into the USA. I was getting smarter by the visit. Finally, when I knew I had enough money to bring her over, I went to this bespectacled shadow of a man at the front desk of Immigration and said, "I want to see your supervisor." He hemmed and hawed but I was insistent.

When he finally called his supervisor, I met a gentleman and a fine immigration officer. He knew the law well and was definitely that kind of government servant who believed in **serving** the citizenry. I explained the situation, and that I was finally able to afford to bring Charity and her children to the United States. He listened quietly and took notes. I think he went out to the front desk and ordered the recalcitrant clerk to produce documentation of the history of my interactions with him, which were now approaching one year. At the end of that meeting, the officer said, "I think this may be a possibility under the K visa provision. Give me a few days to work out the details, and I will get back to you as soon as I have an answer for you." I thanked him profusely and went home.

I am sure there are people who might read this and think, "Why should you have a right to bring an African woman with all those kids to the United States? Won't they just become wards of the state, and a drain on the national economy?" I won't attempt to rebut that here, but I will say that it reflects the coldness of those in our culture who think we are above the needs of the other human beings in the world.

Meanwhile, back at the lab, the work continued unabated. I was quickly learning the trade at the rate of 10 hours per day. I was not paid overtime, but I felt that I needed to prove my worth since my job was going to be the sole support for a family of four... or more. Bill Nearn was a decent fellow and knew what I was trying to do. I think he thought it was kind of nuts, but he was not one to interfere with the personal lives of his employees. He figured if that was what I wanted, as long as it didn't affect my work performance, he was okay with it.

Besides helping me get trained, he was even helpful about letting me get additional work. There was a program at Weyerhaeuser Research called New Business Research (NBR). There were a couple of hot shot MBA grads who were looking into investment opportunities for the company. Being in the tree growing business, Weyerhaeuser wanted to stay close to the crops production end of the economy. They looked into things like wineries, potato farms, salmon hatcheries and honeybees. Bill knew that I had experience with bees so he tossed my name in the hat along with one of the senior scientist who kept beehives himself. We were charged with getting together as much information on the honeybee industry as we could in about one month.

I spent a lot of time on the phone with the US Bureau of Statistics and National Agricultural Statistics. Back then you had to get the information from a statistician employee and they worked regular hours, so I would make up for the time on the NBR by staying late at the morphology lab. The NBR paid for my overtime. When we came to the presentation of the plan to the NBR review board, the data I had provided showed the highly labor-intensive nature of the honeybee pollination industry, and the complex nature of the management of hives. The NBR board decided that it was not a good investment to become involved in migratory pollination contracting all over the nation.

In retrospect, that was a good decision, because the impact of large scale migratory beekeeping has been an important contributor to the decline of the bee industry in the United States. To the point that honeybee hives have to be hauled in from all over the USA just to have enough bees to pollinate the almond crop in California. Weyerhaeuser might have been one of the big players in that process. It was Oliver and Dr. Laidlaw that had convinced me that the relationship between the beekeeper and the honeybee is sacred, a labor of love and mutual respect. The beekeeper that has no respect for his bees will not be a beekeeper for long.

I forget exactly when Bill Nearn was able to purchase the scanning electron microscope (SEM), but that machine greatly increased the demand for the services of the Wood Morphology Group. The result was that the transmission electron microscope was not really used again until I acquired funding to do a project on Douglas fir pollen in 1974. But I will discuss that project later. Meanwhile, the scanning electron microscope lent itself so well to the wood products industry. Most of our specimens were wood or composite products made from wood. The preparation of samples was simple. All we had to do was to secure the specimen to metal mounts, and then draw a vacuum on them and spatter coat them with vaporized gold. This creates a conductive surface layer of gold molecules on the specimen without obliterating the surface microscopic topography. Irregularities in processed paper, milk cartons, and titanium dioxide coatings on copier paper (a division of Weyerhaeuser) were easily exposed by SEM. If a distribution of chemicals on the surface needed to be identified, we would take it to the University of Washington lab where the SEM was equipped with EDX[42].

I spent a lot of time learning to clean the "lenses" of the SEM. Because of the volume of material processed through the SEM scope, debris would frequently collect in the apertures, which were holes in pieces of metal. Technically, the lens is the magnetic coil that creates the electron beam. But the beam is directed through the metal apertures. Biological specimens were a little harder to process. Anything with water in it had to be freeze dried to preserve the structure while removing the moisture. That moisture could quickly gum up the apertures. Another, faster technique was referred to as critical point drying.

The Immigration Officer was true to his word and called me in a few days later to let me know that the K visas for Charity and the kids were to be processed. Notification was sent to the Embassy in Kenya, and I sent the necessary paperwork to Fr. O'Connell. This was before the internet, so even diplomatic mail moved slowly. How can I make the diplomatic morass interesting --.not possible! It was a lot of writing and waiting. As the time came closer for the tickets to be purchased, I made a phone call to Fr. O'Connell. At that time, international calls were very complicated, especially to developing countries like Kenya. I think I started the process as early as possible on the day of the call. I was eventually assigned to an operator in New Jersey. She

---

[42] Energy-dispersive X-ray spectroscopy (EDS or **EDX** or EDAX) is an analytical technique used for the elemental analysis or chemical characterization of a sample. It relies on the investigation of an interaction of some source of X-ray excitation and a sample. Its characterization capabilities are due in large part to the fundamental principle that each element has a unique atomic structure allowing X-rays that are characteristic of an element's atomic structure to be identified uniquely from one another.

To stimulate the emission of characteristic X-rays from a specimen, a high-energy beam of charged particles such as electrons or protons (see PIXE), or a beam of X-rays, is focused into the sample being studied. At rest, an atom within the sample contains ground state (or unexcited) electrons in discrete energy levels or electron shells bound to the nucleus. The incident beam may excite an electron in an inner shell, ejecting it from the shell while creating an electron hole where the electron was. An electron from an outer, higher-energy shell then fills the hole, and the difference in energy between the higher-energy shell and the lower energy shell may be released in the form of an X-ray. The number and energy of the X-rays emitted from a specimen can be measured by an energy-dispersive spectrometer. As the energy of the X-rays is characteristic of the difference in energy between the two shells, and of the atomic structure of the element from which they were emitted, this allows the elemental composition of the specimen to be measured. http://en.wikipedia.org/wiki/Energy-dispersive_X-ray_spectroscopy

had a thick "New Jozy" accent and was understandable to me only because I had watched many old movies. She told me to stay close to the phone, and that she would call me back when she made contact in Kenya. Several hours later, she called me and brought me in on a conversation between herself and a male operator in Nairobi. This was the most difficult part of the transaction. The Kenyan operator had a distinctly colonial British accent, although I am sure he was African, because he could barely understand the woman from New Jersey. At one point she exclaimed in her strongest accent, "What-sup-witch-yew? Can't yew tawk English?" He was dumfounded, but somehow they worked out the details. Then we had to wait several more hours until they could contact Fr. O'Connell and get him to a phone.

When the good Father called, the conversation had to be brief because the charges were $15 per minute. The gist of the conversation was that Charity would be coming by herself. No time for lengthy explanations of why the kids could not come, but it involved the reluctance of the grandparents. Also there was a limited amount of funds to complete the transactions. So that was that! The die was cast; it would be Charity, alone, in a foreign country with only me to interpret for her. This was not what I had envisioned, but the Fates had played their part again?

On the one hand, there was really no time to ponder the situation. Work at Weyerhaeuser and preparations for Charity's arrival overshadowed any deep contemplation of the ramifications of what had just happened. I broke the news to the Honeycomb Fellowship, and they all seemed to support me in this venture. They were disappointed for me that the children would not be coming, but they were "obedient to the will of God." It was harder to explain to my co-workers why I was bringing the mother of three young children to American without them. What made it most difficult was that I didn't know the answer to that myself. Why would I do that? In retrospect my only comment is the old Yiddish proverb:

- מענטש טראַכט, גאָט לאַכט.
  - *Mentsch tracht, Gott lacht.*
  - Translation: Man plans, God laughs. http://en.wikiquote.org/wiki/Yiddish_proverbs

Nor can I explain why Charity was willing to do this. It was certainly a long shot. Getting one person to America is one thing, getting the whole family over was yet another. Still, she was willing to take the chance of traveling halfway around the world, to be with a man, hoping that he would be able to bring the whole family together in America. That must have taken a lot of faith. Well, they say love is blind. I am not sure if "they" say that, but Charity and I certainly did not have an opportunity to discuss it.

Of course, there were still hurdles on the Kenya side. Charity was required to have a birth certificate made, because there was no process of recording births among Africans when she was born. They eventually settled on a date of 1938, which made her 9 years older than me. I had no idea how old she was. I probably should have known that she couldn't have been very young because she already had 5 children, one of whom had already completed nurses training in Kenya. On my side, things were as "lined-up" as I was capable of making it. I had a job, a rental house, transportation of sorts (kind of strange to be driving a 1949 GMC 1-ton in Seattle traffic). I had checked into schools when I thought the children were coming. One principal of the local grade school said that the playground would make or break the kids. If they could hold their own on the playground, they would survive. That was not at all encouraging, and, in that respect, it probably was a good thing that the kids were not coming to the big city. But planning for Charity's personal needs was something for which I could not prepare. Seattle was not an overtly racist area, but there was always the undercurrent. I had no idea how that would affect her. I was beginning to see the logic of bringing Charity first, instead of subjecting all of them to the culture shock in unison.

When I think back on it, it amazes me how quickly the whole direction of my life changed in two short years. I arrived Stateside in October of '71; flunked my induction physical; worked bees for Oliver; attended a quarter at UC Davis in '71; moved to Longview that summer for the Weyerhaeuser 'student' job; moved to Seattle that Fall to take a microscopist's job; arranged for Charity to come to Seattle in Winter of '72; married in March; conceived a child and had my first son on November 28, 1973. That's enough to make any man's head spin, and we were just getting started. The reader might be inclined to have me skip on to "the juicy stuff", but I like to keep it grounded in what was making all of this possible; namely, the job!

Through all of these preparations, things were intense in the Weyerhaeuser lab. Forestry research was becoming a bigger and bigger part of the company. The company was taking its responsibility to be land stewards seriously.... sort of. They were basically being forced into it because open areas of old growth forest were rapidly being depleted but the demand for lumber was growing steadily. Even the harvesting of second growth that had been planted in the early part of the century offered only limited sustainable production. The Weyerhaeuser family realized that if they didn't start scientific farming of the forest, that their days were numbered. They had themselves been responsible for the demise of many smaller companies on their rise to the top of the lumber industry. Now they themselves were threatened by the limitations of nature. I have heard figures that less than 5% of the original northwest forests remain. I would authenticate those numbers, but it is really not important in this context. The point is that all of the timber companies realized that things were changing and scientific forestry was all that they had to fall back on.

I can give you one very clear example. It comes from one of the scientist in the Wood Morphology Group. Dr. Bob MeGraw was a young PhD out of Minnesota that Bill Nearn had hired to look at the genetics of wood quality. He also dabbled in things like non-forest species of fiber production such as Kenaf[43]. If you read the footnote you will see that Kenaf has many uses but it is also a very large plant that can be grown in dense thickets. Furthermore, it is a good fiber source, and Bob was testing its pulping qualities. This would truly be a woody fiber crop that would be grown and harvested as an agricultural crop.

But that is not the example I wanted to give. Bob also initiated a project to test the wood density of trees that were being selected by the company's Forest Genetics Group (FGG) for their rapid growth properties. There was an intensive effort by this FGG to find and propagate breeding orchards of genetically improved trees. This was all before genetic engineering and was based solely on classical genetics (cross-breeding and propagating the best stock). However, in any genetics program, you have to develop selection criterion. Unfortunately, the primary criterion that the company was using was 'rapid growth'. Of course, placing all the emphasis on rapid growth has its

---

[43] **Kenaf** [Etymology: Persian], *Hibiscus cannabinus*, is a plant in the Malvaceae family. *Hibiscus cannabinus* is in the genus Hibiscus and is probably native to southern Asia, though its exact natural origin is unknown. The name also applies to the fiber obtained from this plant. Kenaf is one of the allied fibers of jute and shows similar characteristics. Other names include Bimli, Ambary, Ambari Hemp, Deccan Hemp, and Bimlipatum Jute. It is labeled as Gongoora in Indian, Korean, American food and groceries chains in the United States. Gongoora is from Telugu. For Telugus it is a favourite food leaf. It is cooked with daal and eaten as saag. They even prepare a kind of pickle with the leaves that lasts for one or two years. It is said to be rich in Iron. It is an annual or biennial herbaceous plant (rarely a short-lived perennial) growing to 1.5 to 3.5 m tall with a woody base. The stems are 1–2 cm diameter, often but not always branched. http://en.wikipedia.org/wiki/Kenaf

drawbacks. If you select only for growth, you may end up with a very different tree than you were seeking. Bob Megraw's argument was that they should also be checking wood density in the selected stock of trees to be propagated. If there were fast growing trees that also had greater wood density, they should select those. To that purpose he had built a wood densitometer, and he and his summer intern would collect cores from the trees that had been designated as "superior stock."

Why do I call this a "very clear example"? As with the cherry brown stain, sloppy science can lead to disastrous consequences. It is a perfectly good wood preservative, but someone forgot to check the properties of the stained wood, before they started laminating beams. Likewise, the consequences of sloppy forest science can stay with you for many years to come. If I may digress, I can give an example that is very close to my current home in Hawaii. When the sugar cane plantations along the Hamakua Coast went out of business in the 1990s, a plan was developed to substitute *Eucalyptus saligna* as a forest crop that could be used to generate biofuel for the bagasse-burning furnaces of the plantations. There was also the hope that it could be used for wood pulp. They were in discussion with Japanese companies that send ships to process the wood chip into paper (i.e. floating pulp mills). It sounded like a good idea at first, but these tree plantations have grown very rapidly, and they have not been managed. There was social backlash against contracting the labor out to Japanese workers, thereby bringing no help to an economy that was suffering the loss of the sugar industry. The plan fell through and the business startups pulled out.

Therefore, the smaller trees are beginning to die in the closely planted stands. If they are not cut soon, the likelihood is increasing each year that disease or insects will further damage the stands, or that fire could burn them down. If forestry is to become, quite literally, a cropping system, then standards of intensive management will need to be employed as well. Our ancestors gathered and harvested from the abundance of the natural landscape, but when we took over the landscape we created the necessity to manage it. If we make mistakes, we will be the victims of those mistakes.

I don't mean to become too didactic in this memoir, but these are observations I have made over the years, and it bothers me how oblivious most people are to these fundamental issues of our environment. Not just the wild pristine environment, but the disturbed, manipulated, over-utilized productive environment that we depend on for our very existence. I found a digital copy of the great treatise on the subject, *Topsoil and Civilization*[44] by Tom Dale and Vernon Gill Carter. I think it should be required reading for every college student in the natural sciences.

My part in this grand plan of the Weyerhaeuser Company was a tiny one. Lamination was a big issue, not only because of the cherry brown incident, but also because the company was toying with the idea that all structural wood would be cut into triangular lath and then glued together into boards. As one of the adhesives specialists at the Seattle Lab told me, "Nutz! You can't make a resin that is as strong as natural wood lignin pound for pound, dollar for dollar." Of course you can make a resin that is rock hard, but at considerable expense, and then it does not have the elasticity of lignin. Nevertheless, we see more and more laminated, pressed, composited and reconstituted forms of every wood product. I drove by one large building under construction today in Hilo town. All the siding is particle board. The structural wood is still lumber, made from trees, but I just wonder how those pressed board materials will hold up over the years in the humid tropical environment of Hilo.

These were the very issues that we were presented with in the Wood morphology lab. Is this wood bonding to the metal surface of this siding material? Is the paint application of equal thickness throughout? Is that particle board filled with too much airspace? There were many other questions of like complexity. I used Kirlian electrophotography to solve the issue of the paint thickness. We processed biological samples on occasion too. I was asked to demonstrate the effect of a fungicidal dip on the morphology of the waxy layers on the surface of needles of seedling trees. In SEM micrographs it was apparent that the waxy cuticle was being partially dissolved, and this presents possible hazards for the seedling when exposed to the harsh winter or summer environment. The cuticle is critically important to maintaining moisture balance in the plant in hot weather and frost tolerance in cold weather.

I was once asked to demonstrate that the deposit on the surface of someone's car was not 2-4-5-T herbicide. The company knew that the emulsion was of a consistency that would not drift when sprayed by helicopters, but they had to prove that it was not happening. I used light microscopy to demonstrate that the deposit was mostly alder pollen. I also eliminated the possibility of it being 2-4-5-T by demonstrating that the characteristic fluorescence of the chemical was not present and that there was no oil (emulsifying agent) of the

---

[44] Tom Dale and Vernon Gill Carter. 1955. Topsoil and Civilization. Univ. of Oklahoma Press, Norman Oklahoma.

correct refractive index in the sample. This latter technique I learned because Bill Nearn had paid to send me to attend a course given by the McCrone Institute on the use of polarized light microscopy and refractometry.

I hope I am not boring the reader with all this technical information, but I have always found science very fascinating, and I have low tolerance for those that have no interest in what makes everything around them work, or not, as the case may be. But getting back to the Mshoi family, the problem was not only getting Charity to the USA, but what was going to happen to the children. Samba, Mzae and Samuel Mzee were too young to live by themselves at Mpizini, and I did not think Charity's parents could take them at the homestead. Charity's brother already had too many kids of his own, to be able to support 3 more on a primary school teacher's salary. ed was old enough that he needed to finish his secondary school at Mtwapa. As it turned out, Charity's youngest brother was working at a wood shop Funded by a German development agency in Mwatate. They decide that he should take over the house at Mpizini with Ed.

Gertrude stepped forward to take care of the young ones, but she was in Tana River working at a hospital. Tana River is a very different world than Taita. The kids never talked to me about it, so I don't know if they even remember it. I knew about it because Mr. Moon, the Near East Foundation Advisor, had built irrigation schemes on the Tana River for rice production. It proved to be a difficult environment for the children, although I don't know if the chronic malaria which came to plague Mzae was contracted in Mpizini or Tana River, or both.

Progress was being made with the Embassy in Nairobi, and the preparations for Charity's flight were imminent. The Honeycomb Fellowship was ready to welcome her, and I was in contact with Fr. Fulton at Blessed Sacrament about the arrangements for the wedding. Herb Karnofski had agreed to be my best man, and Emily (Du) Matson was Charity's matron of honor. I can't remember where we got the Kitenge shirts for Herb and me. Charity may have brought them from Kenya, but Herb's had to be altered to fit him. These details are a fog in my mind now. It was such a busy event for me because there were no parents to make the arrangements. It would have been impossible without the help of the Honeycomb Fellowship.

Back in the day, we didn't have terrorists, and you could actually go out to the gate to meet the arriving passengers as they stepped off the plane. There was a whole crowd with me on the day Charity was due to arrive. When she stepped through the doorway, I can't remember if we all cheered, but I remember that Charity was quite overwhelmed. I guess she was only expecting me, so to see all these total strangers crowding around and greeting her, she was not sure what to think. At least, that is what I thought.

I don't remember going down to Customs, so she may have already done her immigration entry at some other airport when arriving from Kenya. Of course, the Fellowship folks were falling over themselves trying to be helpful, carry luggage, etc. As I remembered it, I had driven to the airport in the 1-Ton GMC; I would have wanted to show it off first thing (typical guy thing). Once we were safely in the truck, "away from the maddening crowd", Charity was visibly relieved. I think she was pleased to have finally made it, but I am sure she had trepidations about what she had gotten herself into. Of course, no one departs from a 28 hour flight full of vim and vitality. But now she was too stimulated to just relax and nap. The trip in the big truck probably did not seem daunting to her; after all she had ridden in far rougher and tumble vehicles than this. Lukundu kwa Wose bus would be a far scarier vehicle than my pretty blue truck. But what **proved** daunting were the traffic, and the lights (those cold whitish-blue mercury vapor lamps lighting every street corner). Even in Nairobi, the streetlights are the soft yellow glow of the sodium vapor lamps. Somehow the mercury vapor glares out the stark reality of winter on the 47th latitude. It was February, and the typical cold wet rain that is so characteristic of the Northwest was there to greet her. It was already dark, so she did not notice that all the deciduous trees were bereft of leaves. Of course, she had never seen a tall and elegantly formed Douglas fir tree. Scrubby Cypress pine was the only evergreen that she knew.

I think the heater was still working in the old truck, so it was not an uncomfortable 20 or so miles to the University District, and on the old bench seats Charity could snuggle up to me as we talked about her new life. Of course, this was all in Swahili because she did not speak English. When we arrived in the neighborhood, I had to look around a bit for a parking place (few of the old homes in the district had more than one small parking space, and I had roommates). I think we may have put the luggage in the old house, and then gone next door to Jean and Tom's where Jean probably had some refreshments for the members of the Fellowship, who were all anxious to get to know Charity. Or maybe everyone realized that she just needed to get home and get to bed, as did they. I really don't remember.

I do know that we slept in separate rooms until the wedding. We wanted to start over again and do it according to the Church rules. In the morning, I introduced her to whichever of the roommates were still around when she woke up. I suppose we had some breakfast, but it was not long before I had to make an obligatory trip to the supermarket to find her corn meal so she could make *mswara (ugali)*. She was surprised that the corn meal was yellow instead of white. Mr. Moon had commented at length how much more nutritious yellow corn would have been for the Kenyans, but how most Kenyans would not even have considered corn meal made form yellow maize, much less be willing to eat it. That just shows how habituated we all become to the trappings of our culture. Old habits die hard.

Of course, adjusting from the plain but healthy diet of vegetable soups, beans and ugali -- with occasional rice, and chapatti for variety -- to the spicy, fattening, protein and calorie rich western diet could throw anyone's stomach in an uproar. The plain simplicity of ugali was a countermeasure to all of that. It was necessary to find Charity warm clothes, too. Stocking caps, mittens, a warm jacket, whatever would take off the chill. There was a fireplace in the big old house, but I don't remember if we were able to use it. Charity certainly wanted to build a fire. Of course, I could not stay home with Charity to help her get oriented, show her how to use my checking account, etc.; because I still had to work. Even operating the stove was a new experience for her. Also, she was not able to speak with Jean and the other people in our house. I am sure Jean tried to help her and made her welcome at the Griffith house, but the roommates soon grew uncomfortable with the situation, and began to depart, one by one. So that by the time of the wedding, Charity and I were the only tenants of that huge house…and the rent and everything else was all my responsibility.

# Chapter 6

# The Bonds of Marriage

Go therefore to the main roads and invite to the wedding feast as many as you find. **English Standard Version (2001) Matthew 22:9**

I am remiss in not knowing what preparations I made for the wedding to Charity. I know we did not want for food or celebration, because I think many of the people of the Fellowship helped considerably. All I do remember is that Emily Du Mattson made adobo from the chicken that I bought. I find it ironic that I would remember only that fact. It was not a fancy wedding, but I don't think anyone went away hungry. Herb arrived the day before the wedding, and because the roommates had left, there was a bed for him. My mother also came, and, if I remember correctly, stayed at the house too. It was a big old house, but was still, perhaps, uncomfortable for Charity to have her imminent mother-in-law sleeping in the next room. This was her first meeting with my mother, even though we had exchange tape recordings with my mother from the time I was in Kenya. I thought it was strange that Charity never called my mother by her name, Kay, or Kathy. I believe that from that first meeting, she called her "Mammi". That is not a Kidawida word and it is not Kiswahili. I don't even know where she had heard it before. I don't write it as "mommy" because that is not the same word that she spoke. Kiswahili would be "*mam'angu*"; Kidawida would be "*mao*". I don't know if I can attribute any significance to it, but Charity was determined to use that name for my mother.

I forget what running around I did the day of the wedding, but I know that Herb and I arrived at the Blessed Sacrament church, well within time

75

for the event. It was Charity who brought Kitenge shirts for us from Kenya, but Herb's had to be altered by a tailor to get it to fit. Blessed Sacrament is a lovely old gothic structure, which was the site where I had played music with a fellow seminarian, and later the Charismatic Christians who took over the music because they did not like the group playing "Hey, Jude"[45] in Mass. Fr. Fulton was moved by the Charismatics, and there was a seminal sermon from that pulpit, that we had hailed as the revitalization of the Church. Now 3 years later, Fr. Fulton was still the pastor. I guess the Charismatics were still influential, although my group of friends in that movement had moved on. I think Jim Henderson, who was the flautist, had married a nun and was working in a grocery store in Ballard. As the guests began to arrive I was surprised. Gretchen and her dad had driven up for the event. Phil Gilday from the seminary was taking pictures, and later sent them to me (they were the only pictures we had of the wedding). Even Richard Hopp, also a St. Francis Seminary alumnus, was there. I didn't even know how they had found out about the wedding. I don't think Herb was in touch with them. Plus there were many people from the Honeycomb Fellowship. And they were all waiting for the bride to arrive.

Charity and Emily did not arrive for 45 minutes or more. We all wondered if she had gotten cold feet. Turns out it was all about the flowers. Charity had come with a white wedding dress that she had ordered sewn in Kenya. She did not know that it is not customary to wear white if you already have children. Of course, this was her first actual wedding in spite of having children by two other men. But there were no provisions for the flowers. Apparently, Emily had worked very hard along with Jean and other women from the Fellowship to get the flowers the way Charity wanted them, in a headband... and this was in spite of the language barrier. They arrived at the church finally, and we proceeded with the ceremony. Music was provided, I believe, by the Honeycomb Fellowship. I don't remember anything about it, except that Roy Gillett played my bass.

We returned to our house after the ceremony and a big party ensued.

---

[45] **"Hey Jude"** was released in August 1968 as the first single from The Beatles' record label Apple Records. More than seven minutes in length, "Hey Jude" was, at the time, the longest single ever to top the British charts. It also spent nine weeks as number one in the United States—the longest run at the top of the American charts for a Beatles' single and tied the record for longest stay at #1 (until the record was beaten by "You Light Up My Life"). The single has sold approximately eight million copies and is frequently included on professional lists of the all-time best songs. http://en.wikipedia.org/wiki/Hey_Jude

The house could accommodate because it was about the same size as Tom and Jean's house, which is where the Honeycomb usually met on Sunday. Even Fr. Fulton came, but we had to find him a place in the kitchen so he could sit down to eat. I remember someone had arranged for an African Dance troupe to dance for the occasion. This very much impressed Charity and she thanked them all profusely in a rather long speech in Kiswahili. Of course, the dance troupe was all African Americans, so they did not know what Charity was saying. I tried to translate, so I think they understood that she had been moved.

I think Gretchen and Bob Huffhines did not come to the party, but Gretchen said that she told her dad, "This will not last". The wedding was on February 17, 1973, but I think they were both surprised that Charity and I were still together, when they came to the wedding of Charity's oldest daughter on July 1, 1977, in Tenino. That's when they met all five of Charity's children (plus 1 grandchild) who I had managed to bring from Africa.

I don't think Phil Gilday or Dick Hopp came to the party either. I was so distracted with everything going on that I might not have noticed their presence. It was kind of like being in the middle of a tornado. I couldn't say exactly how many people came to the wedding because we did not have a guest book. We would not have even had photographs if Phil had not brought his camera and made a very nice wedding book for us. Perhaps Phil was at the wedding party; because I think there might have been some pictures of the dancers in that book. Charity still has that piece of memorabilia, I imagine. I don't have any of the wedding pictures, but my mother had one picture of Charity taken the day before the wedding.

I do remember that Fr. Fulton was enjoying the food. He was such a kind old white haired gentleman, sitting there at the kitchen table watching the throng pass by. I remember that he was in a suit and collar instead of the flowing black and white robes of the Dominicans. He was a fixture of the University community.

Joseph Fulton, OP

**Rev. Joseph Fulton**. This man was a good priest. (Photo and eulogy curtesy of Fr. Michael Fones, OP Socius and Vicar to the Provincial.)

Fr. Joseph John Fulton, OP 1912-1998
BEHOLD A GREAT PRIEST
By Fr. William Treacy, Archdiocese of Seattle

On December 12, 1998, a great priest, a bridge builder between separated Christians was summoned to meet the Jesus he loved face to face. Father Joseph Fulton was known as Jack in his college days. As a priest he was known as "Father Joy" because of his constant smile and joy in the Lord.

He was born and raised in Brooklyn. Both parents were devout Methodists and he claimed descent from Robert Fulton the Scotch inventor. His father died soon after Jack was born. He spent the rest of his life looking for his father, and in his search he became a father to many, many people. The homilist at his funeral Mass, Father Finbarr Hayes, OP, asked those in the overflowing congregation to raise their hands if they experienced him as father. A show of hands went up from every pew.

His road to the Catholic Church was an interesting one. His mother and grandmother decided to leave Brooklyn when Jack was 12 and to move to a quieter and perhaps less expensive area adjacent to a good university. After prayer they chose Seattle. Jack was "in Siberia" he said, as he missed his beloved Brooklyn. They settled in the University district.

In his walks Jack saw the tall Gothic spire of the newly built (1908) Blessed Sacrament Church. He was raised with the traditional misconceptions about Catholics. He was told they "worshipped" Mary, paid little attention to Jesus, etc., etc. Overcoming fears he entered one Sunday and was fascinated by the ritual. As a student in Roosevelt High School he became acquainted with a Catholic girl who accompanied him to Sunday Mass. He would also enter on his own to experience the peace and joy that he found in silent prayer.

About the same time, he found a neighbor who was Catholic. This young man, Albert Burke, later to become a Carmelite priest, invited Jack to walk with him to St. James Cathedral to attend Sunday Vespers. His mother heard of his attendance at Catholic services. She was one of the pillars of the University Methodist Temple. She requested Jack to postpone any decision about becoming a Catholic until he graduated from the University of Washington. On his graduation in 1935, he won the President's medal for an outstanding academic record. Prior to graduation he was in St. James Cathedral when the newly ordained Fr. Thomas Gill was blessing individuals kneeling at the communion rail. Jack went forward and knelt. As the future bishop blessed Jack he felt an overwhelming desire to become a priest. In fact he went to the Chancery office to inquire about becoming a priest. He was informed that he should first become a Catholic!

He was received into the Catholic Church in the red brick beloved Blessed Sacrament Church by a saintly Dominican priest, Father Hofstede, later to die ministering to lepers in the Philippines. Drawn to the Dominican Order he was accepted for training and ordained a priest in 1942, taking the name Joseph. He spent some years teaching at St. Albert's in Oakland and served as Provincial of the Dominicans on the West Coast for two terms, during which he invited students from foreign countries to continue their Dominican training in America. On completion of his duties as Provincial he came to Seattle and again became a doctoral candidate in Greek at University of Washington. However, he was asked to become Pastor of Blessed Sacrament in 1966 and he left the academic halls for parish ministry. For seven years (1964-1971) I was his neighboring Pastor in St. Patrick's Church. Since 1962 he was my spiritual director, my Anam Cara (Soul Friend). Following his retirement as Pastor he devoted his time to scripture study, charismatic prayer groups and interfaith ministry. (With permission of Fr. Michael Fones, OP

Socius and Vicar to the Provincial, Western Dominican Province of the Most Holy Name of Jesus) http://www. opwest.org/profiles/f/fultonjoseph.htm

I don't know why the mental picture of Fr. Fulton at the kitchen table stuck in my head. What I do remember is that he and I had a brief but peaceful interlude amid the celebratory chaos. Fr. Jack was a very peaceful man. I was so grateful to Emily, Jean, Tom, Roy, and Herb for making the whole thing work. My mother was there for the whole thing, but I don't know how much she helped. Maybe I was unaware that something was going on between her and Charity that would not bode well for the future. I suppose many people, like Gretchen and Bob, had their doubts about this marriage, but in general, the Fellowship had a hopeful attitude towards our little experiment in intercultural exchange.

Charity on the eve of her wedding (photographed by the author).

When it was time for the newlyweds to depart, Charity changed into a cute Kitenge dress, of which everyone approved, and we were lead out to the "carriage" through the rain of rice. Of course, the carriage was the old blue truck. I don't remember if they had "decorated" the cab, but I know that when I started to drive off, a great clatter ensued. I stopped to look; there were a conglomeration of containers tied to the rear including a 5 gallon bucket! Having removed the noisemakers, I don't think we were followed, because parking was so difficult in the U District that no one wanted to lose their space. Not that we were going far. Our wedding night was to be spent in a motel on Lake Washington. Honeymoon was pretty much out of the question; I was not in a financial position to fund that. Good thing too, because little did I know that my own son would be conceived that night.

Old Faithful, the 1949 GMC decked out for the Wedding. (Photo provided by author.)

I suppose it was all a bit anticlimactic for Charity, having come halfway around the world. She was alone in a strange world, without her children or her parents or any of her siblings, nothing that had been familiar to her. Yet she seemed to be adjusting to the concept. I don't remember that she complained, although it is possible that she was just so overwhelmed that she could not express her feelings. And then to be pregnant for the sixth time almost immediately, whew! Obviously, she had the IUD removed by a doctor in Kenya. The next few months she spent her time trying to adjust to the life of a US housewife. The man goes off to work every day, and the little woman is left to occupy her time. Fortunately, Jean was around most of the time taking care of her own brood of five. Still Charity did not know English; that was a major barrier.

Not too long after the wedding we found out that there was a Tanzanian professor at the U. of W. who taught Kiswahili. He may have heard of Charity because of the African dance group that performed for our wedding. I may have gotten the wild hair brained idea that Charity could learn English by sitting in on Kiswahili classes. Follow me on the logic here. Yeah, I know, it's a crazy idea, but believe it or not, the *Mwalimu* (Professor) agreed. So Charity would walk over to class on campus and audit the class. This was not official, but I think the professor was glad to have her for the conversational parts of the class. He was not concerned about Charity's English. Rather, he was using Charity to give the other students exposure to a native speaker. I guess he thought he was offering us thanks when he invited us to dinner at the end of the class. Unfortunately, he served tripe stew. Charity enjoyed this ethnic dish, but I have to say I think he was testing me. I did eat some, but not much.

Most of our activities after the wedding were fairly mundane. When I would come home at night (which could often be fairly late), Charity would be waiting, sometimes with dinner, but often with frustration about all that she was not able to do that day. That is not surprising because she did not have the language skills to negotiate the neighborhood. It was not far to the University Ave where all the businesses were, but Charity definitely needed help wherever she went. So I spent most of my off-work time trying to meet her needs. We shopped together, did laundry together, went to Church together, even to the doctor together. She was under the care of the University of Washington hospital, which was a relief because it was relatively close and I was confident that her care would be the best.

I think Charity was encouraged by the spring with the flowers blooming and trees beginning to put out leaves. She did not have garden space to plant, and she was not inclined to reading and study. She was not very comfortable in the late winter because of morning sickness, but by spring she was doing better. After all, she had been through the experience of pregnancy five times previously. The doctors were careful to watch her health, since she was probably 35 years old. That was pushing the limits of safe pregnancy with the technology available then. We did the Lamaze classes together in the evenings.

I was having difficulty keeping up with the cost of the house rental and additional cost of taking care of Charity and the preparations for the birth of our child. I was still selling honey… slowly. And I decide we should try to sell some imported items at the public market on Pike Street. I had some African souvenirs, and I had asked my roommate from UC Davis, Fernando Medrano, to send me material from Guatemala where he was living with his wife. I sent him $50 and he returned some nice woven material. We sold some, but the cost of renting the booth in the Pike Street Market made it less than lucrative.

One interesting thing happened at the Pike Street Market. The oldest sister of my grade school friend, Lyle Shabram, recognized me and came up to talk. I did not recognize her at first, until she explained that she was living in Seattle, but the family was still living in Carmel, California. They were all doing well, except that the parents had lost their youngest child in a swimming pool accident. Our encounter was brief but, of course, introducing Charity opened the whole conversation about Peace Corps.

I was anxious to try the beekeeping venture again, so in April, or thereabouts, I contracted Oliver and asked if he wanted to let me try running the honeybee colonies on the Toutle again. I think the thing that encouraged him to let me do it was that his brother-in-law was preparing to start his own apiary of 400 hives in the Cowlitz Prairie area. To that end he was planning to hire a tractor trailer to deliver the hives to Washington. I guess Oliver figured if the brother in law was going all out to the northwest that he could spare some bees for me to try my luck again. So Charity and I took the old blue truck down to Willows, California. She was by that time quite pregnant, and it was probably not an easy trip for her. But she was curious to see the west coast, and gladly agreed to make the trip. I had taken my vacation from Weyerhaeuser, so I worked for Oliver a few days while we shook bees for the brother-in-law's hives, and then he loaded me up with 50 hives, and we headed for the northwest. We had to drive straight through, because there was limited time to get the job done, and I didn't want to have to sleep along the road with a pregnant wife. She helped me stay awake for the grueling drive, and we made it to the Toutle River.

My Dad and Elizabeth had not come to the wedding, and I can't remember if they had met Charity before this trip. In either case, they welcomed her, and I noticed that Charity was much more comfortable with Elizabeth and my Dad than she had been with my mother. So while they got acquainted, I Delivered the bees to the yards that I had previously lined up along the Toutle and up into the foothills of Mt. St. Helens. We had not had time to go on

83

down to Galt on that California trip, and I don't remember that Fr. Carl drove my mother up to meet us in Willows. It might have happened, but I don't remember it. We were not on a joy ride. We were trying to make some extra money, so we could get the kids over from Kenya.

While selling imports at the Pike Street Market, I ran into one of the guys from the band we had formed to play at Blessed Sacrament. I had previously thought he was a hippy from California, but it turned out that his father was a greengrocer who had operated a market stall in Pike Street Market for many years. I am not going to name him, but we began to talk about produce. One of the young students and the Honeycomb Fellowship was from Kennewick, WA, where his father owned an apple farm. His father had asked him to try to set up a market in Seattle, so that he could bypass the packers who always paid minimum price for the apples. So we decided to run the truck over to Kennewick and bring back a load of apples. We took orders through the fellowship, and folks at Weyerhaeuser requested boxes of apples as well. Also the friend at Pike Street Market said he would buy apples from us.

The trip to Kennewick was quite an adventure. I can't remember the young man's name now, but I am going to call him Kurt, for convenience, and because I cannot contact him to get his permission. He was a strapping red headed youth, who majored in Political Science, but ended up going to work for an insurance company when he finished at the University of Washington. He was a farm boy at heart because he had been raised on the Kennewick orchard

The three of us, Charity, me, and Kurt rode over to Kennewick in the old blue GMC, but when we got to his dad's orchard, the apples were not ripe enough to pick yet. So they figured a day or two might make a difference. So Charity and I decided to go on to Milton Freewater, OR, where Floyd and Mary Moon had retired. We called ahead, and Floyd, although surprised, said, "Come on down, I will show you my place." When we arrive, Floyd seemed most pleased to see us. Even though he had made every effort to try to prevent Charity from coming to America, he was now quite accepting of the fact that she was here, and he was most anxious to make her feel welcome. Floyd had gotten me started in beekeeping, so he was interested to hear all about my efforts to run an apiary. He also was most anxious to show me his garden where he kept one hive to pollinate the myriad of vegetables and fruit that he was growing. In spite of his age and difficulty with his back, Floyd was not a man to sit still for long; nor was I. The Moons fed us some dinner, and we headed back to Kennewick. We stayed in a motel that night and then in the morning, we went back to the farm.

Charity was not in condition to pick apples so she stayed with Kurt's parents while he and I picked 200 boxes of slightly green Yellow Delicious apples. We tried the reds, but they were just too green to pass muster. So we loaded up our 200 boxes and headed back to Seattle. Not such a grueling drive, since Kurt could spell me on the driving, and we were able to stop and rest or eat when we needed to. Of course, Charity needed to stop to relieve her bladder fairly often with the baby growing daily. I don't know if Charity considered these as hard times, but I can tell you frankly, she had endured much harder times back in Kenya. Plus, she was getting to see some very beautiful parts of Washington State: the eastern fruit orchard country and the beautiful mountain pass with Mt. Rainier in plain view.

When we returned to Seattle and after we had sold all the apples, it was clear that all this extra effort was not enough to keep up with the rent on the big old house. So, I answered an ad in the newspaper for a travel trailer which was in Central Seattle. It belonged to a retired couple that was intent on buying a newer, larger motor home for their trips. They needed to sell their 19 foot Shasta in order to do that. I forget what they were asking, but I figured we could save considerable money by living in this trailer. I also don't remember how I paid for it, but after having a trailer hitch custom welded to the truck, I took it over to the seller's house. The old man had just returned from a near tragic accident with his wife. They had gone ahead and bought a twenty-four foot travel trailer. On its maiden voyage, the trailer jackknifed when they were trying to brake. It totaled their trailer and damaged their truck. I made mental note that trailering could be dangerous. The old fella was, however, still determined to sell the Shasta, and was quite helpful showing me how to wire the truck up for hauling a trailer. This included installing an electric brake and running lights. By that time I had already arranged to rent a space in a trailer park in North Seattle, and we proceeded to haul the rig up and install it in the trailer park.

The move to the trailer park was not difficult because we did not have that much to move. All the furniture at the old house belonged to Tom and Jean. The 19 foot trailer was fully self-contained. There is an amazing amount of storage space in a travel trailer if you know how to pack it. I had acquired a couple of 4x4x3 foot wooden boxes from the Weyerhaeuser refuse pile and had constructed water-proof lids for them. These acted as storage boxes for things we could leave outside the trailer. Let me describe the change from wandering around a big old drafty house, into a small compact, gas heated trailer. The back end of the trailer was the bed with overhead and under-bed storage compartments. The center of the trailer was kitchen refrigerator and stove on one side and bathroom and small shower on the other side. At the front end of the trailer was a dining nook that could actually seat four people "comfortably", and could be folded down into a bed if needed. Under the seats was all storage. I don't remember exactly when we made the move, but winter had already set in before Charity's pregnancy came to term.

The summer of 1973 was a busy one. I was deeply involved in work and trying to get down to the Toutle to maintain the bees on my days off. At some point that year Bill Nearn had agreed to let me work four 10 hour days (4 per week), since I was always spending 10 hours or more per day at work anyway. Charity would go with me on these trips to the Toutle and would stay with my Dad and Elizabeth while I went up to work with the bees. Elizabeth had a weaving machine and tried to show Charity how to use it. In general, things went better with the bees in 1973. There were no bear attacks, and although I do not remember harvesting honey, I must have separated the supers of honey from the hives before I brought them back to California, so that I could extract them at Oliver's honey house. That way there were only 2 hive bodies on each hive when I delivered them. I am speculating about this because I really don't remember whether it was a good honey year. I must have kept the bees until the following spring, but I will reveal the reason I know that in the next chapter.

Early that year, Oliver's brother-in-law shipped the 400 hives to Cowlitz Prairie. I met him and Oliver near the Winlock freeway off-ramp and helped them unload the beehives. The fantastic thing about the whole affair was this: Oliver stood on the bed of the tractor trailer rig, and proceeded to lift down the hives that were stacked 3 high (2 hive bodies for each hive). He would pick up the approximately 100-pound hive, lower it to the bed of the trailer, then pick it up and move it to the edge of the bed, where the brother-in-law and I would take one hive and move it into the field. This meant that what took two of us to move, Oliver downloaded by himself. After we completed off-loading the brother-in-law's bees, we left the brother-in-law to take care of his colonies, and then I drove him to my folks' house to have some lunch. He was not very talkative, because he had been awake since the day before. I don't think he had driven the semi to Washington, but rode with the driver from California. This was the first time my folks had met Oliver Hill and I think they were impressed. His brother-in-law came to pick him up and, I believe, showed him around the area for a day or two before he went back to California.

As Charity came closer to term, she was more and more uncomfortable and could not make the long trips in the old GMC. Also the weather was turning colder, and she was not used to the climate. According to the doctor, the pregnancy was proceeding quite normally and the newly-developed ultrasound was showing the fetus to be developing rapidly. Speaking of which, I actually know one of the engineers that developed ultrasound imaging. He was a member of the Honeycomb Fellowship. He had been employed at Boeing. It was period of economic downturn in Seattle because Boeing and other major corporations had scaled back. This engineer was one of many who were laid off from Boeing, but, after a few anxious months of unemployment, he was hired by the Medical School at University of Washington, and his job was to help develop the ultrasound imaging system. It proved to be a very useful tool, particularly since Charity finally did come to term. I say "finally" because I was on pins and needles about the birth of my first child. On the one hand I was working my hardest to make money to support us and save enough money to bring the family over from Africa. In addition I was Charity's translator, chauffer, accountant, shopper, and social director. When I think back, I am amazed that I was ever able to pull it off, albeit not perfectly.

I think it might have been that fall that Charity and I attended the Centralia-Chehalis County Fair (C-CC). I don't remember why we were in those towns, but Weyerhaeuser had its Forestry Research Center there, and I might have gone to do some work for that group. I mention this little excursion to the fair because it was the only time in my life or Charity's that we flew in a helicopter. It is the kind of thing we would have liked to do with the kids, but we didn't have them with us. It was one of those small bubble 'copters with open sides and you could see the earth below you right between your feet. The price was right. So we did it! Charity was a trooper, and went along for the ride, but I don't think she was comfortable. I suppose her motherly instincts were working overtime, as she thought to herself, the life of my unborn child could be at risk here. That had not even crossed my mind. I very much enjoyed the ride and the aerial view of the town that would eventually become our residence. I have lived in Hawaii now for over twenty years, but you will never get me up in a tour helicopter. During my time in the islands, there have been 30 or more helicopter accidents with and without fatalities. So I look back nostalgically at the flight Charity and I took at the C-CC Fair.

There was a kind old lady who lived in a vintage 30 ft. motor home across the street from our trailer in North Seattle. Charity and I became friends with the lady, who took care of her granddaughter quite often in the mobile park. As I said, winter had set in with a vengeance that year, and the weather turned very cold. We were comfortable in the trailer, but the lady across the street could not afford to fill her propane tank. So one morning I woke up early to go to work and noticed out the window that the woman's car was running and putting out a cloud of cold steam from the exhaust. I thought that was unusual so I went out to check. Here were the woman and the granddaughter unconscious in the car with the engine running. Apparently, the woman had thought to keep them warm with the car's heater, but the exhaust leaked into the passenger compartment, and was threatening to kill them with monoxide gas. I quickly pulled the little girl from the car and took her into our trailer. Then I went back to try to wake up the elderly lady. I finally managed to get her to our trailer, and she slowly recovered her senses. She was very apologetic for bothering us, but we were just glad we had found them both in time.

I could not understand how the parents of the girl would be so oblivious to the situation of the grandmother in whose hands they had entrusted their child. They arrived a little later that morning, and once the situation was explained to them, I think they made an effort to see that the grandmother would have heat in her motor home. Charity was quite shocked that such a thing could happen in America. She thought life was rosy for everyone in this country. Now I think she understood better that, like everywhere in the world, there are the haves and the have-nots, and little attention is paid to the latter.

Charity was rapidly expanding after we moved to the park. She was capable of riding the bus now and did so with me from time to time. But she seldom ventured out on her own, unless some friend from the Honeycomb fellowship would come to pick her up. By that time Martha, my Pentecostal friend, was still participating in the Honeycomb Fellowship and made an effort to make Charity feel welcome in this country. One of Charity's fears was the dogs that seemed to be everywhere you went on the street. She and I were out for a walk one day in the cold icy evening, when a large Irish setter barked at her and, if I remember correctly, jumped up and pushed her down. The dog was actually just being over exuberant and friendly, but Charity was terrified. She could not understand how people would let such large dogs run loose in the street.

There was another young couple that lived in the mobile park, and we became friends with them. I remember them, because the young man was a budding photographer, and offered to take photos of our child after the birth. Otherwise we did not get well acquainted with the residence of the mobile park. The manager and his wife were nice folks, but a lot of the residents were either old timers or itinerants. The old timers probably had misogynistic ideas about interracial marriage and the itinerants were not there long enough to get to know us. Of course, I was gone so much of the time when I was working, that I did not feel like spending my time getting to know the residents of the park. I viewed it as a temporary situation, but it continued into April of the next year.

That winter, we developed a friendship with another new member of the Honeycomb fellowship. She knew Tom professionally and only came to the fellowship for a party. Doris was a professional black woman and a single mother of two boys. At the time she had a restraining order on the boys' father and was having difficulty. It was not long before she asked us to come to stay at their house to help deter her husband. I don't remember the details but I think we also house-sat for Doris, when she took the boys on a trip. Since she was the only other black person, Charity was happy to have an African American friend. In fact, I think Doris appreciated my help with a number of issues including the boys. They were a handful and were starting to act out because of the confusion of the divorce. I should have paid closer attention, because I would find myself in a similar situation with my own children. Doris and her boys became friends of our family.

About that time, when Charity was in her last trimester, Dr. Jess Daniels came up to the Seattle lab from the Forestry Research Center in Centralia. Bill was negotiating a contract to work on pollen viability problems that the Forestry Genetics Group was having within their breeding orchards. Because I had the training in pollination, I had become very involved in this issue. They brought stored pollen samples with them and ask us to develop a viability test and try to determine what might be causing the rapid loss in viability. Up to that time they had generally air dried the pollen and then refrigerated it, until it was used in the breeding orchards the next season. They were getting very low seed set in the cross-pollinations. I was happy to do this, because my first love is botany, and working entirely with dead wood samples did not challenge me to deal with issues of plant physiology. This was my chance to work with a living organism.

I dove into the research with a vengeance. I was determined to discover what the problem was. We started with standard microscopic procedures.

We observed the pollen in water and found that some pollen would expand into a cigar shape (and often burst), whereas other pollen would not. This indicated that the bursting pollen was taking in too much water and the unexpanded pollen was somehow damaged and could not take in water by osmosis. A big help in this process was a trip to the Forestry School at the U. of W. Dr. Reinhard Stettler was the contact person to whom I was directed, because he had a graduate student who had written his thesis on Douglas fir pollen. Dr. Stettler, who was himself Swiss, followed the European concepts of the doctoral dissertation, which included reporting the details of every experiment conducted. It required writing explanation of the results and why the experiment had either succeeded, or why it might have failed. This student, whose name was G. K. Livingston -- I presume -- had produced a tome[46] that year but had graduated and moved on. The dissertation was most helpful because it gave the details of all the procedures Livingston had used, including radiation treatment of the pollen.

Bill Nearn was anxious to get the transmission electron microscope back in action again, so I subjected the pollen to a fixative, embedded it in epoxy, and proceeded to thin section the pollen for TEM. The result of our efforts was that we were able to show that the damaged pollen had undergone damaging peroxidase activity which created tannin globules in the tissue. The expanding pollen, on the other hand, showed no sign of abnormal organelle development. From that we could assure Jess Daniels that there was viable pollen in the samples, but we needed to track down the cause of the peroxidase activity, and the loss of viability.

In late November, just before we were to go to bed, Charity's water

---

[46] G.K. Livingston and R.F. Stettler Received 18 June 1972. Available online 29 November 2004 Radiation-induced stimulation of pollen-tube elongation in Douglas-fir. A thesis at the College of Forest Resources, University of Washington, Seattle, Washington 98195, U.S.A.

Abstract: Radiation Botany 13, 65–72, 1973.-Mature pollen of Douglas-fir (*Pseudotsuga menziesii*) was subjected to gamma radiation from a 60Co source at exposures of 4, 8, 16, 32, 64, 128 and 256 kR and incubated on an agar medium in vitro. Whereas germination per cents remained constant regardless of treatment, pollen-tube lengths at 48 hr of incubation were positively correlated with radiation dose. The same results were found with X rays. Irradiation seemed to both speed up germination and increase the rate of elongation. Oxygen uptake, as measured by a respirometer, increased proportionately to dose up to 64 kR but declined at higher doses. At the microscopic level, the two highest doses caused an exfoliation of the outer layers of the intine at the time of germination. It is suggested that the observed stimulation of pollen-tube elongation is brought about by an enhanced metabolism at the lower doses; but by a physical change in cell-wall properties at the higher doses.

broke and I rushed her to the University of Washington Maternity Unit. The doctor put her under observation in the pre-birthing unit. She was there for the remainder of the night, as they continued to measure her cervix. It did not seem to dilate at a normal rate. The doctor suspected that the hospital environment had made Charity apprehensive and she had inadvertently shut down the birthing process. After ultrasound indicated that everything was normal with the baby, the doctors decided to put Charity on pitocin to induce contractions. That was successful, and not long after, they moved her into the birthing room. As the contractions became more intense, Charity made it clear that she wanted no more of the Lamaze foolishness, and wanted a spinal block, STAT. So much for the "natural birth"; even though she had probably had five kids without anesthetic, she was in America and she wanted all the help that technology could offer!

Although it was not yet customary for the husband to be allowed to be present at the whole birthing process, this case was unusual, in that Charity did not understand English, and the U. of W. Hospital was progressive. Therefore, I was asked to be present for the whole procedure. I accompanied the nurses to the wash-up station, followed the ablution procedures and donned the surgical cap, mask and robe. In retrospect, I suppose I should have been thinking, "Well, this is the end of the honeymoon". What I actually was thinking was "Oh God, what's next?"

# Chapter 7

# The Bonds of Birth

When a woman is giving birth, she has sorrow because her hour has come, but when she has delivered the baby, she no longer remembers the anguish, for joy that a human being has been born into the world. **English Standard Version (2001) John 16:21**

What was I in 1973? Twenty six! About the time when most young men are just thinking about having a family. In my mind, I already had a family of seven. Now I was assisting the birth of my own son, first of my seed. The hospital maternity people were all matter-of-fact, but I was in a mental state. I can see why they didn't used to let husbands in the birth room. But they put me to work coaching Charity to breathe. In typical fashion, she pulled it off without a hitch, and probably didn't need any coaching from me. The baby was huge (8 lb.10 oz., 21 inches long). That was hybrid vigor, I presume. The head was too big for the canal, so Charity tore. But **he** was healthy and began to cry as soon as they cleared his throat. The staff brought him to us to see after they had cleaned him up a bit. Charity was pleased but she was exhausted. She did not say anything that I can remember after her 32 hour ordeal.

After sewing Charity up, they took her to a recovery room. Now the excitement, and stress and sleeplessness began to hit me. I went to see the baby in the maternity ward. By that point there were no visitors, because no one knew that Charity was in labor. We didn't have cell phones to spread the news, so I used the pay phone at the hospital. I called my mother first, and then someone at the Honeycomb Fellowship. That person passed the word around. The hospital staff knew that I was also exhausted, so they told me to go home and get some sleep. They made it clear that I would need it!

Yeah, like that was ever going to happen. When I got home to the trailer, I heard the ominous sound of rushing water. When I opened the door water gushed out. The air accumulator had burst under the seat in the breakfast nook. I didn't even know this device existed, and it took me some time to actually track down after I shut off the water supply. This is also the place where we stored much of our linens. So the floor was covered with water, the linens were soaked, and I had no water. Finding an air accumulator was not too difficult but figuring out how to install it myself was a trick. I managed, and now the emphasis was on trying to dry everything out before the wife and baby were to come home. Needless to say, I did not get any sleep that day. I think I had the gas heater up at full bore and had either borrowed or bought a space heater to increase the heat. I guess I am lucky I didn't burn the Shasta down, because I left the heaters on when I went back to the hospital. Of course I had to take all the linen to a Laundromat and dry them, because we were going to need them.

When I got back to the hospital all the Fellowship folks that had come to see the newborn were oohing and ah-ing. They and I were surprised that black children are born with blue eyes; the pigmentation takes a few days to develop. They were also quite surprised at how big the baby was, and that he had a nearly full head of hair. He even had hair on his back which the doctor called Mongolian, but it is actually called lanugo.[47] Charity is a relatively small woman, and not the kind you would normally expect to carry an 8 lbs. 10 oz. baby to term. But Charity was good at this childbearing stuff. I don't know if hospitals encouraged breast feeding as they do now, but Charity knew all too well how to breast feed. The staff would have had a hard time trying to prevent her from nursing her new baby. My son recently asked me why he was circumcised, so I had to explain. Then, circumcision was a standard practice in western hospitals. They obtain permission from the parents, but they recommend the procedure. It is painless to the infant and consists of placing a plastic band around the head of the penis, which causes the foreskin

---

[47] Some newborns have a fine, downy body hair called **lanugo**. It may be particularly noticeable on the back, shoulders, forehead, ears and face of premature infants. Lanugo disappears within a few weeks. Infants may be born with full heads of hair; others, particularly white infants, may have very fine hair or may even be bald.

to drop off within a few days. So, within the first hour his fate was sealed, he would be a circumcised half-breed.

Flowers gifts and cards began to flow into Charity's hospital room, but the one gift that I appreciated the most was the diaper service that the Honeycomb Fellowship, or members thereof, bought for us. That was the most helpful thing of all for a young family living in a 19 ft. trailer. Of course, I cannot forget Martha Patton's very kind offer to stay with Charity when she returned from the hospital. It would take Charity a little while to recover from the stitches and the stress of childbirth. It was a great relief to me to know that someone would be watching over the baby and Charity while I was at work. This was before they had anything like paternity leave, and even maternity leave didn't exist in most private businesses. If you took the time off to be a parent, it was on your own dime. And since I didn't have any dimes to spare, Martha was a Godsend.

The issue of naming the baby did not take long. Charity was culturally conditioned to having the firstborn named after the *abo* (Kidawida) or *babu* (Kiswahili) or grandfather (English). To that I agreed, because it was the name of my stepfather, the name of my maternal great grandfather, and the name of Charity's oldest brother. I also wanted his middle name to be in memory of Fr. Kevin, the saintly rector of St. Francis Seminary who had died of brain cancer too few years before. Of course we called him Jimmy when he was young, but over the years he has insisted that we use "James." Ironically, he listed his Facebook name as "Kevin Mshoi" until he closed the FB account. He greatly values his privacy.

I can list many instances in my life where a person's name seems somehow fateful in their life choices. For example, I know an entomologist named Bob Bugg, and Gretchen knew an orthopedic surgeon named Bonebreaker. In my son's case, the connection is more subtle. His middle name, Kevin, is not a stretch: it derives from 'Kenneth' which means either "handsome" from Gaelic *Coinneach*, or "born of fire" from Gaelic *Cinaed*. My wife Gretchen calls him a 12 on a scale of 1 to 10, and he almost got killed by a runaway forest fire in his 15th year as a fire fighter. The name James is really more involved. It derives from the Hebrew name, Jacob, meaning "one that takes by the heel" (Gen. 28:12). The modern interpretation of that expression is, "the supplanter" or "one who takes the place of." The irony is that he is assigned to the National Forest, which had been logged by the Shevlin-Hixon company. James' great-great maternal grandfather laid the foundation stakes for the Bend mill, to which the majority of those logs were shipped to make lumber.

I myself was raised until I was 4 or 5 in Shevlin-Hixon logging camp. That logging camp was in the Chemult Division of James' assigned forest, the Freemont-Wainema. And the reason I was in the logging camp, was because my step-grandfather, was a logger and subsequently a supervisor on that forest cutting operation. When my son finishes his education at University of Montana, his job will be to try to restore the forests to the condition that the Native Americans had maintained for centuries (by controlled burning of the undergrowth). If you ask me, I think that is quite a circle of life. From one perspective, I guess you could consider it the sins of the fathers being visited on their offspring. However, from another perspective, you can consider it an opportunity for the young to rectify the mistakes of their ancestors.

They kept Charity in the hospital an extra day, but by the third day they were anxious to have the room back. So we bundled Charity and the baby up as best we could and took them home to the trailer park. Fortunately, the trailer was toasty warm, and the moisture had pretty much dried up, so it looked like we were going to survive this ordeal. Charity was nursing, so neither she nor I got much sleep. Charity was not in any condition to be changing diapers, so that was my job. I had already taken time off from work to deal with the whole birth, so I did not have leave to stay home with the family. Consequently, I trundled off to work, and Martha, true to her word, stayed with them. I don't know if Martha had cared for an infant before; I think she was an only child like me. I always wondered if this was, indeed, her introduction to child rearing. She did not have any children of her own at that point, and I often wonder if she did eventually have her own family. Unfortunately, I have never been able to trace her through the internet or the folks of the Fellowship.

I will spare the reader the typically boring part of rearing an infant. Of course, to the parents, these are the most important events in the world at the time. Focusing the eyes, laughing, cooing, following a moving object with his tiny eyes. These are what occupy the imagination of a young parent. I will try to stick to the more humorous incidents that I can remember. On one occasion, after the mandatory stay-at-home period, we were taking James to the University District with us, probably for a Fellowship meeting. I headed out the door with James in a little plastic carrier that stood up at a 45 degree angle on a wire stand. Just as I got out the door, Charity called me back for something. I set James, who was all bundled up against the frosty cold, down on the lid of the storage boxes we had sitting outside the trailer. I stuck my head in the trailer to answer her call. When I pulled my head out and started to pick up James again, I realized that he was gone! It was like an icicle had stabbed me in the heart. I thought, OHMYGOD, I have misplaced my son! I was frantically thinking what could have happened, and I looked furtively around for any culprit that might have tried to snatch my son. As I was rushing around looking for James, I realized that the carrier was lying on the ground upside down. Had the kidnapper stolen the babe and thrown the carrier on the ground? But as I reached to pick up the carrier, I realized that James was still in it. The carrier had slid off the storage box because the metal lid was covered with ice. He had fallen, face down, into a patch of dirt at the edge of the concrete slab on which the box rested (phew!). He had not uttered a sound. I guess he was so startled by the fall and the feel of the frosty dirt on his face that he was stunned. He was fine, no bruises or bumps, but you can bet Charity did not let me live that one down for a long, long time. I guess it was just the first sign that, as the joke[48] goes, James would grow up to be "rough and tough and used to hardships."

---

[48] There once was a man named Isiabettiesviennascevitch(sp?) (pronounced, Eyes-a-betty-vienna(like the city)-scev-itch, all one word) who decided to work on a whaling ship in Lake Michigan. Anyways he was new to the job and foreign, and the rest of the crew didn't like him much so they gave him the most dangerous jobs.

One day he was mopping the deck and, from out of nowhere, a wave comes out and sweeps him off the deck. Everyone is sure that he's gone. Then they see him, grabbing on to the sides of his boat and climbing up, finally he gets to the top, grabs his mop, and gets back to work. Everyone is amazed! they say "Isahbetty Isahbetty, are you all right, are you OK?" He just looks at them with scorn and says. (with strong Russian accent) My name is Isiabettiesviennascevitch! And I am Rough! And I am Tough! and I am used to hardships!"

A week later they decide to let him steer for a while, suddenly, a storm comes out of nowhere, and a freak bolt of lightning hits him! He just stands back up though, extinguishes a few fires on his clothes and wipes off some dust, and gets back to work. Once again everyone crowds around and says "Isahbetty Isahbetty, are you all right, are you OK?" Once again he just looks at them with scorn and says. (with strong Russian accent) My name is Isiabettiesviennascevitch! And I am Rough! And I am Tough! and I am used to hardships!" (You may add more if you are feeling creative or mean)

A week later he is on the crow's nest, looking for whales. Suddenly there's a strong gust of wind (they get a lot of freak weather) and Isiahbetty is literally blown off the crow's nest, Down he falls and Crash, through the first floor, Crash, through the second floor and then DONG! he hits the iron bottom (I'm aware it was wood earlier, it's just a joke). Everyone is sure he is dead; a crowd gathers around the first hole and people take off their hats. The captain is about to say a few words when someone gasps, they see Isahbetty start to climb up through the hole his body made in the second floor, and then up back onto the deck. Everyone is amazed and says "Isahbetty Isahbetty, are you all right, are you OK?" He just looks at them with scorn and says. (with strong Russian accent) My name is Isiabettiesviennascevitch! And

96

Another time I actually slipped on the ice while I was holding James, but I managed to keep him from crashing on the ground that time. There wasn't a lot of room for him to get into too much trouble on his own when we lived in the trailer. He had a tendency to chew on the headboard by the bed, but it didn't seem to have done any permanent damage to him. We had to be careful to keep him away from the little stove when cooking. Of course, that was after he became mobile. I guess to an infant, the trailer was a great big world. He did have his mother to entertain him all of the time, and I think that was good for his development. I played with him a lot when I was home too, so he got a lot of attention that first year.

He began to fatten up pretty good; you know, what they call "baby fat". The young couple in the mobile park liked to play with him, and the husband took some great shots of him (which I still have). In them he was all roly-poly and drooling over his pet duck, or was it a penguin? He was a cute kid, but of course, he grew out of the baby fat as soon as he became mobile. I think those pictures were some of the very few we have from those days, but the fellow printed up 8 x 10 inch blow ups of the already close-up pictures. I cherish those. I have one other Polaroid of Charity and me in the hospital with James newly born. I don't remember who took that picture. Maybe the hospital staff did?

As James was graduating to solid food, I was getting ready to present the results of our exploratory project on Douglas fir pollen. Apparently the presentation went well, because the Forest Genetics Group Funded the Wood Products Group to a $17,000 grant to step up the project. We used a number of the techniques that had been used by the graduate student, Livingston. We decided not to use radiation, because there was too much chance of inducing genetic anomalies into the breeding process. We did develop a media and a viability testing procedure to determine how much of a batch of pollen was surviving. We also developed quick tests for viability. Fluorescein di-acetate proved most useful to determine if enzyme activity was still intact. We also did oxygen probe respiration trials and began to investigate what procedures could be used to try to preserve the viability of the pollen.

---

I am Rough! And I am Tough! and I am used to hard ships!" Tallayan10-05-2003, 07:33 PM
http://boards.straightdope.com/sdmb/archive/index.php/t-215284.html

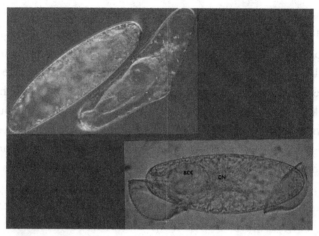

Pollen of ***Pseudotsuga menzeisii.*** (Micrographs produced with a Zeiss microscope by the author at Weyerhaeuser Forestry Research Lab. Centralia Washington)

What we were not able to do was induce the production of an actual pollen tube, which happens readily in the megasporangia (equivalent to stigma) of the fir cone. There was some missing chemical signal that Livingston was able to circumvent by the use of the radiation. This was perhaps a protective mechanism for the gymnosperms (evergreens). The microsporangium (pollen anther) of something like Douglas fir is very sensitive to moisture. It will not open and release its pollen until the humidity reaches an acceptably low level. This is because the pollen itself is very sensitive to water, and will absorb water too quickly, leading to rupture, which is lethal. So the plant strategy is to release the wind-born pollen under low humidity conditions. When the pollen arrives on the megasporangia, which is turned upward to receive the pollen at the time of pollination, the stigmatic surface provides a media that not only allows the pollen to hydrate without rupturing, but also stimulates it to produce the pollen tube that will grow down to the embryonic tissue.

Microsporangium of ***Pseudotsuga menzeisii*** (photographed with a Wild Heerbrugg stereo microscope by the author at Weyerhaeuser Forestry Research Lab, Centralia Washington)

What I am leading up to with all this information is the reason why I was offered the job at the Centralia Forestry Research Lab. It would require us to move away from Seattle and the fellowship of the Honeycomb. This was a big step for Charity, who was only now beginning to adjust to city life in this oh-so-foreign land. The position was supervisory and was to take up the running of the pollen research project for the Genetics Group. This was a pretty big feather in my cap, because I was only the holder of a bachelor's degree, and although I had started graduate school, this was like taking a PhD's job. There were two PhD geneticists on staff, and later a Forestry student with a master's degree was hired to facilitate improvements in the breeding program. Nevertheless, I would be put in charge of developing pollen handling procedures and do further research to improve the preservation of the pollen.

I had several practical reasons to want to take the job in Centralia. The housing prices were cheaper, there was the possibility of buying land, the salary was better, and I fully expected the schools would be easier than in the city for the African children to adapt. That Seattle principal that had told me the kids would either succeed or be broken on the playground worried me. I met again with Dr. Jess Daniels, and he was asking for a commitment. The project was growing rapidly, and they needed staff quickly.

The Funded pollen project at the Wood Morphology Group ended in March, and I accepted the new assignment to begin in April. There was a lot to do in a relatively short time, and a newborn to care for. The move gave me an excuse to spend more time in southern Washington, keeping my bees and looking for property on which I could place our trailer. I did not find the property I wanted, so we ended up renting a space in a mobile park in Centralia. Moving the trailer to Centralia with the old blue GMC was a tricky proposition, but it went off without a hitch. No, I mean without a problem; of course we had to have a hitch welded on to pull the trailer.

I know that I had the bees until the spring of that year, because I remember taking James with me to the mountains to a bee yard when he was still too young to walk. This was before seat belts were mandatory, and child car seats were uncommon and certainly not mandatory. Can you picture James riding along on the bench seat of an old GMC truck sans restraint? My habit was to stretch my arm over him whenever I was slowing down. How ignorant we were then; as if I could have restrained him if I had been involved in a collision. Still, I did not drive fast in the old truck and we were big enough that people stayed out of our way. When we got to the bee yard I parked a little ways away from the hives, but I needed to keep an eye on James, and he would not be content if he could not see me. So I left the door of the truck open. He just sat there and watched as I donned my bee veil and went to work. I know it was before he had started to crawl, because, once he started to move around, I could have never gotten away with leaving him like that. Of course, James doesn't remember this at all, but I remember it distinctly. I was taking my first born son to the mountains to see what nature has to offer. Who knows? Maybe that influenced his psyche, because he too became a person of the mountains, much more so than me. He had assumed his position beside me in front of the stick shift, and that would be his position for the remainder of the time we had the GMC. Later in his life, he would be driving his truck into the mountains and hiking into the high lakes.

That spring was beautiful, the flowers bloomed profusely, and the weather was warm and welcoming as we moved into Centralia. I don't know if Charity felt the same way, but I was most anxious to get to a place where we were closer to the land. The mobile park that we occupied was on a street that ran out of Centralia and was very near properties which were big enough to have large gardens from which the residents sold produce. So we were soon able to buy fresh corn and other vegetables, as well as berries and early varieties of apples. The Forestry Research Center (WFRC) was less than a mile from the park and I did not have to spend an hour in traffic every day to get to work. Speaking of which, I used to get so mad at the people who would sneak into the bus lane while crossing the Lake Union locks on I5 in Seattle. They would try to squeeze back into traffic as the bus lane veered into the tunnel. They knew there was a cop at the other end of the tunnel to catch them and issue citations for violation of the bus lane. I would stubbornly follow close behind the car in front of me so the cheaters would not be able to squeeze back into the traffic flow. I don't know if I ever forced anyone to get a ticket, but that is what I hoped. But in Centralia traffic jams were to be a thing of the past.

Unfortunately, Centralia had a very minimal bus system. So we were back to square one as far as Charity being able to get around the town of Centralia. She could not walk far with James because he was growing so fast. So Charity and James were pretty much relegated to the mobile park and the trailer, even though the weather was much nicer. Charity did not seem to mind much because she could get outside on the cement slab in front of our trailer, and I think she was even able to plant some plants in the strip of dirt along the edge of the slab. Of course, I was not content to stay in those quarters for long. I was embarrassed to be trying to raise a child in a trailer.

I don't know why. The people in the trailer park were certainly not critical. They were an interesting mix of widows and old loggers and few young people who were also trying to make ends meet. One old logger told me of the days when the chain saw was first invented. He said they were paid by the board foot, but they could fall so many trees that they were making big bucks. The company soon got wise and put them all on salary. They couldn't have the sawyers making more money than the salaried men, now could they? Although the residents of the park were all white I did not feel any racial stigma from them because Charity was black. I will tell later of the history of Centralia which was founded by a black man named Washington. I guess my embarrassment was with my fellow employees. Most of them were owners of their own homes, and I felt the pressure to purchase that proverbial piece of land that I could call home.

The Seattle lab had been a bit impersonal. The only person who ever invited us to dinner was Bob McGraw and his wife Jan, who live near the University District at that time. I think we reciprocated, in our little trailer. Bill Nearn was kind to us, but the Group never had parties or group events. Maybe that is why Bob was interested in forming a family friendship. He and his wife had not had a child yet, and I think Jan enjoyed meeting James and Charity. But otherwise the Seattle staff lived all over the greater Seattle area, and there was very little cohesion between the various groups within the Research Department.

Centralia Forestry Research Center was a different story altogether. There was a great deal of group cohesion and a lot of effort on the part of the leadership to build a group identity. They were a relatively new part of the Weyerhaeuser family, and money was being poured into the group for the reasons I described earlier. However, I found it very interesting that the eight million dollar annual budget of the Forestry Research Group was the same amount of money that Weyerhaeuser spent on their first purchase of Super Bowl commercial advertisements. You know, "The tree growing company." Jess Daniels was actually upstaged by a crow in one of the spots (that took 2000 ft. of film to capture). To build cohesion, the group would have almost monthly luncheons (staff meetings) at company expense. Consequently, everyone knew each other fairly well, and the families did more together. The wives of some of the scientists took quite an interest in my little African family, especially Mrs. Tanaka, who was also an instructor at Centralia College. I believe. She was the Caucasian wife of Dr. Yasu Tanaka who was one of the Weyerhaeuser scientists. They started inviting Charity to events, and even asked her to give demonstrations of African cooking and such. Some of these were church get-togethers, and since we did not have a church, other than the Catholic Church (St. Mary's on Washington Ave.), Charity was happy to have some fellowship.

I spent as much of my free time as I could driving Charity and Jimmy around to look at property. We went to one house along the railroad tracks in south Centralia that looked okay but was crawling with fleas. It was as if all the fleas had hatched and were just waiting for the first Red-blooded victim to wander in. We also looked at an old, one-room schoolhouse on the way to Cowlitz Prairie. It had its own well, and the one room was pretty large. It sat on an acre of land, but there were no facilities (the school had an outhouse). We considered a mobile home, but I wanted land. There was a chicken farm just off the Winlock exit from I5. It would have been a long drive, but I had visions of turning the unused chick house into something else, like a mushroom nursery, or a rabbit farm. That also did not pan out. The house would have been plenty big enough, but the owner wanted to be bought out, and I could not get a loan to do so.

The **Tenino homestead**. My mother is tickling Jimmy sitting in her lap. (Photographed by the author)

Finally we found a little place on four acres out of the town of Tenino[49]. It was the homestead house of the grandparents of the Lukenbills. They had water rights to a spring up the road, which was the abandoned part of highway 507 S that had been realigned. The nearest and only neighbor was 200 yards down the road, and the backside of the property was all Weyerhaeuser land. It had been recently clear cut, so it would not be harvested again for at least 40 years. A small creek ran through the property near the house, and another at the far end of the property. It was a small house, with two bedrooms, but the Lukenbills had been remodeling it and had put in a beautiful brick fireplace in the center of the house, with a combination electric/wood burning range in the kitchen. The Lukenbills had put new cedar plank siding on the exterior and retiled the roof as well as installed insulation. However, the interior of the house was, not finished. There were bare old Douglas fir floors, and no wall paneling. To me this was the ideal location. It was only 12 miles from Centralia, and it had an acre of tillable land, woods for firewood, water, and privacy. It was not as nice as the house we rented in Taita, but I could see potential in the place. Most of all, it was being financed by the Lukenbills and they took and immediate liking to us. They required a small down (I think it was $2000) and payments of $220 per month with a fixed rate mortgage. I couldn't pass it up, but it took a lot of persuasion to convince Charity that there was potential.

---

[49] The picture shows the Tenino house the way it was when we bought it. My mother is sitting on a log with Jimmy in her lap and she is tickling him.

I did not think I was asking a lot of Charity to accept this purchase. I knew that we were not going to be able to get anything fancy and still be able to bring the family over. I also knew that I was not going to be able to support the whole family on my salary if we did not have some other resource for earning money or at least producing our own food. So we signed the mortgage agreement, and I began the process of trying to fix the place up to a livable condition. We remained in the mobile park until I was able to obtain some wall paneling and cover the front room and part of one and one half of the bedrooms. The kitchen was still unfinished when we moved in, but Dad and Elizabeth came up one weekend with a load of drywall, and some 1x12 inch lumber for kitchen shelving. Dad showed me how to hang the dry wall and came back later to help build the kitchen shelves. Then I sanded and varnished the floors before we hauled the trailer from Centralia to Tenino and moved in!

The other thing that I really appreciated from Dad and Elizabeth was a refrigerator. They had purchased a new one, and they let us have their older Frigidaire; what a work horse that old refrigerator was! Up to that time we were living out of a tiny little refrigerator in the trailer. We couldn't buy food when it was on sale to freeze. There was hardly enough room in the freezer compartment for ice trays. Now we had a double door refrigerator-freezer… what a luxury. And it was a cost saver, because for the little amount of electricity it used, and the cheap rate on the kilowatt hour, we could score some sales of meat and other perishables and come out ahead. Of course, Charity had never had a refrigerator in Kenya; everything has to be bought fresh and used immediately or jerked or dried to preserve it. I told the story of the New Year's Eve when Jim Smith had brought a whole leg of Kudu to the party in Mgange, and we spent the remainder of the evening jerking the meat and hanging it around the wood stove in the little kitchen.

With regard to electricity, the thing that would be a great drain on our resources was the water pump. The Lukenbills had installed a new pump with a very small air-accumulator, but the problem was that there was no reservoir for the water. That meant that the pump would turn on and off constantly, because there would be no pressure in the line. Also, if the supply of the water from the spring was drawn dry, the pump would lose its prime, and that would cause the pump to run dry, which could ruin the bushings. I didn't understand any of this, but I did my best to try to figure it out. Finally, I concluded that we had to have a reservoir for the water from the spring. So I bought a wheelbarrow and a hoe, bought some pipe and a valve, scarred up some used plywood, and proceeded to build the form for a reservoir. I didn't actually have any plan, and the dimensions were pretty much determined by the 4 x 8 ft. plywood. I couldn't build it too high because it had to all be below the level of the spring or the water would have just backed up the pipe when the level of the spring was reached. I think it was about 8 x 4 x 2.5 or 3 ft. So I assembled the form, mixed, and poured the cement, and waited for it to set up.

When I went to remove the form wood, I realized I had made a huge mistake. I had not allowed for the compression of the inner form, such that I could not free it from the structure. I eventually cracked the reservoir trying to bust out the forms. I hoped this would be a temporary setback, so I went to the hardware store and found a compound called grout sealer. It said it would seal up cracks in the mortar. I don't know how many times I applied the sealer, and filled the tank, only to find that it still leaked. This is where Charity came to the rescue. She was so tired of not having water, that one day, when I was at work, she took a trowel, mixed up mortar, and plastered the whole inside of the tank with mortar. I was dubious but impressed that she would take the initiative. I forgot that she had watched her father, who was a builder, plaster houses. Her work solved the problem and a good thing too. The sealer that I was using had asbestos in it, and had she not covered it up with mortar, I might have been exposing my family to asbestosis and mesothelioma.

That entire operation still did not solve the problem of the pump switching on and off, but at least now it would not loose prime, and we always had water. Eventually, we ended up just leaving the pump off, and depending on the gravity flow from Charity's reservoir. I built a cover for the reservoir but it was not tight enough to keep little creatures out. At least we did not get sick from the spring water. Even shutting down the water pump did not resolve our high electric bills. In the end, I suppose it was the fact that our hot water heater was in the basement, and there was no door on the basement. In retrospect, I think the problem was that the hot water in the tank would flow up into the plumbing under the house, and there, if not used immediately, it would cool and run back into the tank. I insulated the pipes, but it was not enough. Our electric bill would run as high as ±$300 in the winter; this was unheard of for a household with the very cheap electrical rates in the northwest.

All of this was going on in my spare time because I was also very busy at work. I came in fairly late on the pollination season of 1974, but there were many preparations needed to do the research to be ready for the following year. Since we were not in full swing with the pollen handling, Jess included me on various other duties, such as going into the mountains to measure the girth and take bores on test plots of trees in the Cascades. Now that was a cold, wet mother of a job. We were all half frozen when we would drive home from the hills. I also travelled up to the breeding orchards in Sequim, Washington to learn how they processed the pollen and how they handled the pollen when doing the breeding cross pollinations. At the same time, there was pollen from that season that needed to be stored and then tested for viability. At least Sequim is in the rain shadow of the Olympic Mountains, so it gets 132 sunny days per year, and 25 inches annual precipitation.

It was still a good time in James's life, because while I was running around doing all this, James basically had his mother's full time attention. She would come with me to the Tenino house when I was working on the interior, but her job was mainly to take care of James and prepare the meal. I don't think we tilled the garden that spring, and I don't know how I would have taken care of it if we had. I did start to find sources for wood and brought in rough cut lumber that I later used to build rabbit hutches and chicken coops. I might have gotten raspberry starts that summer and planted them behind the house. The area around the house was mostly bare. I don't know if Lukenbill had scraped it with a caterpillar before he started the remodel, but it was quite available to plant things around the house.

I think we probably planted the strawberry and the fruit trees that summer. I also cleaned out the brush around three spindly apple trees in mid-property and a thicket of plums at the top of the hill where the open field would be ready to plant the next year. Also we were able to pick and can blackberries, and there were some wild apple trees down the road from which we made juice. I bought a utensil called a triple boiler. It was made in Finland and consisted of a basket, which fit inside a drip pan which drained juice into a spout. These sat on top of a boiler pan. The steam from the boiler would draw the juice out of the fruit, which could be drained directly into jars and sealed. The juice was at the temperature of steam so it was sterile. After the juice was collected, the fruit could be pulped in the basket and used for leathers, sauce or what have you. I still have that steamer, but the last time I used it was for making Lilikoi (passion fruit) juice. I think that was a mistake, because the triple-boiler was made of aluminum alloy, which I think leeched into the very acidic passion fruit juice. I have never had time to sand down the triple-boiler and try it with something less acidic, like guava. And I never got around to doing that because my third wife sold it in a garage sale.

# Chapter 8

# Bearing the Burden

Therefore an overseer must be above reproach, the husband of one wife, sober-minded, self-controlled, respectable, hospitable, able to teach, not a drunkard, not violent but gentle, not quarrelsome, not a lover of money. He must manage his own household well, with all dignity keeping his children submissive...
**English Standard Version (2001) 1ˢᵗ Timothy 3:2-4**

It is really hard to believe, looking back at it, how much happened in 1974. Not only did I pull off a $17 K project at Weyerhaeuser in 3 months, but I moved my toddler son and wife to Centralia, started a new job, bought a fixer-upper house, fixed it up, started a farm, and brought the additional 6 members of Charity's family to Tenino. I almost have to ask myself if it all really happened. But I know when the kids arrived on March 5, 1975; we were in the Tenino house.

I remember that we spent a lot of time at Yard Birds, which was originally an army surplus store that had grown into a large business (I guess you would call it a department store), but very local style. You could find the strangest things in the surplus section. There was one contraption that I tried for the longest time to figure out; finally I realized that it was an experiment version of an ultra-microtome that had been hand-built by someone in the military, probably when transmission electron microscopy was first developed and they needed a way to slice specimens thin enough to transmit an electron beam through them. Mainly the reason we frequented Yard Birds was because it was the cheapest place in town for most things.

Across the street from Yard Birds there was a permanent swap meet. Now there you could find literally **anything.** I found an old rabbit plane in good condition; that's how they made joints and groves before there were electric routers. I even scored a hydro-ram pump, from a seller who didn't even know what is was. I knew about the concept from the Peace Corps manual. It is an incredibly simple mechanism that has pumped water to the Taj Mahal for centuries. It consists of an air accumulator (vessel which holds air), and two clapper valves. On the water-inlet side you need flowing water; it doesn't have to be much but the faster the flow the more water you can pump and the higher you can lift it. The water flows through the pump and out the other side, but when the water reaches a certain velocity, it forces one of the valves to close. That forced the other valve to open, and that pushes water into the air accumulator. When the pressure equilibrates, the valve on the accumulator closes, and the valve restricting the outflow opens. So how does that pump water, you ask? Well, the accumulator tank has a delivery pipe attached to it, and each time the valves go through their motion, the water is forced into the accumulator and up the delivery pipe to wherever you want it to go. Unfortunately, the ram pump that I bought had damaged clapper valves, and I didn't know anyone that could fix them. I struggled for days trying to get the thing properly adjusted. We had decent water flow in our stream, but we needed water up on the high field that we eventually tilled for garden. The Peace Corps manual had a diagram of how to build one out of pipe, and if I were smart, that is what I should have done. Instead I ended up hauling water in a 55 gallon drum with a little drum pump to fill and discharge it. I wasn't the handiest fellow for homesteading, but I tried.

The forgoing being 'guy stuff', I realize that most readers of the female persuasion are probably glazing over about now, so I will get on with the family situation. Fr. O'Connell was still on the job regarding getting the family over to America. I am not sure but what he might have saved some of the money I sent him previously. Now he was waiting for more money from me and orders to go ahead and send the family out. I did not realize that the plan that I had envisioned was being changed. I thought it would probably just be the three youngest kids that would come. Instead, Fr. O'Connell thought they would need Gertrude's help getting through the flights. Now Gertrude also had a son, so that would mean 5 people coming. Ed was not included at that time because the grandparents wanted him to stay to help the family and finish school. I think Ed probably lived with his uncle Wilson and his wife in Mwatate or Mpizini; I am not sure. But Gertrude was anxious to come to American. I guess she was not that happy with the position in which her education had landed her, and now she was a single parent. I hoped they would not all assume that America was heaven, because they would have a rude awakening.

**Charity and Jimmy** were enjoying their first snow together in 1975. (Photographed by the author.)

Our first winter in the homestead was fairly pleasant. We did not have all the conveniences, but we had firewood, and blankets, and a wood stove to cook on and give heat. I think Charity was warming to the idea of living "back on the farm". I think I got a Sled for Jimmy, and we made the hill to the upper field a sledding slope for the few days that we had sufficient snow. I have a few pictures from those days, and the smiles seemed genuine.

Also we had decided to attend St. Peter's Catholic Church in Tenino and then St. Columban's in Yelm, a little town on the way to Olympia. I think we switched back and forth because St. Peter's was a mission and only had a visiting priest and one Mass on Sunday, whereas St. Columban's was a parish and had more services. In both places we met people who were very friendly. Dave (the local Game Warden and Deacon of St. Peter's), and his wife and two sons were very cordial to us and invited us to Bible study. Olli and his wife in Yelm had one daughter about Samba's age. Tina was their child, but they had been foster parents to 72 children. Also the Bardsleys, who lived just down the road from us, had two daughters, one of whom was a Native American foster child. They also had raised a number of foster children. Somehow that gave us some kind of connection, because as they spoke to us, they learned that we also were soon to bring children over from Africa. In a kind of true Christian spirit, they almost made it their project to welcome

109

the family. This reminded Charity of the way she had been welcomed by the Honeycomb Fellowship in Seattle.

I don't remember if it was before or after the kids came from Africa, but it was particularly cold that winter, and the Bardsleys' pump house froze, so they did not have water. On the other hand, we had plenty of water, but to keep if flowing we needed to run a hose from the outside spigot down the driveway to keep the pipes from freezing. The Bardsleys knew this and so they asked us if they could collect water from the hose. Of course, we had no objection, and were glad to help them out in neighborly fashion. It was a little thing for us, but they were so appreciative that Mrs. Bardsley brought me a real mincemeat pie (I mean the kind made with venison). It was the last piece of real mincemeat pie that I ever ate in my life. It was sooooo good! The crust was made with bacon grease, and the filling was rich. Definitely one of my very most favorite pies, bar none! Neither Mrs. French's kidney pie nor my mother's peach pie could hold a candle to it. Even Mary McCrank's in Chehalis, Washington, (which is famous for their pies) doesn't make mincemeat in the traditional fashion.

The Bardsleys had another problem with their water supply. Their well tapped into an aquifer that was inhabited by *Thiobacillus*, which oxidizes thiosulfate and elemental sulfur to sulfate. It is not dangerous, but it made the water smell like sulfur. Where I was raised in McCloud, California, we had what they called a soda springs (*Thiobacillus* creates a "carbonation" of the water). The McCloud residents considered it a health drink and would collect it for making lemonade. Nestlé's Company actually made an effort to buy the McCloud Spring but the community refused. However good it might be for you, if your tape water always smelled like sulfur, you might tire of it. So after that cold snap, I told the Bardsleys that they could get drinking water from our spring any time they wanted it. Our water was sweet and abundant, so they did.

When I was finally able to send enough money to arrange for the family to fly to America, I was desperately trying to arrange the detail of how we would live. This is how unprepared I was for the coming of the family. I didn't even know how I would get them from the airport to our house. I could not possibly carry all 5 of them in the truck all the way from Seattle-Tacoma Airport in the middle of the winter. I don't remember anyone else in Tenino offering to transport them. I still don't remember how I pulled it off, but I know we didn't go in the Gimmy. My mother kept notes in her photo album, and she has the date as March 5 of 1975. I have a picture of the whole family, also taken in 1975 soon after they arrived.

**The family** visiting the University of Washington in 1975. Bottom left to right: Sam, Samba, Teddy, Charity, Jimmy. Top left to right: Gertrude, Mzae, and me. (Photographed by the author.)

I don't think we had time to arrange a welcoming committee for the family's arrival, but if the Honeycomb Fellowship people came, it has been locked in the deep recesses of my memory. I do remember that none of the members of the Honeycomb Fellowship every came down to Tenino to visit us except Doris and her two sons. I will describe their Thanksgiving visit later.

My first retrievable memory of the kids in America was in the house in Tenino. When they arrived from the airport, it was the first time that James had seen any of these "siblings." At first he did not act startled, but I remember noticing that amidst all the hustle and bustle of the occupancy of the house going from 3 to 8, James was a little overwhelmed, to say the least. Soon after we arrived at the house, Sam was immediately all over James' toys, and that would lead to some conflict in the near future. Sam had been Charity's golden boy in Taita, and now he was ready to resume his place in the pecking order. James would have objection to that, even though he was only starting to be able to express himself in English and some Kidawida. On top of that, they were all gibbering away in some strange tongue, of which he could only understand the occasional word

It goes without saying that the reunion of *Mao* and her *watoto* (children) was warm and tearful. Gertrude had done a credible job of keeping the family together and relatively healthy, and for that, Charity was most grateful. She was also visibly relieved to finally have people around who spoke her native language. To be honest, Kiswahili was not the native language of either Charity or me, and she was not learning English very quickly. Given the demands on my time and mental resources, I really could not afford the time to slow down every activity by explaining it in English, and then translating it into Kiswahili. Some of our communication issues may have stemmed from that fact. I noticed right away that Charity and Gertrude began a running, private, Kidawida commentary on everything that was going on around them starting with that first night at the little house in the woods, in the winter, in Washington, all the way 'round the world from Taita.

Where to start? So many things had to occur as soon as the kids arrived; it is hard to know how to describe it all. Let's start with church. I think the first trip we made to church was to Yelm. I figured we would need some supplies, and there was Food Co-op in Yelm, so we made a day of it. It was quite a site to see, all these little round black faces in a sea of white. There was actually one other black family in the parish; Charles and Oti. They had a son and a daughter (she was about Samba's age), but the father was a disabled veteran. He had served 20 years in the army, and was on his last tour in Vietnam, when he was injured. It wasn't in combat; he was an instructor, and while he was demonstrating hand grenade use, one exploded at close range. He was severely burned and deformed facially as well as on his limbs and torso. But he could get around, he could use the parts of his hands that were left, and he **never** complained. They lived on a farm in Yelm when we first met them. I don't know if they introduced themselves that day, but it was not long before we got acquainted. Oti was a woman of substance both physically and politically. She was running a non-profit of some kind when we met them. The first time we went to visit them at their home, the African kids were shocked by the geese. Oti had a small flock, and they were bigger than any bird the kids had ever seen (I don't think they had seen an Africa ostrich by then). Not only that, but instead of the kids chasing the birds, the geese would chase the kids; that was a big surprise to kids who had grown up with docile chickens.

Just after the kids came, my mother called and told us that if I would come to California, Fr. Carl would deed the Rambler Ambassador station wagon over to us. It was a classic, which Father had maintained for many years, but now he was ready to move to something smaller and less of a gas guzzler. The first oil crisis[50] had convinced him. They knew we would need

---

[50] The **1973 oil crisis** started in October 1973, when the members of Organization of Arab Petroleum Exporting Countries or the OAPEC (consisting of the Arab members of OPEC, plus Egypt, Syria and Tunisia) proclaimed an oil embargo "in response to the U.S. decision to re-supply the Israeli military" during the Yom Kippur war; it lasted until March 1974. With

a bigger vehicle for the family. The blue book on the Rambler was so low it wasn't worth trading in, even though it was in near perfect condition. The irony was not lost on me that because of the international oil crisis a car called "Ambassador" would be transferred to a family just off the plane from Africa.

My mother's album indicates that Samba and I went to California in June of 1975, but I think it might have been earlier. I think we must have gone to Davis by train and Fr. Carl and Mom picked us up. I don't really remember any of this, but I know that Mom and Father did not bring the Ambassador up to us. There is a picture of Samba with Mom and Father. Also there are two other pictures that I took of Samba with snow covered hills of Northern California in the background. Those must have been taken in the early spring because the deciduous foliage had not bloomed yet. This process is like a crime novel, I have to piece together the evidence!

Gertrude, being an adult, was given the 19 ft. trailer as her "room" to share with Samba. I think it was not what she had expected from America, but it was certainly no worse than what she had known in Taita. It was important that she begin work as soon as she was able. What she wanted to do was go to school. I explained to her that we could not afford to send her to school and if she wished to pursue it, she would first need to get her financial house in order. In order for her to work, she needed to be able to drive, so the first order of business was to help her get her license. She did find a job at a nursing home in Centralia right away. It was not a registered nurse's job (her training did not match the requirements in the USA), and it did not pay very well. Nevertheless, her credentials were in order, and they need staff desperately. At first she had day shift, so she was able to ride with me to work, and practice driving at the same time. The Ambassador must have been with us before June

---

the US actions seen as initiating the oil embargo and the long term possibility of high oil prices, disrupted supply and recession, a strong rift was created within NATO. Additionally, some European nations and Japan sought to disassociate themselves from the US Middle East policy. Arab oil producers had also linked the end of the embargo with successful US efforts to create peace in the Middle East, which complicated the situation. To address these developments, the Nixon Administration began parallel negotiations with both Arab oil producers to end the embargo, and with Egypt, Syria, and Israel to arrange an Israeli pull-back from the Sinai and the Golan Heights after the fighting stopped. By January 18, 1974, Secretary of State Henry Kissinger had negotiated an Israeli troop withdrawal from parts of the Sinai. The promise of a negotiated settlement between Israel and Syria was sufficient to convince Arab oil producers to lift the embargo in March 1974. By May, Israel agreed to withdraw from the Golan Heights. http://en.wikipedia.org/wiki/1973_oil_crisis

because Gertrude's Driver training was all in that vehicle with the automatic transmission.

I just noticed how many times I used the word "order" in the previous paragraph. I wonder what subliminal messages there was in that? I guess I was on verge of ordering Gertrude around, and as I would later learn, she was not accepting the direction with docility.

The driving lessons were a bit awkward, because, of course, I needed her to sit next to me on the bench seat so I could operate the pedals and she could steer. Understand that she was a lot closer to my age than Charity, and an attractive woman. I don't know what went through her head, but I know I was not attracted to her. It was strictly business for me. After she learned to steer, I let her sit behind the wheel and I sat close on the bench, so I would be able to take controls if needed. She was a quick learner and was able to pass her driving test well within the one-month grace period. After that, she was able to take the car to work herself when she needed to work swing (3 to 11 PM) or graveyard (11 PM to 7 AM) shifts.

Having the station wagon also gave her the liberty to do whatever she wanted to do in town. It took some of the pressure off of me, because she could also take her mother places that they wanted to go. Of course, there was always the issue of the cost of gas, but now that Gertrude was working, not paying rent, eating some of her meals with us, and otherwise having few expenses, I figured she could pay for her gas. It wasn't too long before she bought her own car, a secondhand Chevrolet. There is a picture of her with the car and an Afro-American friend in my mother's album.

Meanwhile I was trying to figure out how to feed and clothe 8 people on an income of a Technician II. That was probably less than $1000 per month when I started. The only record I have of my salary was the $1440 I earned after I was promoted to Technician Specialist, but it took me a few years to get there. I applied for food stamps, but it was so immediately apparent to me that the process was going to be way more work that it was worth. Therefore, although the family was approved for food stamps, we never used them. I did find a grocery wholesaler in Centralia who made it possible to buy in bulk. His name was Mr. Sorenson (I mentioned him in the last book); he had a fantastic ability to add numbers. I heard he had musical talent as well. I never heard him perform, but he was known in the community for his music. My stepmother knew him because she had audited him for the Internal Revenue Service, and it wasn't the only time he was audited. I guess the IRS couldn't believe he had so little income, but I could believe it, because his prices were very low. By the way, he passed every audit, because the only records he kept were his sales receipt books. He had whole room full of every receipt he had ever written. The IRS agents would take one look at the receipt books, piled to the sealing, and would give up!

I had already bought some Barred Rock and ode Island Red chickens when someone asked us if we wanted a flock of Banties.[51] I thought, why not, but I did not know some of the great characteristics of a Bantam hen. So I built some cages and we drove up to Winlock with the cages. We were told to come at night, because they were not in a chicken coup. They were all roosting in the low hanging tree on the owner's property. It was quite an interesting experience trying to capture 20 or so Bantam hens and roosters, but the kids were enjoying it. They knew chickens probably better than I did, and Charity figured out how to outsmart the wily birds. We finally managed to get them all in cages and took them home.

---

[51] A **bantam** is a small variety of poultry, especially chickens. Etymologically, the name bantam is derived from the city of Bantam, once a major seaport, in Indonesia. European sailors restocking on live fowl for sea journeys found the small native breeds of chicken in Southeast Asia to be useful, and any such small poultry came to be known as a bantam.

Most large chicken breeds have a bantam counterpart, sometimes referred to as a miniature. Miniatures are usually one-fifth to one-quarter the size of the standard breed, but they are expected to exhibit all of the standard breed's characteristics. A true bantam has no large counterpart, and is naturally small.

Bantams have become increasingly popular as pets as well as for show purposes because they are smaller and have more varied and exotic colors and feather patterns than other chickens. They are suitable for smaller backyards as they do not need as much space as other breeds. Bantam hens are also used as laying hens, although Bantam eggs are only about one-half to one-third the size of a regular hen egg. The Bantam chicken eats the same foods as a normal chicken, chickens in the wild eat more insects and vegetation than grains. In commercial situations they are feed grain based foods because this is convenient and efficient for the producer. In contrast, the Bantam rooster is famous in rural areas throughout the United Kingdom and the United States for its aggressive, "puffed-up" disposition that can be comedic in stature. It is often called a "Banty" in the rural United States.

Many bantam hens are renowned for hatching and brooding purpose. Bantams clutch a variety of eggs from quail up to two goose eggs, and are known as fearsome mothers, with a high success rate in rearing any egg hatched. http://en.wikipedia.org/wiki/Bantam_(poultry)

**Bantam rooster:** Old English Game Bantum, (from Morningshores.com (CC BY-SA 4.0)) https://morningchores.com/old-english-game-bantam/

I have a great deal of respect for the Banties. As the footnote states, these birds have a phenomenal ability to protect their brood. Prior to obtaining the Banties, I was constantly fighting weasels, and losing the battle. The adults could fend off the varmints, but the chicks were dropping like flies. Later we were given some White Leghorns, which were great egg layers, but the flock of whites never grew. In contrast, the Bantam flock multiplied and multiplied. They would not roost in the coups that I built for them but would run off in the woods to lay their eggs. We very seldom found their eggs, but neither did the weasels. Soon the hen would come back to get scratch trailed by a clutch of chicks. What the original owner of the Banties did not tell us is that the flock was cross-bred to Silkies. The most notable characteristic of a Silky, as far as I am concerned, is that their Red muscle is kind of a blue grey color, and their blood vessels are blue-black. You have to think twice about consuming the meat from a Silky.

We also started to acquire rabbits, and soon we had 20, and then 40 and so on. It became a race to keep them fed and to provide adequate housing so that the baby rabbits would not die. Sometimes when I would run out of feed, I would make the boys, particularly Mzae, cut greens for them. I imagine Mzae will never want to see a rabbit again in his lifetime. I do still have a hat made from a rabbit pelt when we were still in Kenya. I think we ended up selling some of the rabbit pelts that we stretched and dried. But we certainly ate a lot of rabbit and chicken as well. The cheapest meat I could buy in the grocery store was beef liver. It was forty nine cents a pound, and we ate a lot of it. I'm surprised that the family did not revolt. I didn't like the liver, but at that time I thought of it as a very nutritious food. In later years, we learned that liver could concentrate all manner of bad chemicals being used on the feedlot cattle. So far, no one in the family has contracted cancer, but I keep my fingers crossed.

The next essential item was to get the kids in school. Sam was still young, and could have skipped kindergarten, but Mzae and Samba both needed to go to school. I did not really know how they would fare in the American school system, but the school tested them and placed them pretty close to their age level (or at least that is the way I remember it). Sam was a different case. The Tenino School psychologist actually called me in to monitor the aptitude and intelligence test they were giving him. He tested low, but I observed that it wasn't that he didn't understand what he was supposed to do; he just thought he had a 'better idea'. I remember distinctly one diagram in which he was supposed to draw it to match. He drew the identical drawing, only backwards. Still they relegated him to Special Education. To this day, I don't know if Sam really did have a mental handicap or whether he just did things the way he wanted to. That was usually not the way anyone else wanted him to do. I am told by his brothers that there is not much you can do about Sam. He does what he wants to do. I was probably too hard on Sam in the years we were together because he was a stubborn one. He wasn't mean or sullen or vindictive. He was happy go lucky as any kid when it came to having fun. But when it came to doing what he didn't want to do, he was a master avoider. What he was is stubborn. And that may still be true. I recognized the problem because I was much like that myself as a kid. I buried my homework in a snowbank and such, but I didn't have the nerve to incur the kind of punishment that Sam got from me. In one way, Sam was defiant, almost to the point that he would not cry when I spanked him. Now, I certainly realize that corporal punishment is not an effective disciplinary tool. But then we didn't know there was any other way to raise children. Spare the rod; spoil the child, as the adage went. And I won't say that the absence of corporal punishment is necessarily effective either.[52]

Samba was always a very sweet girl, and always very helpful to her mother and her siblings. She seemed to be happy about going to school, and I think she did pretty well, but I think the social adaptation was hard for her. At first the kids went to Tenino School, but there was a reorganization of the

---

[52] My own daughter was raised sans spankings, but she has had a hard time adjusting to the real world; I always have to wonder if a little more discipline (not physical) would have helped

districts, and they were assigned to a school closer to Olympia (I can't really remember the name of the school but it was in Tumwater). That transfer was inconvenient for everyone. The kids had to board the bus earlier and came home later, and the parent visits were more difficult to arrange and attend. One of Samba's teachers was Japanese, who had been raised in the internment camps of WWII. She seemed to take offence at the fact that Samba had a smoky smell. She had apparently hated the fact that the camp stoves made everyone in the camp smell of smoke. Unfortunately, her approach was to tell Samba to clean herself better. Of course, that was not possible, because we heated the house with wood. Finally we had a meeting with her, and I explained that we would attempt to keep Samba's clothes clean, but that we could not guarantee that the smoky smell could be corrected. I think this became a permanent embarrassment for Samba and set her apart from the more affluent children in that school which had a high proportion of suburbanite sons and daughters of parents who were better-off than we were. Attending the school in Tumwater made it difficult for the kids to form friendships. In Tenino and Yelm there were children for Samba to play with. Knowing Oti and Charles helped, because their daughter became friends with Samba, as well as Olli's daughter Tina. Oti's son was also friends with the boys, so we tried to maintain those contacts as much as possible.

Speaking of thing that worried me about Samba; I felt so sorry for her. In order to insure that the kids would get their vitamin C, I brought frozen juice. But the only juice that we could afford to buy was lemonade and occasionally grape. I refused to buy the artificial juice, and those kids probably didn't even know what Kool-Aid was. The problem for Samba was that she developed sores on her tongue which were aggravated by acid foods. She could not eat fresh tomatoes without her tongue breaking out with sores. I think we had Dr. Park take a look at her tongue but I don't think he ever had an effective remedy.

Since I mentioned Dr. Park, I should say that he was a fine general practitioner, who treated my family with respect, and saved my son James' life (which I will explain later). He was a pillar of the Centralia community and bought a landmark hotel and converted it to a residence for seniors. His X-ray machine was ancient, and his clinic was "no frills", but the medical facility he built next to the Central Park was expanded and is still operating as the Washington Park Medical Center.

Mzae was the brightest of the younger children. I knew this from Kenya because he could learn songs and such skills very quickly. He was sort of my "golden boy", in the sense that he was the most reliable and helpful of the boys. And here I have to confess I need to apologize as well. Because of his helpfulness, I relied upon him to tend the rabbits and other chores. I even made agreements with him to share the proceeds from the rabbits, to encourage him to put out the effort. Maybe that is why he ended up with a Certified Public Accountant degree. He probably thought he didn't get his fair share of the proceeds from the rabbits. What I did not realize about Mzae was that he was suffering from malaria. It was a semi-dormant case, but as time progressed it got worse, and I was not paying close enough attention to realize that his listlessness was not intentional. When I finally did realize that he was seriously ill (basically because he collapsed) we got him to Dr. Park, who determined that it was malaria and put him on a treatment regime. That was a wake-up call to me, and I realized that this business of raising kids is no joke. Bad things can happen quickly, and a parent has to be constantly vigilant. I had not mentioned it in my last book, but an accident occurred in Mgange that involved Mzae. We were making chai one morning before we were to attend Charity's brother's wedding. Everything was kind of rush-rush, and I was in the kitchen with all of the little children because Charity was dressing. Something startled me, and I turned quickly with a pot of hot water in my hand. It hit Mzae who was right behind me and spilled over his face and hands. I didn't realize immediately how hot the water was, and Mzae did not cry out. It wasn't until a huge blister developed on Mzae's face that I realized how serious the burn was. Of course, I rushed him to a clinic and they bandaged him up. I think I had dropped Charity on the way, so she could attend the wedding with the other kids. Needless to say, Mzae and I did not. I felt terrible for him, but he was very stoic about the whole thing. I wonder if he is as internal as a husband and father, as he was as a child.

The youngest of the immigrants was Teddy. To this day, I don't know who his father was, but he definitely needed the influence of a father. He was a good boy, but very thin when he came. He was close to the same age as James, so they soon became a team which they have remained until this very day. Ted is in the Army, has been to Iraq and will be heading back to Iraq for a second tour. He and James have stayed in touch, and recently met briefly in Portland, Oregon before Ted is shipped out again. As I have said before, I will let James explain their relationship when he writes his memoirs, but let it be adequate to say that they have been more like brothers than uncle (James) and nephew (Ted). They were still too young for school, so they spent a lot more time together than the other kids. As I remember it, Teddy stayed with us when Gertrude moved out of the Tenino house.

It was a great place for a little kid to grow up. Because we were off the main highway, we did not have to worry about traffic, so the kids could basically roam, just as my cousins and I had been able to roam in McCloud, as well as Bobby Van and I did in Camp Pondosa. There were chickens and rabbits to play with, and of course the usual haunts of little guys: the shallow creek and the woods. Of course, they were still too young to do much of that at the beginning, but they grew into it. One peculiar thing that happened was the language. All day long they would hear Kidawida from Charity, and Teddy had, of course, been raised to that point on Kidawida and Kiswahili. But as the older kids attended school, they started to talk in English. Very quickly both Teddy and Jimmy picked up on the fact that English was the "in" lingua franca, and within that first year James lost his ability to even speak anything but English. He could still understand his mother and Gertrude to some extent, but in his mind, English was what he needed to know. And Teddy and James have been "conspiring" in English ever since.

**Teddy** (left) and **Jimmy** (right) horsing around at the table in Tenino. (Photographed by the author)

I think the friendship between Teddy and James was a great asset to them. By that time Sam had reclaimed his favored status with *Mao* and would have been able to lord it over Teddy and Jimmy (because that is what we all called James then). However, there is strength in numbers. T & J incorporated could stand their ground and not let Sam push them around. Also, in the resolution of a dispute, T & J had their stories in sync, so there were two witnesses to one before the parental tribunal. It probably balanced out the situation, because Sam's pull with the mothers was counterbalanced by the weight of corroborated testimony. Oh how difficult the lessons of childhood!

Finishing this chapter is going to be tough because my recall is not chronological. I was going to start talking about the impact of Alex Haley's *Roots* on the family, but when I looked it up I found out that that was aired in 1977. I guess I won't be writing about that soon. Therefore, at this point, I must apologize to the reader. Up until now, if I jumped around chronologically, it was intentional. Now, with very little documentation upon which to rely, I may be jumping ahead or backwards without "pre-authorization", so to speak.

I can see from a picture that I took of Jimmy and my mother that she must have visited us very soon after we bought the house. The grounds around it were bare and the trees were leafless. She was holding him in her lap tickling him; he was obviously not big enough to walk. I am sure that she came up on the train, and we picked her up in Centralia. There is another picture of Charity and Jimmy, standing on his own, in the woods at our place, in snow. I am sure that was taken before the other children came from Kenya. Like I said, it was a peaceful time for Jimmy. He got all of the attention of his mother, my mother and me. Putting this scant evidence together and remembering that Jimmy was about a year and a half old when the kids came from Africa, it would have been spring when that happened.

# Chapter 9

# Chinks in the Armor

For from now on in one house there will be five divided, three against two and two against three. They will be divided, father against son and son against father, mother against daughter and daughter against mother, mother-in-law against her daughter-in-law and daughter-in-law against mother-in-law." **English Standard Version (2001) Luke 12:52-52**

We had steeled ourselves against the buffeting of a harsh winter, a harsh society, a harsh reality. We were trying to do something against which so many had advised. Some had been persuaded; some had been honesty helpful; some were in full support, but those were few. Fr. Sean O'Connell had helped us over the great divide, and even Mr. Moon had softened his attitude. I mean, what are you going to do with a young buck when he is determined to defy the best advice of his elders? Seemingly, with the help of the fellowship, and my parents, and even the neighbors, we were making it work. Even the people at Weyerhaeuser appeared to understand. As a family we did not have close personal relationships with most of my fellow workers, but there were no overtly negative attitudes towards us either. Any friction that occurred had more to do with my working relationship with individuals than with the fact that I was married to an African and had a household of eight to support.

What I encountered at the Genetics lab at Weyerhaeuser was a group of mostly local women. Except the geneticist, Jess Daniels, the only other man in the group was Liang Hsin, himself also a PhD in genetics, but hired as a technician. The women that worked at the lab were all long-time residents of the Centralia-Chehalis area. I am not sure that any of them had a degree. There were three that worked year round and then there were temporary staff that worked during the pollen season, and then on into the seed-collection and processing season. They worked long enough to collect unemployment in the off season. My presence was a kind of imposition on a well-established pecking order that had resolved itself long before I came. Under Jess, Liang was the organizer who planned the breeding crosses and managed the evaluation of the breeding stock. He was tireless, as have been most of the Chinese immigrants that I have known. He was himself from Taiwan; there is an extremely well developed work ethic on the Formosan Islands just as there is in mainland China.

On the seed production and processing side, there was an obese woman, who smoked. She had worked herself into the position of record keeper. This was an extremely important position in a breeding program, particularly since computers were only coming into common use, and all of the breeding records were kept on cards. These were then sorted using a set of pins.[53] When I looked this up, I was amazed to find out that this system had only been patented the year I started work at the Weyerhaeuser Research lab. So this woman was the master of a brand new "technology", which I had assumed predated computers by at least a hundred years. I guess that will be a lesson to me not to assume, but it also typifies the status of human knowledge. Some of the simplest concepts take millennia to develop (or reinvent). Conversely, something as complicated as digital electronic computer could be developed between the span of two short wars (in historical perspective). This one, rather unhealthy, lady, whom I will call the Keeper, was the master of the gold reserve, which was the breeding record for the company. She knew she was in the driver's seat and maintained authority on that basis. The younger woman, who did all the field work, harvesting seed and directly supervised the seed processing crew, was clearly at the mercy of the older woman. The temporary women were content to sit all day separating seed from the premature cones (in the sense that the cones had to be picked before they had advanced beyond

---

[53] United States Patent 3688900. **Apparatus for sorting** and retrieving information printed on cards is disclosed, where the information is classified into predetermined categories and the classifications are arranged to correlate with edge-punched holes and notches, and the entire apparatus is compactly structured for use on a desk or tabletop.

Inventors: Wayne L. Wanous, 34 12th Ave. N. (Hopkins, MN 55343)
Appl. No.: 05/141,641
Filed: May 10, 1971

the point where they would release their winged seed). The seed was then X-rayed and resorted to remove the "empties" and "eddies"; then it was stored for planting at the breeding orchard greenhouses.

In the pollen department, there was only one woman, and her I will name. Mildred was a patient lady and had carried on the collection and processing of the pollen catkins (microsporangia) probably as long as the Forest Genetics lab had been in business. She was the one who would be most heavily impacted by my presence, because I was hired to reassess and reorganize the pollen handling procedures. She retired (I think she was pushing 65) not long after I came to the Forestry Lab. I always hoped it was because she was ready to retire and not because of me.

I found Mildred much easier to work with than the Keeper, and fortunately most of my interactions were with the former. Jess, in his wisdom, placed the Keeper and me side by side with a wooden panel in between our desks. Her desk was always cleared and neat by 4:10 PM in preparation for her departure at 4:30 sharp. My desk was virtually never clear, and I often did not leave until 6 or 7 PM. I really can't remember if she was still allowed to smoke at her desk at that time, but she was always very irritated with me because she thought that I stole pencils off her desk. Of course, I would not admit to it, but if I did, I am sure I was not the only one. You see, she had the only phone in the lab on her desk. So if anyone answered the phone when she was not there, they had to 'borrow' a pen to take notes or messages. Right?

When seed processing was in session, the women seemed quite positive about the whole thing. It was a manual job that they would execute swiftly but they could converse with equal ease. The only time they complained was when we painted the seed processing room a nearly fluorescent green color. That in combination with the fluorescent lighting was driving them to distraction. I can't remember if we ever remedied that situation; nevertheless, I tried to stay out of that room. The seed processing foreperson, whose name I cannot remember, was usually the one with whom I was obliged to interact in that room. On more than one occasion I would say something that had all the earmarks of a Freudian slip. All the ears in the room were attuned, and the moment I uttered the unintentional double *entendre*, they would all laugh uproariously. Usually this precipitated my embarrassment and alteration of complexion. I think they all took great delight in so unnerving this 27 year old married fellow with four young kids and a grandchild.

I won't say that the aforementioned foreperson and I did not have some interesting field trips together. These were during the pollen shedding season, and we were assigned to use a cherry-picker man-lift to collect fir catkins (microsporangia). She, being the lighter, would ascend in the basket, while I was the safety assistant on the ground. At the lunch break we needed to eat in the orchard, so she would bring a bottle of wine and some crackers and cheese. It made the remainder of the balmy late spring afternoon quite pleasant. Who would think wine and cheese could have such a civilizing effect? All perfectly above board you understand, but definitely a more civilized way to work. I hear that beer is served on the job in Germany. Perhaps that is a factor explaining why Germany's economy did not plummet with that of the rest of the western world in 2008?

Mike Carlson was another member of the Forestry Genetics group, but he did not arrive until sometime in 1975. He had just graduated from the University Of Washington School Of Forestry with a master's degree in Forestry. He was a student of the aforementioned Dr. Reinhard Stettler and I believe Mike's emphasis was in forest genetics. He did not come to Weyerhaeuser until after we were well into the research on pollen handling. His job was to improve the efficiency of the controlled-crosses in the breeding program, and he did an excellent job. Prior to his coming, the record keeping system was largely a matter of handwritten notation. What he brought to it was a sort of bar coding system. The bar code reader was not in use yet, but he devised a series of labels (some were soft metal tags with two or three tear-off water-proof labels attached). The metal label was tied to the branch of the tree containing the megasporangia (cones) to be pollinated; and the tear-off labels were designed to be torn off at various stages of handling. These all contained the code for the particular cross, and spaces were provided to add information such as date, time, etc.

These tags were then brought to the computer terminal at each breeding orchard to be entered into a database. All of this technology probably already existed in research programs elsewhere, but Mike brought them to Weyerhaeuser. He may have added his own improvements along the way, but in either case, it was a very efficient system. Therefore, when this quote from the British Columbia Ministry of Forestry website says that Mike's career started in 1983, they overlook the fact that Mike started making his mark on forestry 8 years earlier:

125

Michael Carlson PhD. (photo and bio used with permission of M. Carlson and the Canadian Ministry of Forestry)

Mike began his career with the BC Ministry of Forests and Range Research Branch in 1983 as the geneticist for lodgepole pine. Bringing ideas, energy, and enthusiasm, Mike quickly advanced the lodgepole pine breeding program with his pragmatic and field-oriented approach. Mike's energy carried him into leadership roles with western white pine, poplar, and birch programs, plus a wide variety of other projects. Mike's ability to generate enthusiasm and cooperation in others has led to him making major contributions to forest genetics and forestry in British Columbia. Mike also served as chair of the Interior Technical Advisory Committee and as a member of the Forest Genetics Council from 1998 to 2008. Never to be held down, Mike has continued to work as hard as ever in a scientist emeritus position since his retirement in March 2010.

Even though I have not seen Mike in many years, I consider him a friend. More than anyone else at Weyerhaeuser, including even my boss, Jess Daniels, Mike took a personal interest in my little experiment in international diplomacy. I don't exactly know why. Maybe it was because he was the only other employee with small children (he had two daughters). Or maybe it was because we were young bucks starting our careers. I won't say that we had a lot in common. Other than the job, and the fact that we were both establishing our own little homesteads. We did not have the same religious beliefs or circle of friends or backgrounds. I won't even say that our wives or children were that interested in each other. I guess it was just like they say in the above quote: "he generated enthusiasm and cooperation in others." I genuinely liked the man.

The first thing that we did together, outside of work, was to take the kids to the mountains to play in the snow. At that time, Mike had a utility van, so we piled everyone in the van and headed for the timberline snow. The children in my family were not well dressed for the occasion. After a great deal of joy riding and inner-tube through the powdered snow for the first time in their lives, they shivered the whole trip home. Mike's van did not have a very good heater, and the kids were all huddle in the back trying to stay warm. I think Mike might have made us some hot chocolate when we got back from the hills, and none of the kids suffered ill effects from their first encounter with the white stuff.

Mike Carlson also knew that it was difficult for me to feed the large family. One time he acquired a large number of chickens (I don't know how but I think they were white Leghorn egg layers at the end of their commercial service). He asked Liang and me to come to his house to have a chicken slaughter. Now my idea of slaughtering a chicken was rather crude. I did not know about breaking their neck, and I was under the impression that you just cut their head off with an axe. It's quick, but they flop around wildly. On the other hand, Liang was a master. We would catch a chicken and bring it too Liang, and he would proceed to hypnotize them by some oriental stealth (involving holding their beak to a line on the ground), and then ever so gently bleed them from the neck. As they expired in their unconscious state all the blood would be pumped from their bodies while the chickens were seemingly unaware. Liang said that the Chinese believe this makes the meat better because the alarm pheromones of the stress are never released. Mike divided the chickens between us, and we all ate well for a time. I kept mine on the claw so to speak (I took them home alive). When they stopped laying eggs altogether, Charity dispatch them with a wring of the neck.

On another occasion a buddy of Carlson's, who was a forester, invited him to cut poles in the Gifford Pinchot Forest. Some stands of naturally-seeded timber are so closely grown that they become tall and spindly. They either have to be thinned, or if the stand is just too dense, they have to cut everything down and start over. Mike asked me to take my truck so we could load it with poles. It was a big job bucking the poles up to 16 ft. lengths and bearing them out of the field mostly one man one pole at one time. We cinched the first load down with trucker's hitch knots. Now, you have to understand that the bed of the truck was 10 ft., and the duel wheels came under the bed about

3 ft. from the back end of the bed. That would make 9ft of the 16 ft. load extend over the rear axil. It was like driving a boat. A slight turn of the wheel and you could feel the whole load shifting around from side to side. The bow of the truck was way up in the air, and the truck was so close to fishtailing that I had to go very slow.

We dropped the first load at my house, and then we headed back up the mountain to grab a second. It was getting late in the afternoon when we finally brought his load to his home 10 miles south of Chehalis. We had passed through a windy stretch of road and three towns, with our bow high in the air, and our stern swaying along reluctantly. How we escaped the detection of the police I will never know, but I am positive our load was not within regulations. The irony of all this is that I, with the same load of logs, built a 10 x 26 foot awning along the back side of our house, which I later enclosed and poured a cement floor. Mike, on the other hand, built a two story three car garage with a second story floor. It always amazed me how Carlson was able to build such a large structure with the same amount of wood. I guess some of my poles were burned in the fireplace over the winter, which may partially explain the discrepancy. But I have to admit his structure was very impressive.

There are other occasions when Mike was of great help to me. In general, we worked fairly closely, although I will give him credit for bringing a level of efficiency and order to the breeding process that had previously not been there. Liang was a good genetics man, but his ability to work with the staff was limited. Most of the staff were not highly trained and were unaccustomed to foreign accents; I don't think it was a race issue; it was just a matter of simple communication. If there was one thing that Mike Carlson did well, it was communicate. He actually brought enthusiasm to the job. I think that the people that worked with Mike actually received a sense of purpose from him that might not have been there previously. He was well liked by the orchard crews, the lab crews, and we all liked him. Jess depended on him, and Mike and Liang worked together like hand and glove.

As the spring brought back the green and the flowers and the sun, the family began to enjoy the outdoors. The apple blossoms appeared on the three little trees and the plums bloomed in the field above. I needed to get the field plowed, so I started looking at the want ads. I found an old fellow about halfway to Yelm, who brought his tractor up the hill to our open field on the northeast end of the property. Turned out, he was a very interesting guy. Loved his Yellow Fin potatoes, and spotted our plum tree right away, when he plowed our field. He asked if he could pick some plums when they were ripe, because he remembered the plum jelly that his family used to make. We didn't trade plums for plowing, but he did give me a good rate. The soil was beautiful, rich, and deep; a consequence of having been fallow in grass for very many years, possibly not since the Lukenbill's ancestors had homesteaded there. It was a panoramic place, with one side of the field facing the clear-cut Weyerhaeuser land, and the other side surrounded by trees which grew along the slope leading to the clearing. We spent many hours on that patch of ground, which was, in almost all respects, perfect. The one thing it lacked was water, but the soil was so friable and rich that, once established potatoes and vegetables had no trouble sucking up the moisture stored in the deep soil. Land is a good thing, and Charity was glad to have some, although I don't think she realized what it would take to keep it.

What surprises me is that no one had ever built a home on the hill. The homestead house was in a low area next to the road and the stream. Most likely the stream was the determining factor. Back in the day, proximity to water was critical, and even though the Lukenbill's ancestors had discovered the spring up the road, they still needed water for bathing, cleaning, and the like. It was a lot easier to haul buckets of water from the stream than from the spring. And the spring was small, which is why I built the tank to hold a reservoir of water. In the whole time we lived on the homestead, once the tank had been built, we were never without water at the house.

That is not to say there were not problems associated with the water. At the risk of repeating myself, I would like to explain further. Because the pump could not build enough pressure in the accumulator, to cause it to switch off, it would run constantly. Consequently, we had to switch it on and off when we needed water. Eventually, it got so irritating (and expensive) that I finally determined that we would not use the pump at all. After that, with the low water pressure we had to use a bucket to collect enough water from the tap to bathe. It was like being back in Kenya, bathing out of a bucket. In retrospect, the irony is that it was not the pump that was running up the electric bill; it was the hot water tank in the basement. A word to the wise; if you have your hot water tank in the basement, then be sure to insulate the pipes! The hot water rises into the pipes, cools, and then drains back into the water tank. Consequently your hot water tank is heating constantly. Poetic justice has since occurred. I have a good friend who is a plumber. In my house in Hawaii, he installed a passive solar system. The sun-heated water flows up into the water tank and waits for us to use it. That will eventually repay all the loss from the house in Tenino, but we could have used the money then more than now. Fortunately electricity in the Northwest was many times cheaper than in Hawaii. Nevertheless we installed photovoltaic panels, too (something that had not been invented by the 1970's).

In a place like the Northwest, it never ceases to amaze me what difference sunshine makes. Not only is the natural process of tree budding and crocus blooming accelerated, but the very steam from the ground is an elixir that quickens the step and warms the heart. And if it has that effect on people who were raised with four seasons, imagine how it would affect Africans who had never known frost or winter. Our house was small, so when the out of doors became a place to play, the youth were out of doors all day. For the school aged among them, the classroom hours were interminable. I remembered that feeling from McCloud Elementary, with seeds germinating between two glass plates on the windowsill, bird twittering in the chartreuse foliage outside and the sultry spring air wafting in the open classroom windows. We children could not wait to get out and soak up the last rays of sun; nor could the Africans!

Charity's spirits were lifted, too. She was happy to have her children around her, and she was even happier when she was able to garden again. To a woman who grew up on a farm, the chance to plant and to grow crops is a rewarding feeling. Getting out in the sunshine, feeling the warm sod between your fingers, making the rows of tomatoes and squash and carrots grow; all of these things are good for the soul. And now the sound of playing children, the picnic lunches on the hill under the shade of the ripening plums on the trees, planting the Pontiac Red potatoes, hoeing the weeds and gave meaning to our lives. I have never felt as alive as when I had a garden to tend, and I think Charity shared that love of growing things.

Unfortunately, spring turns the heart to love. I know that sounds almost curmudgeonly, but for a young buck I had a rather prudish bent. Gertrude, on the other hand, did not. She began to be quite involved with the young men. This would be our parting of the ways so to speak. You must understand that Gertrude was sleeping in the trailer with her sister Samba. The latter was young and impressionable. So imagine my surprise one morning to find one of Gertrude's "boyfriends" coming out of the trailer when I went out to feed the chickens. Now, at my ripe old age, I would have probably been more tolerant. But as a 27 year old stepfather responsible for the proper upbringing of five young and impressionable youth, this was just too much of an affront to my authority.

I confronted Gertrude immediately. I don't know if the young man had even left the premises by the time I reprimanded her. In retrospect, I am sure she must have wondered who I thought I was, having been "living in sin" with her mother and all of those children for two years. Now suddenly I was acting like the God-given patriarch and guardian of purity. I don't remember the conversation exactly, but I am sure she must have retorted with something like "I am an adult, you can't control what I do." I probably said, "Well, I can if you are doing it in my house (trailer). She was mad, and I was mad, and Charity was mortified. I am sure she was hoping that for once she could live peacefully with all of her children around her... and Ed had still not been able to come. I think she was depending on Gertrude for companionship as well as help with English and adjusting to the demands of the new culture. Now I was presenting an obstacle to the plan. It was a tense situation for all of us. Up to that point, most disputes were minor and could be resolved with discussion. But this presented a unique problem.

I don't know exactly how quickly I decided to take the trailer back to the mobile home park in Centralia, but the intention was to have Gertrude move back to Centralia with the trailer. Of course, it must have taken at least a few days to find a spot in the park. As it turned out it was the same spot that Charity and I had occupied the first year in Centralia. It was not very far from Gertrude's work, so she was set. I did, for all intent and purposes, give her the trailer. I can't remember if she ever even sold it because I don't remember giving her the title to it. I do know that it never came back to the homestead in Tenino.

Now, Gertrude was on her own recognizance. She worked to support herself, and I think she attempted to go back to school, I can't really remember. Charity, James, and Teddy would sometimes come to town with me when I went to work, and would stay at Gertrude's trailer, until I got off work. Once Gertrude got transportation, she would visit us, but she was not available to Charity like she would have been if I had not laid down the law. I can't say that was the cause of our eventual demise, but I am sure it helped to lay the foundation.

Meanwhile, Samba had to move back into the house, and since we only had two bedrooms, that meant she had to sleep with her brothers. James slept in a large metal hospital crib in the room with Charity and me, while Samba, Mzae, Sam and Teddy slept in the room next to us. I had built a bunk bed out of pine board and 4x4 posts, and this was used by the boys. It was a strange shape; nearly 8 foot long and 3.5 ft. wide I can't remember whether Sam and Teddy shared one bunk, but Samba did have her own bed. I think

Gertrude took Teddy with her to Tacoma before he got too big to share a bed with Sam. As I remember they all had sleeping bags (except possibly Samba might have had sheets). I had been raised in a sleeping bag, which is actually a very comfortable way to sleep. The kid's bedroom was very cold in the winter, until John Bardsley, our neighbor, volunteered to dry-wall the closet in that room. That prevented the draft from the ship lap siding that had been the only barrier between the room and the outside. So Gertrude had her gas-heated self-contained trailer to herself, and the rest of us were packed into the little homestead on the creek. She was even free of the day-to-day responsibility for Teddy. I guess it was sort of payback for having taken care of her brothers and sister when her mother flew off to the other side of the world. Now she was on her own, she could have "visitors" as she pleased.

The best feature of the house, which I may have already mentioned, was the central fireplace into which the wood stove in the kitchen also exhausted. Of course, like any fire burning arrangement, the heat rising in the chimney would suck cold air in from the cracks and crannies. We would often all sit on the large hearth in the evening to keep warm. But when the fire would die down, the brick of that large fireplace would act as a great heat sink, and radiate heat back into the room at night. We may have had a two or three baseboard heaters, but we tried not to use them because of the cost of electricity. We depended very heavily on the wood stove for warmth. It does not often get bitterly cold in the that part of the Northwest, and there was a moderating effect of the nearby Lake McIntosh, such that even in cold winters, our area was slightly warmer than more exposed areas. However, it was very damp, and that was another wonderful thing about the wood stove; it kept things dry. I did add insulation above the living room and kitchen. There were things I could have done to improve the efficiency, such as insulate, seal cracks, and put a heatilator grate in the fireplace, but now I know why the pioneers didn't always take Ben Franklin's frugal advice about heating efficiency. It all takes time, planning, effort, and most of all money, which we did not have.

In spite of the Spartan living conditions, we all stayed relatively healthy, with the exception of Mzae, who had suffered from the malaria that he had brought with him from Kenya. Mzae's conditions improved once Dr. Parks properly diagnosed treated him. The only other heart wrenching medical incident that we had was an illness that took hold of James. I came home from work one evening to find James in bed with a fever, when I took out the thermometer, it read 106 °F. I knew we were in serious trouble; so I rushed to draw a cool bath for him and phoned desperately for Dr. Parks. I think he had me bundle James up and take him directly to the Centralia General Hospital, where he was observed and admitted. They could not figure out what he had, but Dr. Parks put him on intravenous fluids immediately. Those were tense days. It wasn't the cost of the medical care because Weyerhaeuser provide medical insurance. What was difficult was the lost work time and the worry and getting the family back and forth to visit James. He was uncommunicative at first; obviously his body was fighting hard with the invader. But after a couple of days, he began to regain his jovial personality. He was very popular with the nurses (a harbinger of things to come!). After a week, Dr. Parks discharged him, but when I asked what the cause of the illness had been, he did not know. He had assumed it was some species of virus which, fortunately, James' young body was able to fight off with the help of lots of rest and a good medical team at Centralia General.

I attribute part of our good fortune health wise to the simple diet that we ate. As I said before, there was not money to by fancy food; although on rare occasions I would take the family to Shakey's Pizza, or very rarely the Country Cousin Restaurant. Mostly we had African foods like *kimanga* and *chapati* with *supu na mboga*. At first we bought our cabbage and potatoes and tomatoes, but eventually we were able to raise much of our own food. We also collected wild apples, plums, elderberries, and blackberries and canned juices and jams, and preserves. I know I have mentioned this before, but it bears repeating, since few people are aware of a most useful addition to our kitchenware, the triple boiler. This is a fascinating invention of the Fins[54], which consisted of a boiler pan on the bottom, on which sat a juice collection pan, into which fit a basket for the fruit. The boiler pan would generate steam which would cook the fruit and draw the juice out of it, and then there was a spout to collect the juice into jars. The jars (if pre-boiled in a pan of water, didn't need to be pasteurized because the liquid content was over 112 ° F when entering the jar. One could bottle a lot of juice quickly, and the fruit pulp could then be strained into sauces. We never tried to make fruit leather, but one could do that. Usually the sauce was consumed so quickly it did not need to be preserved. Add some cinnamon and sugar, and you had a readymade

---

[54] As a fruit grower of Finnish descent, Newenhouse recommended the "Mehu Liisa" Finnish juicer - a triple boiler that makes processing fruit easy. It can be found through garden supply houses that sell canning supplies. http://www.wpt.org/garden/details/index. cfm?content=newsletter2&N_ID=11&body=lead

treat. I still have the Mehu Liisa, but have not use it in years. The last time I used it, I tried to process lilikoi (passion fruit). The problem was that the passion fruit was so acidic that I believe it leached aluminum out of the triple boiler. Now I am afraid to use it again.

Among the other things in our simple diet was chicken and eventually rabbit. The chicken was always free range, and the rabbit was feed on grass cuttings and vegetable trimmings as well as pelletized feed. I tried unsuccessfully to hunt deer, but only once did a wounded deer wander into our yard I had not shot the deer in the first place, but I put it out of its misery with one shot between the eyes from my old single-shot Remington 22 ca. rifle. That was after we had acquired a freezer and that venison held us well for the winter. Ernie and Trudy Sonier gave us pork because I helped him slaughter some pigs (disgusting job!). We mostly bought our milk, except when we had the one goat that we managed to raise; she gave us rich thick milk that was excellent in coffee or hot chocolate.

We would have had mutton, but the one sheep we raised came to a flamboyant, or perhaps I should say flambéed end. We had sheared the sheep, so Charity was glad to have her wool, but I was intent on smoking the mutton. I don't even know if you are supposed to smoke mutton, but you definitely don't want to do it the way I did. I had visions of building a smoker out of a very old dysfunctional refrigerator that had been at the house when we bought it. The compressor was built into the top of the refrigerator, so I proceeded to dismantle the thing from the top. I accidentally cut the fluid line, and some green solution spurted from it. Then I removed the compressor which left a kind of chimney hole at the top. There was a slide out drawer at the bottom, which I figured would work for a fire box. I drilled a series of holes in the bottom of the refrigerated compartment, and, of course, there were already shelves on which to lay the meat I wanted to dry. *Voila!* I had a smoker.

So I thought I would smoke the whole carcass of the sheep buy hanging it in the box, and lighting a fire in the drawer below. What I didn't realize was that there is a tremendous amount of fat in a well fed sheep. The fire was too hot, and the fat melted and ran down into the fire box. Net effect, I had what looked like an upside down rocket trying to bury itself in the ground. Fortunately, it was far enough away from the house that the column of flame did not start the siding on fire. Unfortunately, the thing burned so hot and violently, that I could not get into the box to try to remove the carcass. The whole thing burned into a pile of ashes. I don't know if the sheep would have preferred cremation but that is what happened to its remains; except, of course, the wool, which remained in a plastic bag for months and months. I am not sure it was ever used to spin any wool.

I think if the reader expects to have stories of the joys of homestead life, this is probably not the book to read. Don't ever let anyone tell you that the pioneers had it easy. However, with regard to food, they probably ate a healthier diet than we do now, in spite of our technology and access to a wide range of agricultural resources. The difference is simplicity. The food was from the earth and the earth was not heavily contaminated with pesticides. You will never taste an apple from the store that is as crisp and sweet as an apple picked from the tree after the frost has turned the leaves to gold and red. All of the resources of the plant are stored in that apple, except the sap. That has been shunted into the roots to sustain the spring bloom. And that is probably why cider became such a widely consumed beverage in pioneer time. People consumed what apples they could, but left the unused apple on the tree until the frost. They knew that the trees would continue to invest sugars and food value into the apples until the frost broke the cycle. Then the people would harvest the apples and put them to press. Cider is easy too, because if you don't drink it soon enough you will have some apple jack, and it only gets better as the winter progresses. If you wait too long, you will have vinegar, and that is a useful commodity too. Only now are scientists beginning to identify the important food value of berries (flavonoids and anthocyanins) and nuts (low cholesterol oils) and fresh vegetables (antioxidants, vitamins). Even the occasional glass of wine or other alcoholic beverage can be beneficial.

The dilemma was that we were becoming more and more attached to the land, but the social milieu was drawing the family away from the simple pleasures of farm life. Movies and television and other trapping of modern society were attracting the children -- and the adults. I did finally get an old black and white television, but the reception was terrible. We had an antenna in the yard, and sometimes I would have to go out and rotate the antenna while the family would call to me and let me know if the reception was improving or deteriorating.

There was no question that Charity would commiserate with Gertrude about the hard life that they were leading, and the fact that I had driven Gertrude from the home was a source of mutual irritation to them. The resentment built slowly, but it was undermining the happy acceptance of the life I was able to provide. In perspective, it was a far better life than they would have had to live in Africa, but somehow we so easily forget the pains we have suffered and reevaluate our life in comparison with the culture around us.

# Chapter 10

# The New Recruit

For all the firstborn among the people of Israel are mine, both of man and of beast. On the day that I struck down all the firstborn in the land of Egypt I consecrated them for myself, **English Standard Version (2001) Numbers 3:13.**

We had not forgotten Charity's oldest son, Ed Amon Mshoi. I don't remember what year we were finally able to get him over to the United States. It is all foggy in my mind, but he proved to be an agreeable addition to the family. I think he was 18 or 19 when he came. As I described in the last book, Edward had not lived with his mother for much of his life. When she went to Mombasa to work, he stayed with his grandparents in Taita. When she returned to Taita, she had given birth to three children. It must have been strange for Ed when they moved into the small house of the grandparents. Later, when Charity and I met, and she moved to Mgange with me, only the younger children came to live with us. I don't even remember how aware I was of Ed. He might have been living with his grandfather and Uncle Wilson in Voi. I had not met him when I lived in Wundanyi. Maybe they were trying not to overwhelm me with the news of so many children? After we had been in Mgange for quite a while, the subject of Ed arose. I do not remember who requested that he be allowed to move to Mgange to go to school. He might have requested it himself. As I discussed in the last book, it was a learning experience for him and for me. Now he was willing to make the leap to come to America, and see what fate would bring. I think the one and only visit that Charity's mother made to Mgange was somehow involved in the decision to let Ed join us there. I think she wanted to check me out. After all it was she

136

who had really raised Ed, and she had a vested interest in seeing to it that he would not be led astray.

I don't remember where Ed slept in Tenino. I think, by then Gertrude had been moved to Centralia with the trailer, and he would have had to live in our little two bedroom house. This was not a stretch for him, because he had certainly lived in more crowded quarters in Kenya. I don't think he slept in the kids' bedroom, although they were all still sleeping in one small room. But now he was a young man, with hopes of making his own way. He needed to go to school, and before that, he needed to learn to drive, both of which he was most anxious to do. I forget whether Gertrude had the Ambassador in Centralia or whether it had already given up the ghost (and I was unable to afford the repairs). So Edward's driving lessons were fated to be the real thing.

Now Old Blue was a 1949 vintage one-ton GMC, years before synchromesh gears were ever invented. That meant that one had to double clutch and finesse the gears to mesh. Edward took to it like a duck to water. We had a couple of close scrapes in the first couple of days. I think the Ambassador was running, because I seem to remember pulling the truck out of a ditch with it. That might have been my imagination, but I seem to remember that it was in the winter, and the snow had caused the truck to slide into the muddy shoulder of our dead end road. This is where Edward practiced until he had the confidence to venture out on the highway. He may have started to ride to work with me, and then spend the day walking around Centralia looking for a job. He may have spent some time at the Centralia library trying to better his command of the language and subjects that interested him. It was not long, however, before he was able to take the driving test and passed on the first try.

The speed with which Ed took to the essential skill of driving reflected his whole approach to life in America. He was determined, and consequently he was able to succeed at many things that would have thwarted a lesser individual. After a few weeks he did manage to get a job at the Tenino School in the motor pool. Not as a driver, but working in the shop where the buses were maintained. This gave him some flexibility because he was earning pretty good money. I don't even remember how he got to work every day, because it was a little over 4 miles to Tenino from the homestead. In fact, I remember very little of Edward's time with us in Tenino. As I remember it, his stay did not last very long. I don't even think he was with us the next spring when the gardening started. I know he did not help with the honeybees, and I don't remember ever going to the mountains for firewood with him. Of course, he had been raised on the farm, but I think his intention was to get as far away from the farm as possible. And he did.

He worked for the Tenino School for a few months, but then he decided he wanted to move on. I seem to remember that he moved to Centralia, and perhaps started school there. I don't remember if, or where, he did work, but he did not request any support from us. Later he moved to Olympia, and eventually entered the Olympia Vocational Technical Institute (renamed Olympia Technical Community College in 1976). I believe he studied diesel mechanics, and was later employed with a garage in Olympia. As I said, we did not see much of Edward. He was on the move and seemed to be very self-reliant. When you think of it, he was amazingly successful for an immigrant straight off the plane from Kenya. That was partly due to a very well-developed work ethic, and secondly, he was a personable young man. He had developed a lot in secondary school in Mwatate. His English, while not fluent, was passible. To this day I think he kind of mumbles, perhaps more as an affectation than of necessity. I think he may have very cleverly used it to confuse people; even I can never tell exactly what he is saying and what the truth of it all is. Apparently that can be a good strategy in business.

The fact that we did not see Edward much probably had to do with the fact that he did not have a car. At least in Olympia he could use public transportation. As I said, he was a determined young man, and did not feel that saddling himself with the expense of a car was going to help him get ahead quickly. Instead he concentrated his finances on getting through his training as a mechanic.

I am going to take the liberty to summarize what I know about Edward's life in this chapter. Edward and I have not had much interaction over the years, because once he left Tenino, he went on to try many ventures. He worked as a mechanic for a while, but decided that it was not what he wanted to spend his life doing, so he went back to school, and I believe got a degree. I am not sure if it was an Associate of Arts or a Bachelor's degree. He told me, but I don't remember the mumbled details. What he ended up doing after that was working for and eventually opening his own travel agency. I believe he was located in Tacoma, Washington, for a number of years, and did fairly well, in spite of the dependency of his mother and the family on him. In recent years that business had stopped being a lucrative enterprise because the airlines have taken away the contracts that they used to pay the agencies. Nevertheless, Edward had already moved on to the business of leasing aircraft. This included such things as corporate commuter jets, as well as contract travel excursions. Then he started providing a service of contracting delivery services. He explained that with the example of having airplane parts delivered to remote areas where they were needed and not readily available.

I don't pretend to understand all the details of his business ventures, but it made him self-sufficient, and has taken him back to Kenya on occasion (I don't know how many). He also worked for Sears Roebuck for a number of years in their security department. I believe he was a manager, which led to his current employment with Men's Warehouse. All this time he was working for these companies he was apparently maintaining his leasing service, which eventually took him to Santa Rosa, California, where he met and married his wife.

Apparently Ed was doing quite well in Santa Rosa, and had managed to purchase a house. During this time he became involved with civic activities through the local association of African American businesspeople. He also became interested in Buddhism, and has become a practicing Buddhist. He was also supporting his wife to attend college, much as I supported my second wife at University of California Davis, and then Berkeley. Similarly, James supported the mother of his child to attend her dental training program, which now provides her with a decent income. Sadly, the women of the 20th century seem not to have any sense of obligation to the family unit, as is illustrated by the women who married into my extended family. Edward's wife, once she had finished school, declared that this was not the life that she wanted to live, so they separated. Then she decided she wanted him back, but by then he had given her the house and left Santa Rosa. Having dealt with the ingratitude for so many years, he was not interested in reconnecting. Until now I think he remains single.

As I have said previously, I will not go into the details of my son, James', life, but suffice it to say, after he had gone through a herculean effort to finance his daughter's mother in school, she had no interest in either his education or his employment. Once she had found the security of a regular job, the seasonality of a forest-fire fighter's work became incomprehensible to her. One season, James earned $40,000 supervising a Hot Shot crew in the Northern California woods for the entire summer. When he returned home, the money was all spent. The thought that James would consider finishing his degree in the off season more important than becoming a full time truck driver for Pony Express like her brother), became a major point of contention. And when Pony Express defaulted on his wages because the company was in bankruptcy. Meanwhile James and his pregnant partner were visiting me in Hawaii; it was the beginning of the end for their relationship. Eventually, James was forced to leave her, if for no other reason than to retain his sanity and his Forest Service job. He got an assignment in the Olympic National Forest in Hoodsport Washington. That was a lot closer to the family than California, but that did not resolve all the problems. Unfortunately the custody issues surrounding their daughter have been acrimonious, although they have managed to both play an important part in her life. Of course, this is my view, and may not correspond to James'.

I will not detail my own experience with women here, because it will be elucidated throughout the book. I will say this: both of my former wives impeded my higher education. Charity did not thwart me intentionally, but the next wife is not without culpability. I ended my PhD studies so that she could attend University of California, Berkeley. Having received her PhD when we were together, eventually she became romantically involved with my good friend and fellow technician. She then took my daughter from Hawaii to Maryland, and has never acknowledged the impact that had on my future and the future of our daughter. But why be bitter? Life goes on, hopefully happily for my stepson, Edward, and my own son and me.

While I had my problems with Charity, and Gertrude, I never had any trouble with Edward. He was always his own man, and as I understand, kept a fair distance from the family, as well. I don't think that was always the case. While he worked in Tacoma, I think he was heavily involved in trying to help Charity with the family. Eventually, he found that to be a whirlpool sucking him down financially, which is probably why he moved to California. James bears some animosity toward Edward, which understandably arises from that fact that Edward was a "father" figure in James' formative years, after Charity and I had separated. Perhaps now James can better understand the necessity of Edward abandoning the responsibility for the family that I brought to America, even though he was one of the ones I brought.

As time went on at Tenino, we managed to keep our heads above water. We were not living what you would call a comfortable existence, but we were together, and we were able to feed ourselves and have some semblance of a normal life. We went to church, and the deacon at St. Patrick's in Tenino actually got me to commit to being on the Church Council. What's more he even turned over the catechism class of the 7th and 8th graders to me. I don't know if that was wise. My first class with that ebullient crowd of pre-pubescent youth was pure chaos… until the deacon came in and sat with the class. They knew better than to mess around in his presence. I did continue in the position for a while, and even tried to arrange some field trips and singing groups and such. A core group of kids would attend, perhaps more because of their parents influence than any ability on my part.

This led me to a kind of mini-revival of faith, and I thought perhaps I would become charismatic again. My former colleague from the Weyerhaeuser Environmental Research Lab had taken a job In the WFRL in Centralia. She was also from a Charismatic tradition (although I believe it was Four Square Gospel). She learned that I was conducting a kind of youth program at St Patrick's; she decided to join in with us on some outings. There were some other charismatics in the area, and they were enthusiastic for their children to have this kind of religious experience. One couple had moved from the Los Angeles with their son and daughter because they feared for the health of their children. They bought a beautiful house and property in the countryside south of Lacey, Washington. I don't remember their names. They were Catholics, but had been in a Charismatic group in LA. Their children got along with ours. The wife raised angora rabbits. Charity had never seen angora wool, and was most interested in the process of spinning, which the wife showed her. They may have sold us an angora rabbit to add to our rabbitry, I don't remember for sure. I do know that Charity was never able to get to the stage of harvesting and spinning angora wool.

Nor was the fate of that very kind family a happy one. One day they invited us to their home, and during the visit they showed us where the lightening had struck the electric pole outside their house. This would have been shocking in itself, but what happened next was even more incredible. The lightening went down the guy wire and then jumped across the ground into a fire pit where the family had burned leaves. Apparently carbon was the conductor, and led the bolt to the electrical cable leading to the house under the ground. The lightening proceeded into the house and blew out all the electronic equipment that was plugged in at the time. The father, being of religious inclination, took that to be a sign from God that they were to wean themselves from the electronic trappings of a decadent society. And so they did not get another TV. Their telephones were not affected.

The sad note is that the wife, not long after I left Tenino, was diagnosed with cancer, and died, leaving those two young children in the care of their loving, but bereaved father. Similarly, the wife of the deacon, who had been so good to us when we joined the parish, died of cancer. The deacon, who was a Game Warden, had been transferred to Wenatchee, Washington, so the wife and their two sons moved with him. She had not been in that town for more than a year when she was diagnosed. I think her treatment lasted longer and was a great sadness for the Warden and his two sons. I have not heard from either family in years, but it is so ironic that two wonderful families that were so filled with the spirit of good will and Christian kindness should have to bear that heavy burden through life.

That brings up an even sadder series of events that occurred in the five years that Charity and the family lived in Tenino. The Bardsleys, who I have mentioned, had a very sinister situation in their family. Mrs. Barnsley was a good woman, who had had polio when she was a child, and so believed she could not have children. She wanted children, so Mr. Bardsley had agreed to help her take in foster children. They treated the children like their own daughters (I am not sure if they had taken in any boys). When we knew them, there were two foster daughters in the immediate vicinity. One was already an adult and lived, with her husband I believe, in Tenino town. The other was a Native American girl about Samba's age. They seemed a functioning happy family although Mr. Bardsley did not seem involved in the religious aspects of their lives.

One day, Mr. Bardsley left the family unexpectedly. I remember that Mrs. Bardsley came to our house when she first found out. She was beside herself with anger and fear for herself and the remaining foster daughter. We were all shocked. Mrs. Bardsley stayed on the family property for a short while as the divorce was in progress, but she did not drive, so she eventually had to take an apartment in Tenino. Ernie and Trudy Sonier were a very great comfort and support to Mrs. Bardsley and her daughters during that time, as were many of the church members of the Assembly of God to which they belonged. The importance of community, be it a church or not, cannot be underestimated.

However, the depth with which the secrets can be kept in a community is also amazing to me. I am reading a scholarly book about Taita Hills called *Bewitching Development*. The author, who is now a professor of anthropology at U. C. Davis, lived with the Wadawida in Taita Hills for several years. His name was James Howard Smith, and the way I discovered him was while I was searching for the James Smith who had been a Peace Corps volunteer in Taita Hills. J. H. Smith was doing his research in Taita about the time that Tom Wolf[55] was finishing his Doctoral dissertation on Politics in the Coast Province and Taita. I read Dr. Smith's book. The picture he paints is of a

---

[55] Tom Wolf was the Peace Corp Volunteer that was a teacher in Wundanyi when I arrived in Taita Hills. We were friends for the 6 months that our PVC tours overlapped. I reconnected

culture riddled with witchcraft and secrecy the likes of which I never saw in the two years I was in Taita. Of course, I had heard about *uchawi* (witchcraft), and I know Charity was convinced that our brick outhouse had collapsed because a *muganga* (witch doctor) had put a curse on us. But I did not give credence to any of it, and I personally found the Wadawida to be much like any other culture in the world, full of well-meaning folks, with a lesser element of sinister characters. I can see a young graduate student intent on becoming immersed in the culture being drawn in by the fringe elements. The point is that Dr. Smith's whole perception of the people would be clouded by the superstitions of the individuals who had gained his confidence.

Ernie and Trudy Sonier were very interesting folks, and were good to me and the family. They lived on Old Highway 99 north of Tenino. Ernie worked for a shake mill in Centralia, so he was always letting me know when I could come in for loads of trim. This combination of bark and cedar was good fire starter. The mill also milled other kinds of wood so we were able to collect quite a collection of lumber. I had to haul it up the road leading to the hillside garden plot, and dump it along the road just to have a place to put it. Of course, I could not keep it dry, but I would bring the bark and cedar down to the house and dry it out to use for fire starter. Once you get a fire going with hot burning cedar, you can usually dry wet alder and fir enough to get it to burn.

The other use we made of the scrap from the mill was the rabbit hutches. There were a lot of end-cuts of 2 by 6, 8 and 10 inch wide lumber. These varied from 2 to 3 ft. in length and could be used to assemble rabbit hutches. The rabbits would chew on the wood, but it takes a long time for a rabbit to bore through a 2 inch thick board They were make-shift, but they were cheap and it let us develop a large heard of rabbits. The wood pieces were also good for making "chicken tractors". There was some long lumber in the mix, so I could make triangular frames (about 5 or 6 ft. long). I would then use the short lumber to enclose half of the frame, and the rest would be covered with chicken wire (which was relatively cheap). The floor of the structure was all chicken wire. This "cage" could then be moved around on the grass so that the chickens could eat the grass and scratch for bugs, while being fully protected from weasels and chicken hawks. Also the chickens could not hide their eggs!

Now if the lumber scraps were the only thing that Ernie Sonier did for

---

briefly with him briefly when I was writing the first book of my memoir. He was still working in Kenya.

us, I would have been eternally grateful. However, there was much more that he did for us. One day Ernie hit a deer, or saw one being hit by another car (I think the latter). He called the sheriff and waited for him to arrive. The sheriff told Ernie that he could not get the carcass to a facility in time to save the meat. At that time, deer carcasses were often brought to the juvenile detention center in Chehalis or other facilities in need of meat. Ernie pleaded with the officer to let him bring the carcass to us. The sheriff agreed, and Ernie came rolling into our homestead with a buck. He helped me dress it out, and to the best of my memory, didn't even take any for himself. He probably didn't have space in his freezer anyway, because he always hunted and kept pigs which he slaughtered periodically. I only helped him slaughter pigs once -- the most disgusting process in all of 'carnivoredom'!

Ernie also took me clamming one day in the Puget Sound. We put his boat in somewhere above Olympia and after a brief run to a bar in the middle of an inlet; we spent most of the time at that bar until we had far surpassed our legal limit. We were not digging for geoducks or razor clams; they might have been butter clams or more likely Manila clams (which are now the dominant species in the Pacific Northwest). We took a gunny sack (nearly full) home, and Ernie gave me half of the take. The reaction of the family was comical. Charity fried them up with batter, but most of the children moaned and protested. They were quite put off by this food they had never eaten, and when they would bite into some sand, they would nearly gag. But not Sammy; he loved them. I swear he probably ate most of that half of a gunny sack of clams over the next week or two. Of course, I failed to mention that most of the kids helped shuck the clams, which may have preconditioned them against the crustacean. Sam, as I remember it, managed to avoid all the shucking, so had no similar predisposition toward eating the clams.

Ernie probably would have talked me into hunting, and my father did give me his 30-30 rifle. So one season I paid for a hunting license. Charity was interested, so one Saturday morning we took our dog, Buck, and headed out onto the Weyerhaeuser property behind the homestead. I think I mentioned that it had been clear-cut a few years before and was coming back in grass, alder, vine maple and planted seedling Douglas fir (all good food for deer in winter). We happened to be on the top of a ridge looking down on our dog, which was running through the gully below us. Suddenly we realized that two hunters across the ridge were taking a bead on Duke! Of course, we raised holy hell, and the hunters were dissuaded, but it was a lesson to me. Those people out there are nutz! They can't tell a dog from a deer -- or don't want to? From then on, every hunting season, I made sure that the kids stayed well within our 4 acre property, and kept Buck close to home. I previously described the wounded deer that wandered into our yard. It had been shot with a very small caliber weapon and, as I remember, it was **not** hunting season.

For some strange reason, that reminds me of an eerie incident that occurred on our homestead road. Charity was the first to notice that a man was driving up our dead-end road every day just after I would leave the house to go to work. One day I was late for work, and the man drove by the house slowly. Charity exclaimed, "That's him". Alerted, I came out the front door and the man quickly drove off, heading up towards the end of the road. I don't know if he knew he could not get far because there was a barrier at the end of the road. So I jumped in the Gimmy (GMC) and took out after him. I was just approaching him as he had finished turning around in the narrow space left where the road was overgrown with trees. I positioned my truck in the middle of the road to prevent his passage. I wanted to talk to this guy and find out who the hell he thought he was. What happened next confirmed my suspicions about him. He drove his car towards my truck. I was shocked as it looked like he intended to ram me. Instead he ran his car up on the steep bank and passed by my truck on the left. It is a wonder his car did not turn over because the bank was so steep. Of course he was long gone before I managed to get the truck turned around. Fortunately, it must have put the fear of God in the man because he never returned. But I certainly learned the lesson that you cannot assume that everyone in your neighborhood are well-intentioned people. Of course, we don't even know if he was from our neighborhood. There have been some famous serial killers in the Northwest, and they don't always do their dirty work in the big city. I was learning not to take things for granted.

After Edward left Tenino, we had a good year for farming. I think I already mentioned that man from Yelm who rototilled the garden for us. It was beautiful soil that had been fallow for many years. The frost seemed to have dissipated a bit early that year, and I think we planted the peas in April. Might have been May, but I believe the high school was still in session. One Friday night, after I had spent a hard day at work, I was awakened in the middle of the night. Charity had heard someone drive up the hill to our garden. I don't know if I was still half-asleep or just mad at being disturbed from a deep sleep, but I grabbed an axe handle, and marched up the hill, half-dressed. I don't know what I thought I was going to do with an axe handle, but I was mad, and all the protective territorial instincts of one's dinosaur brain come out at two o'clock in the morning.

When I got to the top of the hill there was a car-load of besotted teenagers laughing and milling around their '55 Chevy that was stuck in the dirt, freshly planted dirt where little pea seedlings were tossed hither and yon. I was pissed! I started hollering at the kids and waving my axe handle around in the air. They were terrorized! I don't know why; they could easily have taken me and buried me in my own garden! But apparently the primitive territorial signals of an irate bull male still registers in the medulla of mischievous malcontents. They quickly begged me to forgive them, and all laid shoulder to the stranded vehicle. Soon they were out of my sacred garden and speeding down the hill, ne'er to be seen again.

Soon after, I purchased Pontiac Red certified seed potatoes at Yard Birds. Charity wanted to cut them in half, but I remembered my horticulture and encouraged her to plant the carefully selected disease free tubers whole. And then it rained. It was a deep and soaking series of squalls which carried the potatoes through to the summer. And a beautiful crop of potatoes it was; I think we harvested 20 gunny sacks full. But that one crop of Pontiac Reds led to so much contention that we never planted potatoes again; or at least that is how I remember it. I think I first gave a bag to Ernie and Trudy. Charity could sort of understand that because she knew we were indebted to them for a lot of things that they had done for us. But then I gave a bag to Olli; you may remember that they were the parents of Tina, and had raised 72 foster children. I don't even remember if the potatoes were for them or whether he was requesting them for some charity that the Catholic Church in Yelm was sponsoring.

Now that was another straw on the camel's back. Charity could not see giving away our hard earned crop to people with whom we were not even close friends. On the one hand, I can understand Charity's feelings. Having been raise in a country where every ear of maize is precious and every crop can mean the difference between survival and starvation, her reaction is not unexpected. I guess I saw it a little differently: 1) I didn't know where we were going to store 20 bags of potatoes, 2) without the support of these friends and fellow Catholics, our survival would have been more tenuous that it actually was, and 3) I always figure every good turn deserves another. And I was vindicated. That fall Olli, came to our house with an apple press and a truckload of apples. They had a nice little orchard, and he could not feed all the apples to his pigs. We spent the afternoon pressing the apples in my newly constructed back porch (made with the poles collected with Mike Carlson). Then he split the apple juice 50/50 with me (we had scrambled to collect enough jugs to hold it all). As I said before, I can understand how fond the pioneers were of apple cider... especially after it fermented. Our portion did not actually stay around long enough to turn to apple jack; I suppose I was as much a culprit as the kids... that cider just kept getting better and better! Elderberry juice is good for you, but tastes just ok. Blackberry juice is very nice, but unpasteurized cider has all the juices beat.

So I was humbled by the generosity of friends and even acquaintances. I would have been in serious trouble if I had given away more of the potatoes, but we did lose a lot of potatoes over the winter to rot and frost. We used the basement under the house like a cellar, but it was neither dry enough nor sufficiently insulated to be a good root cellar. Of course, Charity could not have known the difficulties we faced in winter, but she would learn.

The sad memory that this reminiscence of Olli and his wife conjure was the fact that their only daughter, so full of fun and comical, died in an automobile accident when she was just 15 years old. It makes you wonder what God was thinking. Here these two people had helped 72 children grow into adult human beings, but the one child that He had allowed this couple was taken from them. Almost like Abraham and his son Isaac... but He let Isaac live. Go figure! I remember that Olli, by the time we knew him had large bags under his eyes, much as I do today. I always wondered what worries and struggles had made those visible impressions on his face. I am sure the death of his daughter added to them. These kinds of anomalies have also caused me to reevaluate my faith.

That summer of the great potato planting was a busy summer. The potatoes did not need additional water, but the vegetables that we planted did. So I managed to acquire a 55 gallon drum and a hand-operated drum pump. With that roped onto the truck we would load up and go down to Johnson Creek, which was a little over a mile from the homestead. We would take swimsuits so the kids could play in the creek while I pumped the water in the tank. That would take some time with the little pump. Then I would drive up to the garden and begin pumping out the water into jugs so Charity and the kids could take water to each plant. It worked, until the pump broke. I didn't try to fix it or replace it. By then the vegetables did alright because they had gotten their roots into the deep rich soil.

Jimmy actually became afraid of the water at Johnson Creek. He would play at the water's edge, but he was afraid to go in and put his head under water. I tried to encourage him by taking him out with me. This made him more fearful, and, in fact, he never did learn to swim under my tutelage. He did eventually learn to swim and was required to swim every morning at 6 AM when he was on the basketball team in high school. The coach thought it developed lung capacity. To this day James takes opportunity to swim at the University of Montana. Ironically, one of his dreams is to have a sailboat, and he had me pay to have his daughter take sailing lessons at Gig Harbor. Training his future crew I guess.

Speaking of outings that summer, I think it was on the Fourth of July that we took the family to Mt. Rainier National Park. It must have been when we still had the Rambler Ambassador and I think we went with some other family, perhaps the Bardsleys, or it might have been Mike Carlson's family. I don't remember the trip very well, but I know the kids were very impressed. It is understandable because Mt. Rainier is a majestic mountain surrounded by a skirt of winding valley streams and wooded ridges unlike any the Africans had ever seen in Taita. We stopped at a camping area to have our picnic. While we were laying out our table with food and, as I remember, a big watermelon, someone below us said there was a bear in the lower area of the campground. Well, of course, we all ran down to see the bear... except Sam. I think he thought he was going to get some quick grub while we were gone. But it was not Sam who got the first licks. While we were looking for the bear below, the bear had doubled back and found the table that we had abandoned. When we realized what had happened, we hurried back to check on Sam. His eyes were as big as silver dollars. The bear had come right up to the table where he was sitting and grabbed the watermelon. I am sure the hungry bear must have broken the watermelon open and proceeded to consume it, but as we rushed up the hill making noise, the bear turned into the bushes, with melon still in mouth, and disappeared. So Sam was the first Mdawida to see a black bear in America.

I think Mr. and Mrs. Moon came to visit us in June or July. Apparently Floyd kept track of the berry season, and his intention was to get blackberries. It escapes my memory how he knew where we were living; perhaps my mother had written to him. When we visited the Moons in Milton Freewater, the kids had not come and Charity was still pregnant. I don't think I was very good with the correspondence those days, because I was so busy all the time. This was also the first time Mr. Moon had seen the family since the kids arrived.

I donned my coveralls and led Mr. Moon and some of the older kids down to the berry patch by Lake Macintosh. Mr. Moon was ready with his coveralls as well because the thicket gets so high that you need protection all over your body from the thorns. The berries were plentiful and we brought back all that Mr. Moon had hoped for. Of course we had already canned and jammed and eaten berries to our satiation before our visitors came. Mr. Moon was not interested in elderberries, but ever mindful of the bounty of the earth, he did enjoy his blackberries.

Mr. Moon did not ask many questions nor did we reminisce much about Kenya. I think he was more interested in my job and what I did for Weyerhaeuser. However, we had an enjoyable time picking the berries in the warm summer sun (unusual for that time of year, when it is usually overcast). When we returned to the homestead, Charity had slaughtered a chicken or two, and the girls were making some vittles to send the Moons on their journey with their bellies full. I am sure the conditions of our house were not what they had both expected, but they were polite, and joined us in our repast. The one thing I do remember clearly is a question that Mary Moon posed to Floyd. She kind of put him on the spot, asking if he didn't think that maybe he was wrong about trying to prevent Charity from coming to America. Of course, he had to concede in front of Charity and all the children, but I am not sure he was totally convinced in his mind. And as time would eventually tell, he had good reason to be skeptical, although at the time it looked hopeful that we might make it work.

That was generally a pretty productive summer. In spite of having been abandoned by the older children, and with me at work five days a week, it was tough for Charity to get all the chores and gardening done. So I asked Jess Daniels if I could go on a four-ten work week. I had done this in Seattle, and I was hopeful that it would work for the Forestry Research Unit as well. Of course, in the peak of pollen season there was no way that would be possible because pollen was coming in every day. We even had to work some weekends. But when that died down, then we were in the process of storing the pollen for breeding. During that first summer, we were doing drying experiments and trying to determine how best to maintain pollen viability. I had developed a germination test at the Seattle Lab, and now we were trying to improve the tests with methods for enzyme detection with fluorescein diacetate. It was not until later that summer that it became apparent that we should probably try freeze-drying the pollen. It had been successful with other species, but Douglas fir was unique in having very large pollen grains with very thin walls (a pollen grain consists of an exine or outer wall, and intine or inter wall). The conditions of freeze drying would require that the apparatus have controls that would allow for very gradual processing. We had not yet developed the equipment, and the pollen flow that year was fairly light, so we were pretty much done with pollen processing early in the summer.

So I was able to go on the 4 day work week, which gave me three days to catch up on projects at home. Bringing in the harvest, teaching Charity to can, and use the triple boiler (Mehu Liisa in Finish). Eventually my great aunt Nina offered to give us her large 6 quart pressure cooker, which made it possible to can beans (I don't think we used it for any of the other foods that have to be pressure cooked, although when the tomatoes did not ripen, she learned from Mrs. Bardsley how to make chow chow[56]). Later in the summer, I took orders from Weyerhaeuser workers and people at the church for Yakima produce. I then drove the Gimmy over the White Pass on Highway 12, and purchased peaches, and sweet peppers and other popular commodities that were in season. Of course what we brought back for ourselves all had to be canned or eaten fresh.

I think the family was pleasantly surprised by the peach. Of course, they had never eaten peaches, but how can anyone not love the sweet Alberta peaches grown in Yakima. Juice will drip down your arm if you try to eat a whole one. The peach fuzz was irritating to the kids but I showed them how to par boil a peach so the skin slips off. Of course those kinds of peaches are hard to come by these days. The California varieties are so hard and crunchy, and that is **not** by accident. I was on a tour with the peach breeder's assistant at U. C. Davis one year, and he was showing us various dwarf varieties that they were vetting. Having just sampled a very succulent peach, I asked if it would be among the selected stock. He assured me that it would not. I protested; "but it is so sweet", I said. He said "Exactly, and soft and succulent." Of course, I asked "what characteristics are you breeding for". His answer -- I

---

[56] Chow-chow (Chowchow, Chow Chow) is a Nova Scotian and American pickled relish made from a combination of vegetables. Mainly green tomato, cabbage, chayote, red tomatoes, onions, carrots, beans, asparagus, cauliflower, and peas are used. These ingredients are pickled in a canning jar and served cold.

Chow-chow is regionally associated with the Southern United States, Pennsylvania, New Mexico, the Appalachian Mountains, and soul food. The recipes vary greatly; some varieties are sweeter than others. Pennsylvania chow-chow, known by the Wos-Wit brand, is generally much sweeter than the southern varieties.

Chow-chow found its way to the Southern United States during the expulsion of the Acadian people from Nova Scotia and their settlement in Louisiana. Chow is eaten by itself or as a condiment on fish cakes, mashed potatoes, biscuits and gravy, pinto beans, hot dogs, hamburgers, and other foods. http://en.wikipedia.org/wiki/Chow-chow

kid you not -- was: "We are looking for a peach that turns red when it is still green and can bounce to market". Those were his exact words. The Hawaiians are not very partial to peaches, and it is not a wonder. The only peaches they get are these varieties that are bred to have cell structure like an apple, and are very good for shipping. In fact, on the rare occasion that Costco brings in a shipment of ripe, succulent peaches, the Hawaiians don't like them. They think they are too mushy[57]. They think a peach is supposed to be crunchy and tart like and apple... go figure!

Of course, the Hawaiians and the Kenyans have mangoes, which, in my opinion, run a close second to peaches for sheer eating enjoyment. I remember coming across a wild mango in the savanna when I was in Kenya. It seemed to be out there by itself. I am sure there were people that knew about it, but it was loaded with small green mangoes, which did not even look ripe. But when we cut into them they were juicy and sweet and amazing. What a treat on a hot Equatorial day in the lowlands. The wild mangoes in Hawaii are a little like that, but they are so popular that it is hard to get to them before they have already been picked. Some pick them small and green for mango pickles. There are a lot of new and very tasty varieties of mango as well. My personal favorite is a little known variety called Mapa`ulu. But the thing that the Hawaiians love most on the Big Island is lychee; that is the "peach" of the island residents. Lychees are sweet and plentiful only once a year. I guess that is what makes them so popular. When you have a fruit all the time, it loses its luster, so to speak. What we humans seem to cherish are the things that are hardest to get.

In retrospect, it is hard to think about the life we lead in Tenino without some nostalgia. It was hard, but it was real. We didn't have much, and we lived in tight quarters, but we didn't think we were unhappy. Certainly, the young kids seemed perfectly happy to be in America. The older kids also seemed eager to make their way. I can understand how, after the newness wore off, that Charity might have felt let down by the life in America. After all, she had been pretty important in Taita. She was not only the mother of her family, but she was also the head of the project (farm and household), and had people working under her. She had suddenly risen in her social standing

---

[57] Sometimes the peaches are too mushy, because that is what happens when a partially ripe peach spends too much time post-harvest before it is consumed. Ironically, the same thing happens to apples, especially those that are picked early, stored under nitrogen, and then shipped out of season.

from farmer to an active, if unofficial, assistant to the Peace Corps Officer. Things went hard for her when I left Taita. After they settled a dispute with the landlord, they finally moved to Mpizini. There they had to contend with malaria and the local people with whom they were not familiar. When she came to America by herself, of course her hope was to have the family join her. But after that was accomplished, there was a period of let-down. Life evolved into the daily routine of being a mother again, and the head of a homestead. The difference was that in America, there was no "help." Mostly she was on her own, while I was out trying to make enough money to survive. This would have been true in Kenya as well because many of the husbands have to live and work away from their families. But when you are raised in a mountain culture with extended family all around you, you get used to being part of a bigger society. I am sure America, and particularly the homestead in Tenino was a very isolated experience for Charity.

# Chapter 11

# The Siege

By the waters of Babylon,
there we sat down and wept,
when we remembered Zion.
On the willows there
we hung up our lyres.
For there our captors
required of us songs,
and our tormentors, mirth, saying,
"Sing us one of the songs of Zion!"
**English Standard Version (2001) Psalm 137:1-3.**

As I said, few of the Honeycomb Fellowship ever visited us in Tenino. We went to Seattle on a couple of occasions, but Doris and her two sons were the only Christians from Seattle that ever came to stay with us. This was at Thanksgiving holiday. By then we had acquired a huge turkey, which we called Agnes. Someone had given her to us, and she was, shall we say, not in the springtime of her life. But she was an amenable fowl, and everyone liked her. Agnes would wander around the homestead doing what turkeys do. I was surprised when I looked up gobble in the dictionary; there actually is no definition for the sound that turkeys make. Gobble actually means to gulp down your food, and apparently has no etymology related to turkeys. In fact, the word referring to turkeys is actually the male turkey, or gobbler. The onomatopoeic 'gobble gobble' is, in fact, the sound of the male turkey. But Agnes had her own sort of 'garbled gobble.' She was definitely a female because she actually laid an egg one day... only one! It was quite tasty. But when Doris and the boys came for Thanksgiving, I wasn't sure if we would have enough turkey. We did buy a turkey, but just to be on the safe side, we decided to euthanize Agnes because she was really getting long in the tooth… well, the beak, then.

The family arrived the day before Thanksgiving, so as part of "showing them around," I took Doris, Charity and Jimmy in the cab of the Gimmy, and her boys and our kids piled onto the bed of the truck (with rack around to make sure they did not fall off). We then headed up the hill onto the Weyerhaeuser property behind us. I was thinking we might have a little shortage of firewood, so I was hoping we would be able to bring some back. What a fortuitous trip! We ran across and area where shake-splitters had been making cedar shakes from downed cedar stumps.[58] In the process of making shakes, they only take the high grade splits; the rest of the wood is left behind in a pile. So we loaded up enough cedar kindling to last us the rest of the winter. The city boys found this to be great fun; the country boys were happy not to have to split kindling. The women had plenty of time to gossip about all that had happened in Seattle and Tenino in the last year.

By then my Dad and Elizabeth had given us the old colonial style couch that my mother had purchased for the house in Longview, but which did not fit well in the little house on the Toutle. I believe it was a hideaway bed, so Doris did have a "comfortable" place to sleep. I don't remember if the boys slept in the bed with her, or wanted to sleep on the floor in their new sleeping bags. This was a real country adventure for them. The next day I proceeded to execute Agnes with all the wailing and gnashing of teeth that such a ceremony entails. Although she would be gone, she would not be forgotten! Samba helped me parboil and pluck Agnes' remains, while Charity and Doris readied the store-bought turkey for the oven. I had already conceived the plan as to how we would cook both turkeys at the same time. I had installed a makeshift spit in the fireplace, and brought the raging fire to the level of hot coals. Then, knowing that Agnes could potentially be a tough old bird, I proceeded to stuff her with oranges and onions and herbs instead of traditional stuffing. It turned out to be an excellent plan. I believe that Agnes came out to be the tenderer of the two turkeys, and we all remarked how Agnes had well served her purpose in life, and hopefully was off to the great barnyard in the sky.

---

[58] The base of a cedar tree is too broad and irregular to be good for lumber, so the fallers will cut it off above the irregular base. This leaves ample log from which the shake-splitters can cut their shakes.

The visit went well, and when we said our goodbyes, we invited Doris and the boys to return again. But that was the last time I ever saw them. I think Charity may have visited that family years later in Seattle, or they might have visited her in Tacoma. As I said, the friendships that had formed at the Honeycomb Fellowship seemed not to have stood the test of time and distance. I have in recent years attempted to find the people I knew from the fellowship, and have only been able to find one couple, Roy and Ruth Gillette. Roy is in a nursing home because, as a consequence of his childhood polio, he can no longer swallow properly. But his spirit is well and he still tries to minister to his fellow patients. Ruth lives nearby, but is torn because her daughter has moved to Arizona with the grandkids. One of the ironies of life is how old age leaves us often living very differently than we would have believed we would.

Probably the closest friendship that Charity had in the community of Southern Washington was Oti and Charles. Their daughter and Samba liked each other, and the boys played with their son. Since Oti and Charles were the only African American family in the whole area from Tenino to Yelm, I guess that is not surprising. But other people like Dave, the Game Warden, and his family, and Olli and his wife and daughter Tina were friends as well. When I took over the catechism, other families with seventh and eighth grade kids would join us for activities. When Mrs. Bardsley moved away, we did not see them much, although we visited them and the Soniers on several occasions.

We were holding it together with our little homestead, and though Charity's older children had moved on, we were succeeding in keeping the lights on and the fire stoked. The kids had by then been transferred to the school far off in south Tumwater, so their days were long. They boarded the school bus very early in the morning (I am thinking seven) and did not get home until just before I would get home if I didn't work overtime. Maybe their day was not quite that long, but as I Google it, all the schools were at least an hour and a half bus trip each way. Why the school district did that, I will never know. In Tenino, the school was close; it was easy to get to parent teacher conferences. I contemplated even joining the PTA. But once they were moved to the school south of Tumwater all bets were off. I think I was able to attend one parent teacher conference after they moved. I vaguely remember Sam's special education teacher was very young with a huge head of very curly hair. I remember thinking that she did not seem professional in the way that my grade schoolteachers had been. I honestly don't remember what kind of progress Sam was making. I never met the Japanese teacher that had been so hard on Samba about being cleanly, when what she really objected to was that we had a wood stove and Samba's cloths smelled smoky. What a difference the culture of the suburb makes. At one time -- my time as a matter of fact – most of the kids that came to school smelled smoky. You didn't even notice it because everyone burned wood. Actually, my mother and I left the big house in McCloud that was steam heated, we moved into an apartment that was heated by oil. So we probably smelled a little different because we didn't have a wood stove. It wasn't yet considered a social disgrace to burn wood... or oil.

Sometime that year we had an unexpected visitor from Kenya. Fr. Sean O' Connell had taken some kind of training leave in the USA, and made it a point to visit to see how we were all doing. Charity was very happy to have him as a guest, however briefly. He was pleased to see that we were living comfortably (by Kenyan standards) and seemed to be happily married with a happy family around us. That was the last we saw of Fr. O'Connell. We had one more visitor from the Maryknoll Society, but he was someone we had not known previously. It was Fr. O'Connell that had told him about us. I believe he might have been conducting what the Catholics call a Mission Retreat in the Olympia area. It is fuzzy in my mind now, but I think he might have actually come from Hawaii where he taught at the Maryknoll School in Honolulu.

There was another couple that came into our life, however briefly. He was an American who had worked in the northern oil fields in Nigeria, but he had taken a wife who was actually from Chad. He had heard that we lived in Tenino, and he was desperate to find some African companionship for his wife. I believe that they were living in a motor home in Yelm at the time. She, like Charity, did not know English when she came to the Northwest with her husband, and was very lonely. I will not give their names, even if I could remember them, but I will call her Chica. It was not her name, but it was a similar name. She became very attached to Charity right away; even though they were from opposite sides of that mighty continent, there was an affinity that she was not finding in the mostly white village of Yelm.

The husband and I were not at all alike, except that we had both married Africans. He was a typical "red neck" except for his acceptance of color. And his interests and mine were very different. He liked his whiskey; still, for the sake of his wife he was polite and brought Chica to visit fairly often, and we visited them from time to time in Yelm. She liked the kids, and liked the feeling of being in an African household, with a fire burning and simple hearty food. She had herself obviously been raised on a traditional farm, and had probably only gone to Nigeria to find work. Instead, she found her husband. That would be a fateful decision for both of them.

After knowing them for a few months, the husband got a job out of the area, and so they moved away from Yelm. We did not see or hear from them for quite a long time. Then one day they showed up at our house. By then Chica was all swollen, not from weight gain, but because she had begun to suffer from some serious disease. I still don't know what the disease was, but apparently it was not contagious. It was not Schistosomiasis[59], because I would have recognized those symptoms. Chica's husband needed a place for her to stay while he worked, because she needed help to cook and take care of herself. Charity agreed to help. He would come and pick her up when he got off work, and would bring her back in the daytime. I think she was under a doctor's care but they did not have the resources to put her in a nursing home. Eventually she got worse and he had to take her to a hospital. He did not tell us where, and we did not see them again for some time. One day he showed up by himself. He told us that Chica had died. We expressed our sympathy, but he had not told us in time to go to the funeral. I am sure this was always a disturbing thing to Charity. To die without your friends or family around you is a very scary proposition to an African who had been raised in an extended family. The husband and I shared some whiskey and then he left, and I have never seen him again.

This disturbing event was kind of an omen to me that the world is a cold place and could come closing in on our little homestead. We were lucky that we had only had a few illnesses and no injuries to the children or the adults. Sometimes you just have to stop and say, "thank God." Even the older children seemed to be making their way. Edward was apparently getting his education, and Gertrude had apparently found a prospective husband. What I did not

---

[59] Schistosomiasis (also known as bilharzia, bilharziosis or snail fever) is a parasitic disease caused by several species of trematodes (platyhelminth infection, or "flukes"), a parasitic worm of the genus Schistosoma.

Although it has a low mortality rate, schistosomiasis often is a chronic illness that can damage internal organs and, in children, impair growth and cognitive development. The urinary form of schistosomiasis is associated with increased risks for bladder cancer in adults. Schistosomiasis is the second most socioeconomically devastating parasitic disease after malaria.

This disease is most commonly found in Asia, Africa, and South America, especially in areas where the water contains numerous freshwater snails, which may carry the parasite. http://en.wikipedia.org/wiki/Schistosomiasis

realize was that the very thing that gave us some stability, Weyerhaeuser, was planning a major change that would massively impact our lives.

In the fall and winter of that year, Weyerhaeuser Forestry Research was expanding so rapidly that they thought they needed a new facility. The long term plan was to move to the new Corporate Headquarters Research Facility that was being built in Federal Way, Washington, but I was convinced that that was a long way in the future. Apparently the Director of Forestry Research also believed they would be waiting too long for that move, so he initiated plans to rent what had been the Centralia General Hospital before that facility was moved to its current location across the Chehalis River in 1971. The old hospital was just two blocks over from the Forestry Research Facility on North Iron St. It was being used by a home nursing company, but they could not maintain the rent. I was beginning to learn the hard lesson that life in corporate American is in constant flux. I'm not convinced that the move to the old hospital was actually that necessary, and I see from the Goggle satellite that the original Weyerhaeuser facility is still in use lo these many years after the Research Group was theoretically moved to Federal Way. Who knows if the company is still renting the old hospital?

The move to the hospital involved many modifications of the facility. We had to have the local cooper install a fume hood in the pollen lab. The irony of that was that we eventually had to have it rebuilt because it vented outside of the office window of the lead scientist on of the genetics group. Since the building was not air conditioned, when he opened his windows in the summer, he ran the risk of getting gassed by noxious chemicals. This was just one example of "The best-laid schemes of mice and men gang aft agley" (Robert Burns). I was allowed to redesign what had formerly been the hospital lab, because I was in charge of the pollen processing program. It did give us a much larger space for pollen processing, and I was able to build a special room for microscopy outside of which I had a piece of black vinyl countertop built into the counters for my desk. The rest of the room was lined with counters, drawers, and cupboards with glass doors so we could see what was in them. The microscope room was built to my specifications: A high, deep counter along the back wall and a smaller counter along the opposite wall. On wall over the two counters shallow cupboards were built to accommodate all the stains, and microscope supplies. The microscope room was separated from the room where my desk was by a pocket door that was light tight, so I could develop film or do projection microphotography in the scope room.

Multipurpose **Zeiss microscope** like the one I had at Weyerhaeuser Co. [Photo (CC BY-SA 4.0)]

The acquisition of the microscopy equipment was ironic in its essence. That year, Weyerhaeuser had hired a consultant to interview the professional and the technician staff to determine if they were happy with their wages and benefits. Of course, I was interviewed. Thinking it was a confidential report, I spoke freely, and of course, I did not think the compensation was adequate to support a family of 8. Apparently it was not a "confidential survey", because when I next had my annual personnel review with Jess Daniels, he asked: "why do you think you need a raise; after all, we just bought you a $10,000 Zeiss microscope?" Naturally, I did not reply "How is my family going to eat my microscope?"

Admittedly, it was a beautiful microscope. It was equipped with phase and Nomarski interference contrast as well as incident light lenses so I could do reflective as well and transmission micrography. It also had fluorescence illumination, which was very useful for the pollen research. I also had a Wild Heerbrugg stereoscope with camera attachment, and a rotary microtome. I really did enjoy microscopy, and probably could have stayed in the microscopy group for years. In the Weyerhaeuser personnel directory, I was listed, not as "microscopist", but as a "microcapist." Sounds a little too close to "my crock o' piss;" a typographical mistake, I assure you. At the Seattle lab, we had an old Leitz compound microscope. It was a good scope but Bill Nearn was determined to spend the departmental money on the electron microscopes and peripheral equipment. He did inherit the several small Zeiss incident light microscopes from the cherry brown project, which were handy. When Bill Nearn retired and Bob Megraw inherited the Microscopy Group, he also inherited "my" Zeiss microscope. It was a beauty, and the interference contrast could produce beautiful first order colors[60] which made cell tissue verily jump out at you (see figure 8). I am told that one of those micrographs was on display at Corporate Headquarters for years.

The hospital was not the only building that The Forestry Research Group acquired. The whole research division was expanding rapidly. First the tissue culture scientists moved in, and basically took over the original research lab. They had lots of requirements for growth chambers etc. So soon the Company rented an entire former Safeway store with thousands of square feet of floor space. The tissue culture proved difficult, and the two staff scientists that were working on it, Dr. Zachary Wochok[61] and another, whose name I do not remember, were sort of superseded by a woman scientist.

The young Chinese scientist that was hired on contract to "put these guys to shame" was working at a biogenetics lab in Portland, Oregon. She spent a $1 million Weyerhaeuser fund, but when her day of reckoning arrived, she tried to claim 80% success in creating tissue cultured Douglas fir seedlings. The problem, as it was soon discovered, was that her claim was based on a paltry number of samples; I think about 20. Out of all the effort, she had only been able to produce 20 seedlings and only 16 of them looked like they could potentially grow into trees. Needless to say, Zach was redeemed, although his fellow tissue culture scientist had already left the company. I think he did eventually work out a technique for reliably producing advantageous buds from excised gymnosperm tissue.

Zach left soon after, and ended up a co-founder Plant of Genetics, Inc., in Davis, California. I cited the paper that we published together, where I had developed a technique for using fluorescence microscopy and a photometric devise to measure the bands of the Douglas fir chromosomes.

Later Weyerhaeuser hired a scientist to develop a technique for producing rooted cuttings of gymnosperms. I was called in on that project in October of 1978 toward the end of my time at Weyerhaeuser. They wanted me to

---

[60] The easiest way to explain first order colors is the image of the several distinct bands of a rainbow. The colors (red through violet) in the first band are bright and intense. The subsequent bands are clear but they are less bright. The first band is the closest to single wavelengths of light for each color gradient. Usually we see color mixed with other wavelengths. The rainbow (essentially a prism effect) separates the wavelengths it to bands of different wavelengths. The color gradient appears in each band, but the wavelengths making up the colors are different in each band.

[61] Wochok, Z., Andreasson, J. and Klungness, L. M. 1980. Geimsa banding in chromosomes of Douglas fir seedlings and plantlets. Ann. Bot. 46(3):249

produce micrographs of the tissue in the callous ball from which the roots would emerge. Again, I was probably not going to tell them what they wanted to hear. I did the micrographs and still have them. But I was shocked at how disorganized the tissue was. So I started reading up on graft unions and what I could find about rooted cuttings was not promising. For example. during the October 12, 1962, windstorm, many of the orchard trees in the Willamette Valley were snapped off at the graft union. I thought to myself, a gymnosperm can be a hundred or more feet high, and the only thing that keeps it up there is the very flexible but resilient continuum of xylem and phloem tissue from the trunk to the roots. If a rooted cutting, with an irregular clump of callous developed into advantageous roots, the vascular connection to the stem of the plant would be compromised. I presented the report to the management, and I think it raised a lot of questions. I can't swear that my report was instrumental, but I am told the rooted cutting project was pretty much abandoned for gymnosperms like Douglas fir and hemlock.

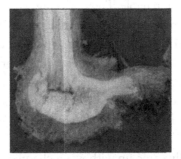

Cross section of a **rooted cutting** of Douglas fir which shows the disorganized callous tissue out of which the adventitious root has grown.(photographed on a Wild Heerbrugg stereo microscope by the author at Weyerhaeuser Forestry Research Lab, Centralia Washington)

But that was something that happened later; the current issues were solving the problem of the preservation of the pollen that had been produced from the breeding orchards that season. We determined how important it was to get the pollen dried quickly, because if it did not desiccate, it would rupture and mold. But this had been easy when there was only a small about of pollen coming in from the breeding orchards. By then, the quantity of pollen was increasing every year, so the task of drying it became more critical. I tried a drying experiment to see if we could use a hydroscopic solution to bring the pollen to specific moisture content. This was actually Jess's idea, but it was my job to work out the logistics. Let me say, up front, it was a crazy idea! We purchase some bowl-like chambers that had a dome over the top and could be sealed with joint grease to insure air-tightness. We started using Drierite, which is a crystalline drying agent. But it did not seem to have enough desiccating strength. The pollen catkins seemed to be more hydroscopic than the Drierite. So then we switched to sulfuric acid. Theoretically you can create dilutions of the acid with water to achieve different relative humidity in the airspace over the solution.

The problem was that, not only do the sulfuric acid molecules enter the air (which is, by the way, why you can smell the acid), but also we were working with an inexperienced crew of women who apparently didn't know about "battery acid". Pretty soon they were showing up with holes in their clothing, and burns on their fingers. That put a quick stop to the experiment, but I think the pollen would not have survived the acid laden atmosphere anyway. There is that ol' Robbie Burns line again… "Best laid plans…."

It became more and more apparent that we were going to need something more efficient, and more reliable. Freeze-drying was the answer, but that is not a straightforward proposition. In normal freeze-drying you freeze the product, and then you draw a vacuum on it, and suck out all the water while it is still in the frozen state. This can be a very violent process at the molecular level, and generally preserved the chemical structure, but tears the cell walls and membranes all apart. So we had to go through a long series of testing to determine the proper conditions for freeze-drying live pollen that would keep it alive.

What we eventually came up with was a chamber freeze dryer in which we had installed a heating plate, devised by our electronics technicians, which could be taken from sub-zero temperatures to room temperature with a timer-controller that could precisely alter the rate of heat exchange. We would freeze the pollen in liquid nitrogen, and then place the vials on the temperature-controlled warming plate, and draw a vacuum on the pollen. If we heated the plate too rapidly, the pollen would begin to "boil" in the vials. That meant that the moisture was being extracted too rapidly, causing cellular damage to the pollen. But if we raised the temperature very slowly, the pollen would desiccate without the agitation, and therefore would be intact viable cells.

It was known that the ideal moisture content of most pollen is around 17%, and this we would test periodically on a Mettler dry-weight balance. Simply put, it was a balance with a heat lamp over it. The sample was placed on the balance and the lamp was turned on. When the weight stopped changing, the sample was dry. The difference in weight from start to finish was the moisture content of the pollen. Of course, freeze drying the pollen below certain moisture content would kill it, so we had to be very careful to set the parameters of freeze drying correctly.

Unfortunately, by the third year of pollen processing in this way, the volume of pollen was just too much to handle by this procedure. The Director was visiting the pollen lab in the middle of all of this, and he asked me whether I thought we could handle the volume. I told him that I did not believe we could. Jess might not have wanted me to say that, but I had to be honest. Nevertheless, I think it was good that I was truthful, because it probably led to some changes that were for the better. Much more emphasis was placed on improving the efficiency of pollen handling at the orchard level, and Mike Carlson was instrumental in improving the tracking process, such that the required breeding crosses were accomplished efficiently with nearest source of pollen. Instead of sending everything to the Centralia lab and then shipping pollen out to make crosses, the system was computerized, so that if pollen was needed from the Ryderwood orchard to make a genetic cross at the Sequim orchard, the pollen was delivered directly to Sequim almost the day it was shed. We continued to freeze dry excess pollen for use where crosses were not possible within a growing season.

During this whole process of developing pollen handling, Jess Daniels was asked to address a convention of allergists. I guess the doctors who deal so much with pollen-induced allergies were interested in what Weyerhaeuser was doing with gymnosperm pollen. Jess asked me to prepare a presentation. That was a heady experience. I probably went into way too much detail about the structure and function of the pollen wall, and how we had encountered the problem of pollen storage. Perhaps that was of interest to some doctors who might have needed to maintain collections of pollen to test the allergic reactions of patients. From my perspective, it was a pretty big deal. Me getting to address a banquet room full of doctors… heady stuff! And the dinner they served was top notch.

Meantime, "back at the ranch", as they say in the cowboy song, things were "rolling along like the tumbling tumbleweed." By the winter of 1977, we were pretty well established on the farm. We had raspberries behind the house, and fruit trees and strawberries about to come into production in front of the house. We had quite a few chickens; now they would be called free-range, but then we didn't know about such 'esoteric names' for un-caged chickens. We also had rabbits and a goat, one dog, and one cat named Zawadi ('gift' in Kiswahili). The latter was a pretty calico, the goat was a female Nubian, and the dog was still Ol' Duke. I think the sheep was already history by then, but the goat was giving milk, and the rabbits were still multiplying. I think we sold some rabbits, and I think I gave the proceeds to Mzae for all his effort. The goat must have come to us after kidding, otherwise we would not have been able to get milk, but she produced for quite a long time. I loved that rich creamy milk in my coffee. The kids were not that crazy about goat's milk straight, but it was good in tea… at least it beat powdered milk!

Keeping the goat tethered was a trick. We did not have fence on the property, and it would have taken more money than I had to build a fence high enough to keep the goat in. So we tethered her. But she was really good at getting loose and every time she would get free, she would head straight for the house. Now Samba did most of the husbandry of the goat, but I don't think that Samba was what drew the goat to the house. This browser preferred strawberry plants and fruit tree bark, with a smattering of raspberry leaf for desert. So Samba was constantly trying to figure out how to tie the goat up in such a way that she would not choke herself or break free or chew her way through the tether rope.

She was a pretty goat, and I think that, of all the animals I have cared for, including the Herford bull, goats are the most like dogs in their intelligence[62]. Sheep are interminably dumb, but goats are wily like the coyote; just a little too smart for their own good. Having watched feral goats on the slopes of Haleakala in Maui, I can see why they evolved that way. Of course, they don't have predators on Maui, other than people, but they have developed the skills of avoiding potential predators. They stick to remote areas that are often too steep for other animals, and men, to reach. They are very sure-footed, although frequently you will see the bones of a goat that was just a little too bold on the cliff's edge. The Hawaiian game department has been known to use helicopters to cull the goats from the cliff areas.

---

[62] **Goats** are among the earliest animals domesticated by humans. The most recent genetic analysis confirms the archaeological evidence that the Anatolian Zagros are the likely origin of almost all domestic goats today. Another major genetic source of modern goats is the Bezoar goat, distributed from the mountainous regions of Asia Minor across the Middle East to Sind. Neolithic farmers began to keep goats for access to milk and meat, primarily, as well as for their dung, which was used as fuel and their bones, hair, and sinew for clothing, building, and tools. The earliest remnants of domesticated goats dating 10,000 years before the present are found in Ganj Dareh in Iran. Goat remains have been found at archaeological sites in Jericho, Choga, Mami, Djeitun and Cayonu, dating the domestication of goats in western Asia at between 8000 and 9000 years ago. http://en.wikipedia.org/wiki/Goat#History

In later years, I was sampling for a parasitoid of a gall forming fly in Maui Pamakani (that is a species of bush native to Hawaii). The goats loved the Pamakani, and would come to eat the galls as they foraged; I guess they thought the colored flagging that I used to mark the galls were fruit. I very seldom saw the goats doing this unless I very quietly approached the little valley where the Pamakani grew. The minute the goats detected my presence, they would immediately disappear over the rocky edges of the gulch.

Goats are curious creatures, and our domestic goat would snoop around the yard checking out the chickens, and other strange objects she had not yet perused. Goats are, of course, browsers, not grazers. Sheep, being grazers prefer grass, but goats prefer bush and broadleaf vegetation. Hence, the old wives' tale that goat will eat laundry and tin cans. Really they don't, but they will attempt to eat anything that chews well. I was very surprised to find out that goat herds are hired around the hills of Berkeley, California, to clear poison oak from the hillsides. The toxic exudate of the plant does not affect the goats, but the goat herder cannot be allergic to poison oak either, because the goats are coated with the noxious oil.

In the spring of 1977, Gertrude had moved to Tacoma and was being courted by a bus driver named Keith Thurman. Charity was holding down the farm, but the gardening efforts had subsided somewhat because she was also taking care of the daughter of one of my co-workers. I can't remember why that woman had been hired by Bill Nearn, my former boss, even though she was assigned to Centralia. I think she was part of a student intern program of which Bill was the supervisor. She was a single-parent black college student, who had the difficult task of commuting from the city (Olympia or Tacoma) every day to work in the Forest lab. She needed someone to care for her daughter, and I suggested that Charity might be able to do that for her. She and the daughter came to meet Charity, and seemed to be satisfied that it would be a safe environment for her daughter. Charity agreed, probably more because she wanted to earn the money than that she needed more to do. The mother, whom I will not name, must have thought it would be good for her daughter to be among black children. We did not charge her very much, because I knew that her financial situation was tight. From our perspective it worked out fairly well, but I don't think that the mother thought the arrangement was ideal. She did leave the daughter with Charity every day that she worked in Centralia.

There was a humorous incident that occurred with this young mother. She had, of course, interviewed with Bill Nearn, but had not seen him after

he hired her. One day in mid-summer, Bill came to visit the Centralia Lab
to see how she was fairing. The irony was that she did not recognize the man
that hired her. Bill cleverly jumped on the opportunity to say, "I know, we
honkies all look alike." We all laughed. Of course, the reference was to an oft
stated racist expression. "Oh, those colored people all look alike." I found that
worked both ways in Kenya, as well. The Danish volunteer and I were always
being confused with each other by the Wadwida because we both worked
in the same district. He was a foot shorter than me and had blond hair and
blue eyes, whereas I had red hair and brown eyes. To them, and especially to
the children, we were just the *Mzungu* (quite literally, the alien). The young
mother did not take offence to Bill Nearn's comment; she could see the humor
in it, but she could also see that there was no maliciousness or racism in the
statement. It was a clear indication that things were changing in America,
and the fact that Weyerhaeuser had made the effort to hire a black student
was a good example.

I am reminded by the memory of this summer student, that the corporate
world is a fickle place to live. By the time she had come to Weyerhaeuser to
work for the summer, the genetics group had already moved back into the
original lab facility. I don't remember the exact reason, but the genetics group
had been shifted back to the first lab, and the administration had taken over
the hospital along with the other divisions of Forestry Research. For whatever
reason, I guess the management had decided we didn't need all the extra
space, and that some other up and coming division was the more disserving
of the space. I was given a room about 10 x 6 feet to adapt for my microscopy
facility, and it was out of that room that we did all the pollen testing. Again
I had remodeled it to provide maximum efficient use of the microscope
and peripheral equipment. In fact, I had developed a technique for photo-
recording the results of the germination tests by direct projection micrography
of the pollen in germination media. The room had been designed to be light
sealed, and there was the original darkroom right next to it. Therefore, I
would take the micrograph of the germination sample, and then transfer it
in a light tight container to the darkroom for development. The 8 x10 inch
prints were easy to use to measure pollen length and width. We had attended
demonstrations of an image analyzing device that could have automated the
process, but the company decided it was more money than they wanted to
invest in the quality control process.

In point of fact, there were many other changes going on at Weyerhaeuser
at that time. The move to Federal Way was looming on the horizon, and

with all the money Weyerhaeuser had spent on the Super Bowl commercials, serious questions were starting to be asked about the cost of the whole research division. Ironically, those commercials had cost about the same as the whole Forestry Research budget that year. I think the amount was eight million dollars. Consequently, rumors began to spread that there was going to be a PIP. That stands for Personnel Improvement Program; which in plain English means people were going to be fired.

People began to get nervous, and some decided their best option was to jump ship. One technician that was working for the Plant physiologist decided he would go back to school. Since Weyerhaeuser was not offering him any assistance with his education, he decided to call in his chips, so to speak. He had worked countless unpaid hours during his time at Weyerhaeuser, but unlike the rest of us, he had the good sense to document all those hours. He was, of course, a management employee, but that notwithstanding, an employer is not allowed to work an employee over 40 hours a week without compensation. That is the Federal law. Of course, management protested, but this fellow was able to verify that the management had known he was working the extra hours, and with his documentation, the Company decided to capitulate and pay the guy time and a half for all the accumulated hours. That was a tidy little advance on his education! Mike Carlson was also looking to the future, and was already applying to graduate schools. As I may have indicated, he ended up attending University of California Davis. Another fellow who was in the Wildlife Management division, got a sweet deal from Weyerhaeuser Co. They gave him a full scholarship, also at U. C. Davis, and promise to rehire him when he finished. He definitely lived the life of Riley at UCD, while the rest of us struggled.

These were the people that left voluntarily, but the only person in our Genetics group that was PIPed was Liang Hsin. Hardest working guy in the group, who had taken on all of Jess' day to day breeding responsibilities. While Jess played the dignitary, Liang was the only guy fired. All the breeding crosses that had been made over the years were planned and implemented by Liang. He and I were not particularly close, but I had a lot of respect for him, and his work ethic. The fact that Weyerhaeuser had so little regard for his work, and the fact that Jess had done so little to defend Liang from the bean counters, cut me to the quick.

Of course, all the talk of transferring to Federal Way had already made me very uncertain about the job at Weyerhaeuser. I knew there was no way that I could buy a house and support a family of 6 (Teddy had by then moved in with Gertrude) in the suburban area of Tacoma. Even though the company was offering to provide a bus to transport the Centralia employees to Federal Way, I did not see how I could keep our homestead going if I was going to have to spend 3 hours on the road every day. The company's Real Estate Division was offering to buy the properties of the transferred workers, and there was a mini-boom in land prices then, but I had no assurance that we would obtain a fair price for our property. In all, the prospects of continuing to work for Weyerhaeuser Company were looking grim.

But the straw that broke the camel's back, as far as I was concerned, was the firing of Liang Hsin. I use the term "firing", but in fact it was officially classified as a "termination of employment due to lack of work." Of course that was not true; there was plenty of work, but at least it gave Liang the right to apply for unemployment compensation. I doubt that he did apply; he was a proud man used to working hard for his living. Liang went on to get a good job with the federal government in Oregon, but that was not the point. A company that had so little regard for the exemplary service of this hard working man was not the company to which I wanted to commit my career. Therefore, I arranged to meet Rex McCullough, who was then the acting manager of the Genetics Research Group, and told him that I thought it was an unwise choice to fire Liang and that I did not feel that I could commit to the company on a long term basis. He seemed to understand, and at that meeting we worked out an arrangement that I would transition to a contractual position as an independent contractor. He indicated that he would set aside $40,000 that could be used to hire me to do whatever tasks for which they needed my skills. That transition did not take place until April of 1978, but it did indeed seal my fate.

Ironically, I am only finding out now that eventually everyone's career was affected by the changes going on at Weyerhaeuser Forestry Research. Rex went on to become Vice President of Timberlands Forestry Research and Development. However, by 2004 he was a Management Consultant, although he was listed in a conference program as having retired from Weyerhaeuser. Jess Daniels, on the other hand, apparently never left Centralia, but formed Daniels & Associates. I found this in a Washington Agriculture and Forestry Leadership Program course publication on the internet.[63] One person who

---

[63] Keeping Our Social License to Farm: A Proactive Approach 4-12-01 Washington Agriculture and Forestry Leadership Program, Class XXII, Group 4: http://www.tricity.wsu.edu/aenews/agforestryg4.pdf

was not able to retire from Weyerhaeuser was me. At the time I separated from the company I had 5 ½ years of service and I would have needed 7 to be vested. What is worse, just the week that I terminated, a call went out to the management staff of the company to request workers for the Longview Pulp Mill, which had just gone out on strike. My friend Herb Karnofski, who had never worked in the pulp mill in all his time with Weyerhaeuser, accepted the assignment and pulled enough overtime to net $50,000 above his base salary that year. I, who had worked in the pulp mill every summer from 1963 to 1968, was not eligible to work there because I had just resigned from management.

You can imagine that I have asked myself many times over the years why I resigned from Weyerhaeuser. Was it idealism, fear, disgust, or just sheer stupidity? I have to say that in recent years, it looks more and more like the latter to me. Here I was the sole bread winner for 6 people and I was pushing my idealistic principles above the simple reality of survival. But what do you have if you don't have principles? Remember, I was going to be a priest, and then I was going to save the world, and now I was looking at being a Weyerhaeuser technician the rest of my working life? One's dreams die hard.

I thought that the company would probably have me doing microscopy or, at least, research. And I did have a few microscopy contracts, such as the one with Zach Wochok. But I had not planned very well for the transition to self-employment. I wanted to be self-employed, but I was counting way too much on Weyerhaeuser to provide the base. I thought I had earned respect and appreciation for my skills and for all I had done for the Company. But, like Liang, I was soon rudely awakened to the fact that Mother Weyerhaeuser is not a term of endearment, but rather a term of sarcasm. Mother W., being a corporation, is really most interested in the bottom line. If the reader takes any lesson from this memoir, it is this: in the corporate world you are on your own. No one has your back, as has been so amply demonstrated by the corporations divesting themselves of their employee retirement packages during the Bush administration. I guess I am lucky that I learned that lesson in my twenties and not in my fifties.

In Weyerhaeuser's defense I will say that they were more loyal to their staff than most corporations, and they did let me sell my stock which the company had purchases for me over the 5+ years. Of course, it was $50 a share when they bought them and $22 a share when I sold them. I think I got approximately $600. Still, providing stock in the company to employees at no charge was a pretty progressive personnel policy in the 1970s. In later years, I attended a documentary showing at the Newman Center in Davis, California. Aside from the shocking statistic that the 400 major corporations in the world at that time would merge into as few as 90 by the year 2000; the only thing I remember clearly from the movie was a comment by the CEO of Dole Foods. Alluding to the inviolable principle that profit is the driving force, he said "If we don't make a profit, we can't help anyone."

# Chapter 12

# The Fall of the Citadel

...but the Lord will lay low his pompous pride together with
the skill of his hands.
And the high fortifications of his walls he will bring down,
lay low, and cast to the ground, to the dust.
**English Standard Version (2001) Isaiah 25:11-12.**

In the last chapter, for continuity's sake, I skipped ahead to the circumstances of my departure from Weyerhaeuser Co. Now I must retrace the circumstances of my family during that fateful year of 1977. I have to admit that I was getting a little strange again about the religious issues. I was having that old conflict in my heart about whether I was doing what God wanted me to do. Since I was a deacon at St. Patrick's in Centralia, I had a key to the church. On my way home from work, which was usually late, I would stop at the church and let myself in. I would kneel at the sanctuary and beg for a sign from God whether I was doing the right thing. What I didn't know then was that, if God answers, he doesn't speak a language I understand.

I don't know if the work had become too routine, or the pressures of family life too stressful, but I definitely had a sense of insecurity about the direction my life was taking. I am sure the uncertainty of my job was not helping, but I didn't feel that I was progressing. It was not that the family situation was bad, but there were little irritations that were cropping up. Charity also seemed less satisfied with the situation. Gertrude had gone on to live in the city, and was on the verge of marrying her boyfriend. When she would come to visit at the homestead, she and Charity would meet in the kitchen and have long discussions in Kidawida. By then, with the possible exception of Samba, none of the other kids could understand their involved discussions. Of course, I did not know what they were talking about, but I suspected it was Charity's opportunity to vent about the difficult conditions in which she had to live. I also suspect that Gertrude was not reminding her how fortunate she was to be in America, living on her own land, with all of her children around her. Who could blame them? I was happy that we were able, at least, to create an agrarian world like the one from which Charity had come. She was perhaps thinking more of her life in Mombasa than on the farm in Taita. How does the WWI song go: "How ya gonna keep 'em down on the farm. After they've seen Paree'."

At one point in the spring, a newspaper reporter from Olympia called to ask if she could interview the family. Of course, we agreed, but I was not there when she came to talk to and take pictures of the family. Later she called and wanted to schedule an appointment with me. For whatever reason I refused, and there never was a newspaper article about us. I wasn't sure if I was ready for that kind of publicity. Who knows what kind of impact, if any, such an article would have had.

Gertrude's wedding date had been set for July of 1977, and Charity was very involved in the preparations, as would be consistent with an African wedding. We were not in any financial condition to underwrite the whole affair, but Gertrude took the initiative to find a church just out of Tenino, and arrange for the invitations, etc. I don't know whether Charity insisted that I invite my friends and relatives, or whether that was my idea. At any rate, my mother scheduled to come at the time of the wedding, and Gretchen and her father also came. I think perhaps Mrs. Bardsley and the Soniers came, too. I can't remember who else. Many of Gertrude's friends were unknown to me.

On other summer visits to the homestead, my mother had come with Fr. Carl, and they usually stayed in a motel. But this trip she made by train, as she had the first year that she visited us. The house being very small, Charity and I gave up our room for her, and slept on the sofa bed. My mother had a way of always being a center of attention, not always in the good sense. With all the hustle and bustle of preparing for the wedding, I think Charity felt that my mother was in the way too much of the time. It was particularly galling to Charity that my mother would prance around in her pink negligée, even in front of visitors. I think that visit drove a stake into the heart of their relationship, which had never been warm.

Gretchen distinctly remembers Charity asking her at the house before the reception: "Would you live like this?" Gretchen, being ever honest, said, "No." I think Bob Huffhines and Gretchen were just surprised that we had survived as long as we had in this marriage, and were now marrying off the oldest daughter. Bob and Gretchen were happy to talk to my mother, even though they had thought her quite nuts for leaving Jim, my stepfather. Noticeably, Gretchen's mother did not come. I think she did not have the same tolerance for my mother that Bob had. All of this inter-racial openness was a bit beyond her sensibilities. I would not call Jana racist, but more proper. She did not like to be in socially awkward situations. Or maybe she just thought it was a shame that I had gone off to Africa, and left Gretchen to her fate. I am not sure which.

As I remember it, my father and Elizabeth were noticeably absent from Gertrude's wedding as well. I don't remember exactly why, although they sometimes would manage a tourist business for friends of theirs in McKinsey, Oregon, during the summer. Even if that had not been the reason why they did not come to Gertrude's wedding, I am sure Elizabeth would not want to have been at the wedding with my mother. This may also have been the reason why they did not come to my wedding to Charity.

The wedding was in the morning and it turned out to be a beautiful day, if I remember correctly. Fortunate, because there were a lot of people and no reception hall at the church, much of the post-ceremony celebration occurred outside the church. I don't actually remember Keith's family coming to the house in Tenino, although we did have a small reception after the wedding at the house. In fact, I had not met Keith's family before the wedding. I am not sure if Charity had met them on her visits to Tacoma before the wedding. Nor did I give away the bride. In fact, I don't remember anything about the wedding ceremony.

I think I had only met Keith once before the wedding. I seem to remember that he needed my truck to move, and I went to help him. He seemed like a decent enough guy, and had a regular job, so I figured Gertrude was lucky to have found him. I did not know immediately that the reason for the marriage was that Gertrude was pregnant with LaQuita.

Because I was delivering Mom to the train station in the Gimmy, there was only room for some of the kids, which was all right with her, because things had turned pretty frosty between my mother and Charity. I could chalk it up to mother-in-law syndrome, but perhaps there were some good reasons on both sides. I know that Charity thought that I deferred too much to my mother, but I also know that my mother was deciphering the fact that Charity was not happy with what America had offered her. Knowing, as my mother did, the sacrifice that all of us had made to get her whole family to

America, she was indignant. It was clear to her that undying love was not at the heart of this marriage between Charity and me.

As Mom kissed Jimmy and Samba goodbye, I think she suspected that she probably was not going to be seeing them again for years. I was, of course, oblivious. To my mind, the family was a permanent unit by God's design. Nothing was going to turn me from my commitment to these kids.

Charity expressed her unhappiness about my mother's visit by refusing to honor the marriage bed. That was a significant change in our relationship. My reaction was not to have sex again, and we did not. Still, I was determined to fulfill my responsibilities as a father, so I was committed to making the thing work. The uncertain future at Weyerhaeuser was worrying me greatly, and I still longed to get back to Africa. I was hoping that contracting would open doors to more international development based employment. I had learned a lot at Weyerhaeuser, but I didn't feel the satisfaction of helping people, other than supporting my family.

So that was the question: how would I support the family if either we moved to Federal Way, or if I separated from Weyerhaeuser. The demands of the job and the farm were just taking too much time to allow me to do the necessary research to explore the possibilities. By the end of the summer, I was convinced that I would not be able stay with the company; but I also could not wean myself from the Mother Weyerhaeuser's teat. I began to look into Foreign Service possibilities. The price of property was good, so I figured if I got a contract in East Africa, we would be able to sell the house and have enough to move everyone back to East Africa. I knew that if we made it back there, I would be able to earn plenty enough as an expatriate to comfortably support the family. I had no such confidence about finding work in the twin city area of Southwest Washington.

When I broached this subject with Charity, she was adamant that she did not want to sell the property or move back to Africa. So that was a great obstacle. I guess I thought I might be able to overcome it, so I continued to entertain the idea. I contacted the United Nations Volunteers, and they expressed interest. Eventually they sent an invitation to a position in Tanzania. The volunteer salary offer was 4000 Tanzanian Shillings per month. That was only about US $600 per month at the existing exchange rate, but we had lived on $200 per month in Kenya. Plus the United Nations offered health care, travel allowances, and, I believe, housing. I figured it would be a good move, but we would need to sell the property.

Charity was completely opposed, even when I assured her that my job at

Weyerhaeuser would be ending. In the same way she had refused to sell the property at Mpizini, when she left Kenya, now she was determined not to lose the property in Tenino. Understandably, land ownership was a very important thing to her generation of Africans who had no such right in Colonial Kenya. And I will grant that some other members of Charity's family have used the property in Mpizini from time to time, but now it is abandoned and falling back into the disrepair in which we found it back in 1970. Charity and I were both unaware that this fateful disagreement would lead eventually to the loss of the Tenino property.

I don't know why Charity was so strongly opposed to returning to Africa. Maybe it was the fact that it was Tanzania. Or maybe she figured that it had been such a major step to come to America that she did not want to step backwards. Or maybe she was beginning to doubt my judgment. Whatever the case, it left me no choice but to try to survive with whatever work I could get in the vicinity. The transition to self-employment did not occur immediately, so we had a few months left for me to try to figure out what to do.

My stepfather and Elizabeth visited us at Christmas time. It was a happy occasion, and from all appearances we looked a happy family unit. But looks can be deceptive. I was still convinced that we would be together forever, but I don't know exactly what Charity thought. Perhaps she was still dedicated to the marriage, but she was certainly not in full agreement with me on the direction the family should go.

**Christmas 1977.** Top left to right: Charity, Mzae, Sam, me, Jimmy and Samba. Bottom: Mzae, Grandfather James and Jimmy, Samba, Sam and Elizabeth. (Photographed by the author.)

I don't know if I discussed the future prospects with Dad and Elizabeth at that time, but it was not long after that they knew that things were shifting for me. I had been in contact with the Zeiss Representative in Washington State, who was at the time Hans Schreider. Hans told me that he was a veteran Luftwaffe pilot, who had immigrated to the US after the end of the war. He had sold me most of the equipment that I purchased for Weyerhaeuser. One day he took me to lunch and asked me if I wanted to make an extremely smart purchase of a microscope. It was a used, reconditioned Zeiss Ultraphot, which was the top of the line in micrography at that time. What is more, he could sell it to me for an absolute steal. The Ultraphot model was being replaced by the Axiomat microscope, for which they had taken the older microscope on trade in. Four thousand dollars for a microscope, which cost several times as much in its day, was a good price. Hans knew of my plans to try to do contract microscopy, and he wanted to help me get a fine instrument to make that possible.

I discussed this with my folks, and my Dad agreed to co-sign on a loan to buy the microscope. However, when we applied for the loan with Weyerhaeuser Employees Federal Credit Union, they refused the loan, because I did not have collateral, and they did not believe I had a viable business plan. That was a very serious blow to me. I didn't know that banks and Credit Unions only make business loans on well-established business models. Who ever heard of a business doing contractual microscopy in the Pacific Northwest? I had already contacted the Small Business Administration, and would have applied for a small business loan. If my situation with the family had not been so financially tenuous, I would have pursued this with vigor. But being turned down by Weyerhaeuser's own credit union took the wind right out of my sails.

I had three months left before my paycheck would be cut off. We did not have any financial reserve, and I was the only one in the family that had a job. Oti and Charles had, by that time, purchased a nursing home and were trying to keep it staffed. Charity would help them out sometimes when they were short staffed. But we lived a long distance from Yelm and we had only the one vehicle. Charity could not drive, so if anyone went anywhere it was with me. I was still on the 10 hour 4 day work week, so I had some time to look for work, and Weyerhaeuser had provided a room equipped with typewriter, job information, a telephone and other things needed for job search. I wasn't the only employee leaving Weyco employment. But in spite of the aid, I was not coming up with any leads.

Through those months before my termination, I don't know what Charity was thinking. I would explain to her that things would have to change, but I did not see any movement towards solutions to the problem. I don't say that Charity was spending money excessively or doing anything to increase our expenses. Of course, she didn't have a lot of options for doing so. Life on the farm stayed pretty much the way it had been. I was having to cut back on credit card expenditures and try to pay off our credit card debt. It was not very large, but to us, it was a great burden. I had used the card to pay basic bills like winter-time electrical bills, and repairs on the truck. But I finally had to cut up the American Express Card.

There are many stories I could tell about the adventures of keeping a 1949 GMC running, but I will not. It would be far too incredible for even the most mechanically minded reader. Suffice it to say, my salvation was an 85-year-old mechanic named Jack Preston. He had owned a shop and a car dealership during his career, but that was before Social Security, and it had not left him with a nest egg to retire on. So he kept his small shop on Tower St. open for business into his golden years. He once even broke his shoulder socket working on my GMC, and actually came back to finish the job after he had recovered. I'll never forget how he came to pick up the truck when it was broken down. He had a 1945 Ford pickup, for which he had built his own tow-bar. It was just a long metal bar through which a bolt could be slipped into a pin assembly on the Ford's rear bumper. The bar was then chained to my truck's front axil. It was nothing like an A-frame tow hitch, but it worked pretty well. I am sure people were shocked to see this little '45 Ford towing that big '49 1-ton GMC. They really don't make men like Jack anymore. Here I am only 64 and can barely get around with my spinal stenosis... Jack was overhauling truck engines when he was 85!

I don't remember much about those last few months with Weyerhaeuser. I do seem to remember that there was a lot of pressure to analyze data and write up research reports on the work we had done over the previous four years. I spent a lot of time with Jim (forgot his last name); he was the computer specialist for Rex McCullough and knew how to do SAS analysis. I had learned to do statistical means and standard errors on my Texas Instrument programmable calculator, but this was another level of technology to which I had not yet climbed. I remember distinctly that Jim confronted me one day. He said, "If you don't at least learn to keypunch your data, I am not going to analyze it for you anymore." What I didn't realize then is how lucky I was; Weyerhaeuser had already upgraded to Texas Instrument terminals, so key punch was no longer the cumbersome process of punching tape or punch cards. You could just type the data in with comma to separate the data points, and then type the enter key to end each line of data. Little did I know that this would save me a lot of grief in the future.

Working 10 to 12 hour day required that I would eat dinner in Centralia. Jim was a bachelor, so he ate out a lot. We would head over to the Country Cousin after work, and he might order a regular dinner. I always ordered the cheapest thing on the menu, which was a cup of soup and salad with a cornbread muffin. I think they charged about $2.50 and a dollar for a bottomless cup of coffee. Last I checked, the Country Cousin is still in business, and so is Jim. When he separated from Weyerhaeuser, he started a Computer Store in Centralia.

When April rolled around, I was actually able to get some contract work from the staff at Weyerhaeuser Co. I had already started working on Zach Wolchok's chromosome banding project, and he paid me $10 an hour on contract until June. That was not full time, and I also did some other small microscopy studies for other scientists during that time.

Fred Moon (no relation to Floyd) was the facilities manager, and the man in charge of the fund that was paying me. He also gave me very different work. The first project was to build shelving for the administrative office being transferred to the old hospital. It was so large that I could not assemble it totally in the company shop. So Fred had me build it in two sections. What is more, it could not be fit in any of the doors of the hospital. I ended up having to hoist it up to the second floor deck outside of the office where the shelving could be passed through the sliding door. Edward, Charity's oldest son, was visiting the homestead at the time, so he helped me maneuver the beast.

Fred then contracted me to do some seeding weights for a big experiment at the Rochester Nursery Farm. The kids came with me in the evening to help do that job, and I paid them for their time, which, of course, I was charging to Weyco. Fred also had me build some tent frames for some seedling sprinkling experiments. And then he had me build an enclosure in the recently acquired Safeway building for the electronics technicians. After that, Fred told me that the funds were being appropriated for other purposes, and he did not have any other contracts for me at the Forestry Research labs.

I wanted to see if I might get work from the Weyerhaeuser Wood Morphology Group, which had passed from Bill Nearn to Bob Megraw when Bill retired. I called Bob, and he said they did not have any work in the lab, but he said he needed a farm manager for the summer in Puyallup. Bob had bought a raspberry farm and he needed someone to manage it. This probably didn't help my contract with Weyerhaeuser, but I had no objection to physical work, and it didn't look like there was any other income on the horizon.

Therefore in June, the whole family became "migrant farm workers." Not in the true sense, because we came home every night to Tenino. But every morning we would depart at 5 AM to get to Puyallup, Washington, so that we could spend the day picking raspberries. My job was to oversee the workers, deliver the berries to the packing houses, pay the pickers, maintain the fields, and keep track of the books. That year, the daughters of the previous owner had agreed to stay on to act as checkers. It was a job they had done for their father, and they had very strict rules for the pickers. All they had to do was stand in the packing shed and punch the cards of the pickers when they brought in a hallock-carrier of berries. Occasionally they would go down the rows of berries to see if some picker they suspected was not picking the rows clean. They could tell, because a gleaner will pick only the fat, easily reached berries, where as a thorough picker will have berries of various sizes in their hallock. They were both gorgeous, but they were also vain. They constantly had a comb in their hair or their hand, and they would not do more than stack the hallocks and tell me when they needed them moved. I would have to load what added up to 14,000 lbs. of berries onto the truck by myself. None of my family liked them, and they were disdainful of my kids and wife, who were picking berries for the first time in their lives.

I am embarrassed to describe how we had to travel, but fortunately the weather was unusually hospitable that season, because the Gimmy only had room for 2 adults and 2 kids in the cab. That meant, like migrant workers, the other kids had to ride on the flat bed. The system we had worked out for that was a 4 x 4 ft. box held on the flat bed with rope. These were the same boxes I had used for storage when Charity, James and I lived in the travel trailer.

If the readers wonder what happened to the Ambassador, it had died, and I could not afford to repair it. In fact, I don't remember much about how that happened or, for that matter, when it happened. I remember the Ambassador died on us in Tenino one day. It turned out that the problem was solved with the replacement of the condenser, but I was forced to leave the Ambassador in Tenino overnight, and some juvenile delinquents busted the rear window while it sat. That led to water in the rear seat well, which caused the interior of the vehicle to mold. I couldn't afford to fix that, and the Ambassador became less and less useful as a transport vehicle. Eventually it died permanently.

Bob had provided an old pickup, and at first I used that to deliver the berries. But then the water pump went out in that truck. Bob repaired it fairly quickly, but I think I started using the Gimmy to deliver the berries because the higher bed was easier to unload berries at the loading dock; meaning I could use a hand truck to roll the stacked flats of hallocks into the warehouse. Of course they all had to be loaded by hand on the truck, but easier to do once than twice.

Driving the Gimmy was kind of an acrobatic feat, because, by then, the 1$^{st}$ gear's teeth were so worn that the transmission would jump into neutral unless I held the shift lever with my right hand. The door latch on the driver's side was also worn out, so when I would make a right turn, I had to hold the door so it would not swing open. To top it all off, the vacuum driven windshield wiper motor was defunct, so if it rained I would have to operate the wipers from inside the dash or out the window. Mercifully it did not rain that summer. It was only possible to reach inside the dash because I had had to remove the speedometer gage when it broke. This was truly what the Mexican migrant workers would call a cucaracha, or, in Hawaiian Pigeon, a chakalaka. Yet surprisingly, that amazing old truck got us back and forth and delivered the berries to the packing house every day for the whole summer.

We took the back road through Yelm every day because I did not trust the Gimmy on the freeway, and if we had ever been stopped by the police, the Gimmy would have been grounded. It was a pleasant ride, but kind of hard to enjoy at 5 AM, and most of the family was too tired to enjoy it on the way back after a full day of berry picking. I don't remember what Jimmy would do all day, because he was pretty young, but Samba and Mzae worked alongside their mother. Even Sam showed some initiative to try to help earn some money. For the younger kids, it wasn't all that different from being at home. They would spend the day in the garden with their mother in the summer most years. I believe I let them all keep their money from the berry picking. I won't swear to that because I don't know if Charity would ask them to chip in on purchase of things needed for the family. But I know that I let Charity control her own earnings. I forget how exactly I was paid. That year, all the berries went directly to the packing house, and they did not pay until the end of the season. Bob had given me some advance to set up an account to pay the pickers, and I might have taken some money out of that. We settled up at the end of the season as I remember, but it was not a large sum, about $2000 plus expenses.

During the berry season, we still had to be able to maintain some crops at the homestead. This was only possible because, on the off days when there were no berries ready to pick, Charity and the kids stayed home to tend to the garden. Of course, I was required to be at the berry farm every day, because on the no-pick days, I had other tasks like weed whacking and tilling the weeds around the blueberries that Bob had planted. Bob also encouraged me to plant corn and pumpkin, and he said he would split the proceeds with me. So that also required attention and weeding. About mid-season, the packing house reported that we had an insect problem. The manager said that if we did not spray, the shipments would be refused. Bob told me what pesticide to buy, and how to attach the spray apparatus to the tractor. The spraying had to be done in the evening on a Saturday, so that the pickers would not come back in the field until Monday. I don't even remember what the pesticide was, but I have pangs of guilt about this until this day. Not the spraying of the pesticide, but that I let Mzae drive the tractor. He wanted so badly to learn to drive the tractor, that I let him do the spraying. I didn't let him handle the pesticide, but he was probably exposed to it going down the rows with the tractor. The spray boom was behind the cab, so it was directed away from the driver, but I am sure there was some drift. I believe he was wearing a respirator and protective suit. At least, he has not developed cancer, and he has since sired a healthy child, so I sleep a little easier now.

Of course, being an inexperienced driver, Mzae eventually ended up driving the boom of the sprayer into a post, and I had to buy parts and repair it. But the upside was that Mzae didn't have to continue spraying. He had done a good job for his first time out, and I think he was proud of himself. Better yet, the spray worked, and we had no more complaints from the packing house, and we didn't have to spray the rest of the season.

Near the end of the season, the corn was ready to harvest, and Bob asked me to try to find local markets for it. Of course, everyone else's corn crop was ready to harvest, too; so the competition was fierce. I did manage to sell some at a couple of local vegetable markets, but corn deteriorates rapidly, and we had a lot left. Bob took the remained of the harvest and put it in the Weyerhaeuser cold storage locker. He had put it in a paper barrel that had been shipped to the Federal Way lab. With its shipping content removed and filled with corn, it looked like part of the regular inventory at the lab. I continued to try to find a market for the corn. But eventually Bob just gave the barrel of left over corn to us for the family. It was already starchy, but Charity and the kids dutifully cut all the kernels off the cobs and froze them. The pumpkins were not ready to harvest when the berry season ended, and I don't know whether Bob was able to sell them for Halloween or not.

We were stocking up for winter, and it would be a long one. I even made them cut up the green tops of the onions we harvested out of our garden to freeze, because I knew they could be used to make *supu na mboga*. That was also the year that Ernie Sonier brought us the deer that had been killed on the highway, so we had venison in the freezer. As the remaining cash diminished, we also decided to slaughter the goat. Samba was sad to see her pet goat slaughtered, but the whole family had not eaten *mbuzi* since Kenya, and they all enjoyed it very much, including Samba. Some of that also ended up in the freezer. Although there had not been time to do as much canning as in the year that we put up 1000 quarts, we still had some raspberry jam, and plums, and apples, and chowchow to preserve. We were really living the farm life that most Americans have never experienced. Of course, Charity knew about producing one's own food. Nevertheless, I am glad that the kids were able to continue to experience the concept of self-reliance in America. Their lives would take a very different course, but at least they can say they knew what people have done for centuries to survive. Some of the world's most successful people grew up in poverty.

Now with the berry season over, I needed to try to find more work. I made contact with Fred Moon, to see if anything had opened up at the Centralia Lab. They had not, and much of the money set aside for contracting had been used elsewhere. They agreed that I would still be allowed to use the microscopy lab, since I had invested so much effort in remodeling it (without compensation), and lobbied for the equipment. So I continued to try to interest local businesses and laboratories (such as the State Photogrammetry Laboratory in Olympia) in my services. At this point, I would have taken anything, part-time, full-time, or contract. But nothing was forthcoming. I estimate that I may have made 300 job applications during that time with no success. I thought Rex McCullough and I had come to an understanding of why I was leaving Weyerhaeuser Co. That may have been an unfortunate assumption because I used Rex as one of my main references. Jess knew that I had quit in protest, so I did not use him. But I did not think Rex would black ball me for quitting. That may, or may not, have been a misplaced trust. The net result was that I was not getting positive responses from any of my job applications.

I had contacted the local community college about the possibility of teaching a course in microscopy. The biology instructor and several other staff were interested in having such a course as a refresher for their own benefit. I also approached Weyerhaeuser about offering the course to the

Weyerhaeuser employees. Ironically, I did not get any students from the staff in the Centralia lab, but the technicians from a field station near Centralia did sign up. Chuck and Debbie Leslie were a couple who were both live-in caretakers and technicians for a Weyerhaeuser field station near Pi El. So between them and the staff from Centralia College, we had just enough students to hold the course.

In 1973, I had been sent by Bill Nearn to a McCrone Institute training course to learn analytical microscopy; that is the use of polarized light microscopy to determine chemical properties of specimens by their refractive indices. McCrone, for the $500 cost of the course, had issued us a comprehensive manual that covered all aspects of light-microscopy theory and practice. I spent what reserve funds I had to order these manuals and a Kodak publication on photomicrography in sufficient quantity for my class. The College was not equipped with any fancy microscopes. They would not do anything more that standard 10 to 400x transmission light microscopy, so it was going to be necessary to demonstrate some of the capabilities of the microscope at my microscope cubical at the Weyerhaeuser Lab. Since it was a night course, I easily obtained permission to do this.

The course was to be held in Fall Quarter, so I spent time preparing the course syllabus and making the handouts and overhead transparencies that I would need for the class. I had not yet reached the stage of panic. Our resources were limited, but I had hoped that this effort might lead to some kind of supplemental income through the college. At the same time I was preparing this course material, I was looking into how I might further my educational skills, because I was beginning to realize that I was not very marketable -- at least if you considered my lack of success in applying for jobs. I had visited the Campus of Evergreen State College, and met Dr. Humphrey, who was the director of the microscopy facility. Evergreen was established under a unique directive. It was to provide educational opportunities to the employed public as well as the typical college student. This led to the concept of directed learning, and the development of a physical facility to encourage independent study. The State must have been flush at the time because they got the very best equipment available for this facility. This included computer, chemistry, and microscopy facilities. The microscopy lab had the best Zeiss light microscopes and electron microscopes. Dr. Humphrey and I agreed upon a directed self-paced program that would explore new techniques in microscopy. I did not actually finish the project until 1981, but I initiated the program and paid the tuition in the fall semester of 1978. What I was developing was a tissue freeze-sectioning technique that employed the newly developed piezoelectric freeze stage of Bailey Instrument Inc. Ironically, at one point during the development of the technique, the owner of the company, R. J. Bailey, was offering to work with me on patenting the technique. My life was in such a state that I did not follow through quickly enough. The offer remained open to cooperate, but all that company was able to do was loan me equipment to work with for six months. I should have pursued the offer, but I was too busy trying to keep the family afloat. Resources are always the make or break part of invention.

The course at Centralia College was conducted, and the students and teachers bought their manuals. That was probably the most valuable thing that I provided because all of the course material was in those two manuals. They would have them references for the rest of their careers, just like I had relied heavily on those manuals myself; sort of the cookbook of good microscopy. I don't know what happened to the rest of the students, but I know that Chuck Leslie went on to get his master's degree in horticulture at the U. C. Davis, and landed a job with the Federal government as a tissue culture specialist. I know you can't do tissue culture without using microscopes, so I claim a very small degree of credit for his success. The course was accredited, so at least I know everyone got college credits for their time.

The teachers were not terribly impressed with my teaching style, so they suggested that, if I wanted to continue to teach this course at Centralia College, I should probably take a course in adult education. It was not an expense that I wanted to incur, but I figured I had better take it if I wanted to teach again, so I enrolled for the winter quarter. Compared to university courses in biology it was pretty Mickey Mouse. I realized than that social science and education courses are not at the same level as science classes. But I did learn something about human behavior, particularly adult behavior. I also learned that education is about jumping through the hoops. I had tried to pack way too much real information into my microscopy course, when in fact; a college course is not about how much information you can pack into a series of classes, but whether the student will absorb enough to pass the exams. I did get kudos for my enthusiasm about microscopy and the professors did try doing some of their own photomicrography.

I was making all of this effort to try to stay in the profession that I had trained for, but the outlook was getting bleaker and bleaker. I have to acknowledge Mike Carlson, who gave me a contract for $120 to produce Cibachrome prints that he had taken of the Genetic Group staff. Other than that, the incoming cash was nil. I was getting pretty discouraged. And can you imagine how I felt when I came home one day to find that Charity had taken Jimmy and left her other three youngest children at home without supervision. There was no indication of where she had gone, and she did not call. I was very upset, and I think the kids were also concerned. Perhaps my anger was their cause for concern, but I huddled with them in a corner where we were all sitting on the floor. I told them then than they did not have to worry and that I would never abandon them. Fateful words, considering what eventually happened.

It was three days before Charity showed up with James, and she did not explain herself. To this day I don't know where she went or why. She knew I was very unhappy about it, but apparently she was also getting very concerned about my unemployment. Maybe she went job hunting, or maybe she went to visit Gertrude, maybe she just had to get away. I don't know which, and never will. It was not a good omen for the relationship. In 1977, *Roots*[64] (the miniseries based on Alex Haley's novel *Roots: The Saga of an American Family*) was broadcast. Charity's whole family watched it intensively. It led to many Kidawida discussions between Gertrude and Charity. I did not mention it when I was describing that period of time, because the impact of *Roots* on Charity was not fully apparent until this most recent absence of Charity and James occurred. I knew that Charity was not happy about things, but I didn't realize that she was beginning to think of me as her "slave master." I had thought I was doing my part to reverse the injustices of centuries, but now, somehow, I seemed to become implicated in the indignities that had been heaped on Kunta Kinte.

---

[64] In 1976, Haley published **Roots: The Saga of an American Family**, a novel based on his family's history, starting with the story of Kunta Kinte, kidnapped in The Gambia in 1767 and transported to the Province of Maryland to be sold as a slave. Haley claimed to be a seventh-generation descendant of Kunta Kinte, and Haley's work on the novel involved ten years of research, intercontinental travel and writing. He went to the village of Juffure, where Kunta Kinte grew up and which is still in existence, and listened to a tribal historian tell the story of Kinte's capture.[1] Haley also traced the records of the ship, The Lord Ligonier, which he said carried his ancestor to America. http://en.wikipedia.org/wiki/Alex_Haley

# Chapter 13

# The Diaspora (Migration)

But he himself went a day's journey into the wilderness and came and sat down under a broom tree. And he asked that he might die, saying, "It is enough; now, O LORD, take away my life, for I am no better than my fathers."
**English Standard Version (2001) 1 Kings 19:4.**

I must admit that the First three months of 1978 are a big block in my memory. I have no idea how we survived. All I can remember is watching the snowy image of the TV late into the night. Christmas had come and gone and I don't even know if we celebrated. I was coming up with nothing in the way of employment or even piece work. I don't even remember if I cut cord wood to earn a little cash. In American culture a man is little or nothing if he doesn't have work, and a man with a large family to feed and no job is a bum. It was hard for me to hold my head up at church; I think I would not have even attended if the family did not depend on me for transportation. We must have been living very frugally because we survived from the end of December until the beginning of April on what we had earned during the summer and the little that I had received for the teaching contract.

I don't remember if Charity had started working for Oti and Charles during that time, but my memory is that it wasn't for very long. By the time April came round, I knew that I had to do something different. I wasn't making any progress in the northwest. I began to think that if I could get back to U. C. Davis, I might have a chance of finding some source of income. I was down to $59, which was barely enough to buy a train ticket to Davis. Why didn't I look into attending a Washington State institution? I can't answer that, although I admit I had not even tried to inquire. I had already started at Davis, and I was hoping that my probationary success (3.7 GPA) would give me a half a chance of getting started again.

I was not leaving the family. In my mind, I was doing the last thing I could do to try to get some kind of job to support the family. I was not leaving the family in a very good situation, but I really had no choice. I was hoping that Charity would somehow be able to get to work at Oti's nursing home, and at least I knew that we had some food stored away. The kids were still attending school, so at least they would be able to eat lunch at school, and did not need to be transported since the bus came to our road. It crossed my mind that the two oldest of Charity's children might have some respect and help her out.

Did I leave because I couldn't take it anymore? Perhaps, but that is not the way I saw it in my head. I was desperate, but I was not intentionally abandoning my family. I was hoping there would be some breakthrough, some shred of luck, which would keep the family together. So I boarded the train in Centralia. I suppose, Edward or Gertrude must have delivered me to the station. I don't remember any goodbyes. As I said, I don't remember much. Perhaps the memories were so painful that I had to repress them. I paid my $50 and I was off to Davis.

The train ride on the Coast Starlight was an all-night affair. I must have been tired because I apparently slept for a good part of that trip. I couldn't afford to eat in the diner, and I don't think I had taken any lunch with me. The train arrived in Davis at six AM. Since I couldn't eat anything, and the campus financial aid office didn't open until 8 AM, I did a little wandering. I noticed that there was a foot path across the tracks to a small enclave of what looked like railroad shacks. It kind of reminded me of Camp Pondosa. So I wandered over and took a look around. Turns out it had been lodging for the railroad workers originally, but had long since been sold to a man who ran the place like a motel. Only most of the tenants were pretty long term. It was, by far the cheapest lodging in Davis, and I made mental note that I would have to come back to check these out if, by some miracle, I was able to get back into college.

I was on the doorstep of the Financial Aid Office when they opened the doors. The woman at the desk protested when I inquired about the possibility of applying. It was already 10 days into the quarter, and most of the financial aid funds had already been allocated for the quarter. You know that sinking feeling that you get when you talk to one of those government workers? The ones who believes that their particular responsibility is to make sure that the government doesn't spend any money on you? I insisted on applying so she relinquished the forms. As I was filling out financial aid forms, I was feeling really stupid for spending my last dime to get to Davis; was I nuts! It was beginning to be a serious question.

But then a man named Terry introduced himself. He said, "I am your case worker; will you come into my office, please." Now let's pause a moment and dissect that innocuous phrase. Any government employee could say that, with little conviction I might add. But there was something very sincere in Terry's manner. The first thing that struck me was "your case worker"; you mean they really assign individuals to "work" for "you"? Next, before inquiring any further about me, he invited me into his office. He had probably seen some paperwork that I had filled out, but he wasn't even concerned that he might have the wrong person. And on top of it all, he said "please." Now that was totally disarming, so it was not hard to unload all the details when he started to ask questions.

As far as I can remember, I had missed all the application and enrollment and tuition deadlines. I don't even know why I thought it was even possible to enroll ten days into the quarter. And on top of that, I had nothing and it had been seven years since my first spring quarter at UC Davis. Apparently, Terry's case load had subsided by that late date because I think he devoted the whole day, with occasional interruptions, to my predicament. He had me running around quite a bit, collecting transcripts, confirming class schedules, checking employment opportunities, and whatever else needed to be completed on such short notice. Most of all, I needed to confirm that I was still one of Dr. C. Y. S. Peng's graduate students. She was happy to see me back, and was looking forward to developing a thesis topic around microscopic studies of honeybee digestion of pollen.

It wasn't until four o'clock that afternoon that Terry was able to call me into his office and present me with the package that he had been able to work out in the short span of 8 hours. Now that is a truly dedicated government worker! Frankly, I have not met one quite like him since. In the course of a day, he had gotten me a federal grant to pay my tuition with some cash to spare and had set me up for work-study. Not only that, but he had also waived my out of state tuition, and pushed through my enrollment in the classes I wanted to take. Those included: Plant Ecophysiology, Advanced Insect Physiology, Advanced Physiology, Culture of Plants, World Vegetable Crops, and an International Agriculture Development core course.

In the process of investigating the courses that day, I had met with Robbin Thorp, who offered me work-study in his lab, and I had enough money to pay a month's rent at what I called the "Squatters Camp" and send enough money home to pay the house payment. It looked like I was going to be staying, and luckily I had brought just enough basic supplies and clothing to pull it off. I hadn't even brought my textbooks and notes from the spring quarter of 1972. The faces were still familiar, and it wasn't too long before my knowledge as a microscopist helped me get contracts with Grady Webster (whose Pollination course I had taken) and Dr. Tucker in the Botany Department. I had one contract come to me at Weyerhaeuser, just before I left for Davis. I actually didn't know how I was going to do it, because it involved embedding and sectioning advantageous root tissue for Dr. Abo El Nil. However, having access to the Entomology lab and their Zeiss microscope was a big help. I finished that last Weyerhaeuser contract in June, which netted me 600 much needed dollars. The good doctor went on to receive a patent for the tissue culture of Douglas fir (*Pseudotsuga mensiesii*).

Sometimes I have to stop and pinch myself, when I realized how quickly things just fell into place to let me continue my education. Whereas I was running up against solid brick walls in Washington State, now I was a very saleable commodity at Davis, California. Maybe there was one other difference; I stopped using Rex McCullough as a reference on my resume. I can't really prove that he ever black-balled me, but I thought it ironic that the work started pouring in when I stopped listing him as a reference. Maybe it is just the difference in culture. At Davis, what people want you for is what you know. Maybe my skills were not in demand in the northwest at that transitional time for Weyerhaeuser and other industries that were in an economic slump caused by the long term effect of the 1974 oil crisis. Who knows? Whatever was the case, my luck had changed at UCD.

I barely had time to get to a bank and set up an account so I could cash the financial aid check. Bank of America was on First Street, and that was on the way to the squatter's camp across the tracks. So I headed from the bank to secure a room at the camp. The manager happened to be around that late in the afternoon, so I checked out a couple of possible lodgings with him. I could not afford an individual cabin, but there was a kind of bunk house in which he had one available room left. The price was right, so I paid my two-month advance. Ironically, the room was about the same price I had paid to share a room in the apartment on 8th St in 1972, and it was a lot closer to campus. Of course, it wasn't as fancy as the apartment; it consisted of a hallway along which there were entrance doors to six individual rooms. At the end of the hallway was a kitchen area that everyone shared. Obviously, there were shared bathroom facilities as well, but I have absolutely no memory of the baño. My room was on the front corner of the building so it had windows on two walls; which was a nice feature since there was no air-conditioning, and Davis gets very hot in the summer. There were also shade trees on that end of the building which also helped keep my room cool. The cooling system for the rest of the rooms was a swamp cooler at the end of the hall in the kitchen. That would not have been so bad, except that the residents insisted on placing the garbage can under the swamp cooler, so it was blowing the smell of pungent spices and rotting garbage down the hall. It nearly took an act of Congress to finally get the residents to agree to move the garbage onto the back porch, and that was not until I had lived there for several months and become one of the senior residents.

The residents of what I will call Central Hall (because it was in the center of squatter's camp) were mostly foreign students. There was a disagreeable West African fellow on the other side of the hall, who communicated very little with the residents, unless he had a beef with us about the kitchen, the bathroom, or the noise level. Most of the residents departed at the end of spring quarter, leaving only the African and me. In the room next to me, a swarthy Indian fellow from Bangalore named Jairus David, son of Rachinyadas, had just moved in. Ironically, it was the Indian who became my good friend, and not the grumpy African. The latter was older, had been at Davis doing his PhD for a long time, and, as I said, not an easy fellow to like. Jairus, on the other hand, was personable, much younger than the African, and had only recently come to America. I came to find out later that he had intended to attend an east coast university (Cornell, I think), but the course offerings were not adequate to his objectives, and so he boarded a Greyhound bus and traveled across the United States to enroll in the Food Science Department at UC Davis. Time would prove that to have been a wise decision on his part.

How Jairus and I became acquainted I don't exactly remember, but it was a little hard not to run into each other when our rooms were side by side. I think what probably got the discussion going between us was Jairus' cooking. Being from Madras Province, he liked his food very, very, very spicy. It was so hot; you could tell just by smelling it; the capsaicin would literally grab you by the nose hairs. I probably mentioned that I had a taste for the hot and spicy Indian food from my time in Kenya. Maybe that commonality made the world feel a little smaller to both of us.

190

As I may have mentioned earlier, if you have never been to Davis, it is hard to imagine how absolutely essential it is to have a bicycle in that town. Therefore, a priority item was to find a bicycle for a price I could afford The Bicycle Barn was a facility on campus (so called because it once was the research dairy barn). There students could take their bike for repairs and it was where 'junker' bikes were recycled. I am not sure if I purchased my bike there, but it is quite probable. Other essential items would be acquired slowly. First, books and school supplies needed to be bought. I don't know what I used to cook that spring. It is possible that my mother and Fr. Carl brought over supplies and a few cooking utensils. Since I did not have transport, I don't think I went to Galt that quarter. As the reader may have surmised from the course list, it was a very busy quarter. The classes were all over campus, so I would have never survived without the bicycle.

Davis is a pleasant town, and in the spring it is actually quite beautiful. All the tree-line streets are leafing out, and the weather is generally favorable. It doesn't get extremely hot until later in the summer, and a gentle breeze comes up the Sacramento River Gorge in the afternoon. At that time, the area around Davis was mostly agricultural. Row crops were everywhere, although the west side of campus was not far from the orchards. There were a lot of almonds in Dixon, to the south, and cherries in Winters, to the west. Woodland, to the north had more row crops. By April those crops were already bloomed out and the cherries would already be forming up for the June harvests. Almonds take longer, but there are also some late blooming varieties of almond. I believe I helped Dennis Briggs do pollination research that spring. One of the tasks was very taxing. In order to determine bee activity in an orchard, you have to count foragers. Dennis had found that standing and counting while one faced the tree underestimated the number of bees in an area. Consequently, he developed a technique where one would lie on one's back and looked straight up in the air. By counting every passing bee against the light background of the sky, one could get a much better estimate of the foraging activity within the standard area of ones field of view. The hardest part of that job was staying awake. Later that summer, my job was to analyze the data that we collected that spring.

Diving into classes 10 days after the quarter began, meant that I had to catch up on at least 3 class sessions for each of the courses. That was tough, but it meant I didn't have much time or energy to fret about what was happening to the family. Nor was I hearing much from them. I had paid some bills and sent them my address, but I did not hear from Charity for quite some time.

In fact, the quarter was a whirlwind. I had only taken 12 credits in 1972, but this was 5 courses for 15 credit hours. Ecophysiology was team taught and very mathematically intense. I thought I was a goner, but in fact I pulled out with a B, and gained a whole new outlook on quantitative biology. Advanced Physiology of cultured plants was of great interest to me, and I busted my butt to produce a huge review paper on "alternate bearing in tree crops" which gained me an A. I can't remember how many professors wanted to copy my bibliography of 113 citations. Dr. Charlie Judd's Advanced Insect Physiology was an easy A, because it consisted of reviewing published papers on the subject. We had to defend our evaluations verbally. World Vegetable Crops, although a mandated undergraduate course for the IAD program, was a tough one. It required lots of memorization of a mountain of facts about cropping systems. If I had not written such a good paper for the course, the final would have knocked me down to a B, but I scraped by with an A-. The famous professor, Masatoshi Yamaguchi, also told me that he appreciated my participation in class. Another famous face in that course was a guest lecture by the name of Charles Rick, for whom the Charles M. Rick Tomato Genetic Resource Center was later named.

The hardest course for me was the core course in IAD. The class was divided into group projects, where each group would do an economic development plan of a government in the developing world. I chose the Tanzania group, but in the end I disagreed with the group assessment, and got permission to present a minority report. Following the lead of President Julius Nyerere[65], my approach was very socialistic. At one point in Tanzanian history, that president turned the college students out of the universities and

[65] Julius Kambarage Nyerere (13 April 1922 – 14 October 1999) was a Tanzanian politician who served as the first President of Tanzania and previously Tanganyika, from the country's founding in 1961 until his retirement in 1985.

Born in Tanganyika to Nyerere Burito (1860–1942), Chief of the Zanaki, Nyerere was known by the Swahili name Mwalimu or 'teacher', his profession prior to politics. He was also referred to as Baba wa Taifa (Father of the Nation). Nyerere received his higher education at Makerere University in Kampala and the University of Edinburgh. After he returned to Tanganyika, he worked as a teacher. In 1954, he helped form the Tanganyika African National Union.

In 1961, Nyerere was elected Tanganyika's first Prime Minister, and following independence, in 1962, the country's first President. In 1964, Tanganyika became politically united with Zanzibar and was renamed to Tanzania. In 1965, a one-party election returned Nyerere to power. Two years later, he issued the Arusha Declaration, which outlined his socialist vision of ujamaa that came to dominate his policies.

conscripted them to work around the country to help with development. He also put the army to work on national development projects. In my mind, he was one of the greatest leaders in Africa. At that time Nelson Mandela was still in jail, but Nyerere was as respected in Tanzania as Mandela eventually became in South Africa. Both men stepped down from power voluntarily. This socialist approach was not a popular view with the lead professor of the team-taught class, because he was one of the post-war international consultants with their capitalistic approach. Nevertheless, I managed to get a B for the course. This kept me just over 3.5 GPA for the quarter. This, when you think about it, was quite an accomplishment for a 32 year old man. Considering how near ruin was my life before I spent my last $59 to get back to Davis.

It was the botany department that had the greatest darkroom, and I spent many hours in that place, developing pictures from my various microscopy projects for various professors. It was through Grady Webster that I obtained an access key to that facility. However, most of what I was doing for Grady Webster involved scanning electron microscopy and that facility was in the basement of Briggs Hall. Bob Schuster was the technician in charge, so I had to get on Bob's good side. Grady had me taking micrographs of the seeds and trichomes[66] of many of the species of Euphorbia. Dr. Webster was world renown as the taxonomist extraordinaire for the Spurge Family (Malpighiales:Euphorbiaciea). They were so fascinatingly varied I have to include some micrographs, although I am sure they have been published in some of Grady's papers (Fig.19).

---

Nyerere retired in 1985, while remaining the chairman of the Chama Cha Mapinduzi. He died of leukemia in London in 1999. In 2009, Nyerere was named "World Hero of Social Justice" by the president of the United Nations General Assembly. http://en.wikipedia.org/wiki/Julius_Nyerere

[66] Trichomes on plants are epidermal outgrowths of various kinds. The terms emergences or prickles refer to outgrowths that involve more than the epidermis. This distinction is not always easily applied. Also, there are nontrichomatous epidermal cells that protrude from the surface.

A common type of trichome is a hair. Plant hairs may be unicellular or multicellular, branched, or unbranched. Multicellular hairs may have one or several layers of cells. Branched hairs can be dendritic (tree-like), tufted, or stellate (star-shaped). http://en.wikipedia.org/wiki/Trichome#Plant_trichomes

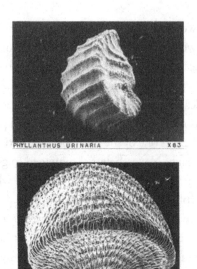

Euphorbia seed sculpture (photographed by the author for G. H. Webster, PhD, Dept. of Botany, Univ. California Davis).

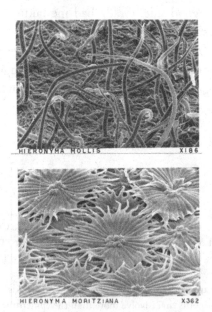

Euphorbia leaf trichomes (photographed by the author for G. H. Webster, PhD, Dept. of Botany, Univ. California Davis)

Dr. John Tucker was the resident expert on oak (*Quercus* spp.) and he had me documenting the species hybrid differences in leaf morphology with SEM.

Oak also has trichomes and epicuticular wax platelets that differ by species, and within hybrids of the species. These structures are all adaptations to dry land conditions, also known as xerophytic. They are generally more prevalent on the underside of the leaf where the stomata are located. If the images look like a weird tropical forest, perhaps on an alien planet, that is intentional. The plant has adapted to create a little "forest" of trichomes and platelets that create a microclimate that retains moisture. Since the stomata will close when the climate is too dry, this helps them stay open longer, and that is essential to photosynthesis. The exchange of carbon dioxide for oxygen is critical to building carbon based sugars which become the building blocks of the plant. Ironically it also is the reason that we exist. Were it not for the production of oxygen by plants and algae, we oxygen breathing organisms would not exist. Not to mention that the carbon based compounds that plants produce are the building blocks of all carbon based organism, like us.

The structure of the oak leaves gives a clear impression of the importance to the Genus of protection of their stomata. I never saw a publication with these SEM micrographs but I did find a paper by John Tucker that had drawings of the trichomes of some of the oaks. Too bad I couldn't have micrographed the whole Genus.

Views of the dorsal side of leaves of three species of **Oak** showing **trichomes** and **stomata** with various amounts of epicuticular wax platelets. (Photographed by the author for J. M. Tucker PhD, Dept. of Botany, Univ. California Davis)

195

I can say honestly that during the whole time I was a microscopist, from Weyerhaeuser and through my master's degree program, I was never bored. In spite of the intricate, technical, and detailed work involved in producing such micrographic documentation, I was constantly fascinated by the beauty and diversity of nature. Now it is so much easier with electronic imaging cameras and computer processed digital photographs. Then you had to get your exposures right, develop the film, keep track of the magnification as you enlarged, cropped, adjusted exposure, and developed the prints. Then, you had to label the prints, by hand or with transfer labels that would stick to the micrograph. For publication, the prints had to be archival quality, and had to be made up on very specific "plates". Then they needed to be photographed at the right exposure and prints had to be made from the photos of the plates. Nowadays, preparing the specimen is the hardest part of micrography. Once you get the lighting right, your automatic electronic camera will take a perfect exposure, which you can then transfer as a digital image to Photoshop*. There you can adjust whatever brightness, contrast, color balance the micrograph needs, and put the image file right in the publication document. This involved pre-electronic procedure I followed to produce the plates in a report that I completed for Dr. Humphrey at Evergreen State College; this was to obtain the credits for my independent study course. I am so grateful that Dr. Humphrey's sent this only copy of the report back to me, because it contains documentation of the all the microscopy work that I did at U.C. Davis, and some of the Weyerhaeuser work. Still, to me, the most appealing micrographs in my small remaining collection are the Nomarski Interference Contrast images of pollen etc. These were taken on Kodachrome, and printed with Cibachrome, and to this day are of archival quality. Kodachrome 35 mm film was discontinued by Kodak, but Cibachrome color printing paper is probably not still available. When the Cibachrome patent expired, it was released under another name[67]. Unfortunately Ilfochrome is probably not commercially available now, which is a great loss to the photographic arts.

Robbin Thorp hired me that Spring Quarter for $7.50 per hour as a

---

[67] **Ilfochrome** (also commonly known as **Cibachrome**) is a dye destruction positive-to-positive photographic process used for the reproduction of film transparencies on photographic paper. The prints are made on a dimensionally stable polyester base as opposed to traditional paper base. Since it uses 13 layers of azo dyes sealed in a polyester base, the print will not fade, discolor, or deteriorate for an extended time. Accelerated aging tests conducted by Henry Wilhelm rated the process as producing prints which, framed under glass, would last for 29 years before color shifts could be detected.[11] Characteristics of Ilfochrome prints are image

Lab Assistant to work with Dennis Briggs, his technician. That was far better wages that the average work-study job at $3/hr. My responsibilities were to performed microscopy procedures for analysis pollen tube growth in almond stigma, and to develop pollen germination analysis for almond pollination experiments.[68] I helped with other field experiments when needed. I also prepared pollen for SEM analysis, and prepared photomicrographs for publication. Because I had been introduced to computer image analysis at Weyerhaeuser, I was able to suggest the use of a Quantimet® Image Analyzer. That instrument was available on campus, and we used it to estimate almond orchard bloom from aerial photographs that Robbin had commissioned. I also developed the computer data recording procedures for use in the Almond Pollination Project.

It was a very busy spring, and by the time the Whole Earth Festival finally rolled around, I was ready for a break! I was still very much in the married father mode, so all the scantily clad long haired hippie women were not a distraction for me. I won't even mention the nubile Davis coeds running around in their short-shorts and tank tops. It was good living in the Squatters Camp, because no self-respecting coed would consider living there, so there was no distracting femininity lounging around on the doorsteps of the little cabins. Central Hall itself was strictly a male stronghold.

---

clarity, color purity, and being an archival process able to produce critical accuracy to the original transparency. https://en.wikipedia.org/wiki/Ilfochrome

[68] Klungness, L. M., Thorp, R. M. and Briggs, D. 1983. Field testing germinability of almond pollen (Prunus dulcis). J. Hort. Sci. 58(2)229-235.

Briggs, D., Thorp, R. M. and Klungness, L. M. 1983. Artificial pollination of almonds (Prunus dulcis) with Bouquets monitored by fruit set and pollen germination. J. Hort. Sci. 58(2)237-240.

The **Whole Earth Festival** was a little late in 1979, happening on the May 4 to 6.(Was available CC BY-SA 4.0 from the Whole Earth Festival archive at Shields Library, Univ. California Davis) http://wef.ucdavis.edu/old/wefhistory/Posters/index.htm

The great things about the Whole Earth Festival were the music -- and the food. The Animal Science department grilled hamburgers for a buck. Wildlife Fisheries and Conservation Biology blackened Cajun style catfish for $2 a plate. Veg Crops served corn on the cob, and other departments made their offerings to Gaia. The International students served all manner of foreign delicacies, while belly dancers, and acrobats, and Polynesian fire dancers entertained. I never got to the herding-dog trials, nor the steam tractor pulls, because I was too absorbed in the music. Wavy Gravy was there too, like he had been since the festival began.

I think I dragged Jairus out of his cerebral cubical to attend Little Charlie and the Night Cats, among other musical offerings. That just might have given Jairus some inspiration to buy an instrument; I think he started with a mandolin. He had music in his bones, and he was missing the relaxation of sitting down to play music. Of course, I did not have the bass with me, but I too was missing the opportunity to play. The headliner bands played in the Quad, and because some of these were hard rock bands, I didn't spend much time there among the sea of humanity. But there were band venues all over campus, and I tended to visit those. Rather than being able to hear nothing but the blaring music, at these side shows you could actually hear yourself talk. But these tended to be the more unusual music. Little Charlie, for example, was a local blues band.

I remember the Whole Earth Festival primarily because it was such a change from the life I had been leading, e.g. class, library, lab, squatter's camp, collapse in bed; that was a typical day. It certainly kept my mind off of the situation with the family, which was good because I wasn't getting much information. I don't even remember how many times Charity answered my letters to her. Admittedly my letters tapered off. I knew I was doing what I needed to do. I thought in the long run the whole family would be better off for it. But I have to admit the whole earth festival was a relief of tension that was getting intense.

The job with Robbin was only funded until the end of the Spring Quarter, so I had to be looking for other work. So in May, I landed another job in the Department of Plant Science at the same rate of $7.50/hr. The Departmental Chair, Dr. Laurence Rappaport, had a post-doc named Jose García-Martinez who needed my microscopy skills. My responsibilities were to performed freeze-substitution and lyophilization of isolate vacuoles of barley for SEM micrography and identification of protoplast fragments by selective binding of concanavalin-A spheres to plasmalemma. Later I performed cryomicrotomy and lyophilization of cowpea epicotyl for morphometry and photomicrography showing the growth effects of gibberellins. This was a variation of a technique that I had developed at Weyerhaeuser, using nitrogen freezing in tertiary butyl alcohol. At Weyco I had used the Bailey piezoelectric freeze stage to microtome the frozen specimen, but I had found a cryomicrotome in the Entomology Dept. which I used for this project. This information was used by the doctors in joint publication. I also made Nomarski interference contrast photomicrographs of vacuole formation as well as a photometric statistical analysis of vacuole dimensions with Zeiss imaging equipment. Both were used in publications.[69]

---

[69] Jose L. Garcia-Martinez and Lawrence Rappaport 1984. Physiology of gibberellin-induced elongation of epicotyl explants from Vigna sinensis, *Plant Growth Regulation* Volume 2, Number 3, 197-208, DOI: 10.1007/BF00124768 Martinus Mijhoff/ Dr. W. Junk Publishers, Dordrecht, Netherlands.

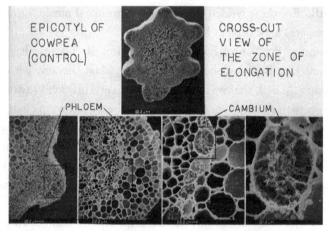

Preparation of **cowpea epicotyl** using my technique which preserves the delicate structure of the cytoplasm of the cambial cells. This had not previously been possible in lyophilized (freeze-dried) or critical point dried tissue. (Photographed by the author for Laurence Rappaport PhD, Dept. of Plant Science, Univ. California Davis)

Unfortunately, I don't think the doctors appreciate the breakthrough that this tissue preparation represented. Their emphasis was on the biochemistry, and although they appreciated seeing inside the cells, they did not grasp how unique the technique was. I really was developing a unique skill. I don't think any technique available at that time would preserve the cellular cytoplasm (as seen in the cambium cells) for SEM micrography as well at as this technique. Had I pursued the patent with Bailey instruments it might have become equipment as widely used as the critical point drier. I had even drawn up the patent diagram for the freeze drying chamber, and had it notarized by a Notary Public. Nevertheless, opportunity was just around the corner, if I would have had the time and energy to walk around the corner. Just like the effort to buy the Ultraphot microscope, I just didn't have the resources to pull it off. I was trying to earn enough in my spare time to keep a family of six housed and fed, although admittedly I was not doing a very good job of that either.

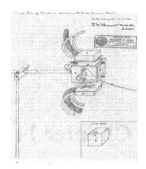

Patent diagram of the freeze drying apparatus that I conceived to facilitate freeze sectioning of tissue for scanning electron microscopy. (Drawn by author and notarized August 26, 1980)

# Chapter 14

# Regroup?

"They are my sons, whom God has given me here." And he said, "Bring them to me, please, that I may bless them." **English Standard Version (2001) Genesis 48:8.**

Over the years, one tends to forget what an uphill battle life can be. In re-examining some of the work that I produced that spring, I see that the effort had been far greater than the reward. The review paper that I had written in Advanced Physiology and Culture of Plants was, according to the professor:

18 Sept.

Mike,

Your paper on periodicity was excellent, and could be published if a lot of work were done on it. It's an unusual collection of ideas and needs polishing. I haven't reviewed the paper for some time but if you are interested in going further please give me a call.

Roy Sachs

The problem: who was going to pay for all this effort? I ran into similar problems with Dr. Rappaport. I spent countless hours on the draft of a manuscript on the SEM of intact tissue organelles isolated from the tissue of *Hordeum vulgare*. Granted, it was in fulfillment of the requirements for a Bixby work learn contract, which had paid some money. But in the end, he decided that it was no longer relevant. Jose Garcia-Martinez went on to get his PhD. But my efforts netted very little, except the satisfaction of having done a credible job.

Speaking of unproductive ventures, I even tried to get an article published on the short alphabet that I had used to take all of my notes since University of Washington. I went to a professor in the linguistics department, and she expressed some interest, but it never materialized. Just for the heck of it, I am going to include a picture of the script as roughly scribed on a Wacom tablet. The script is not that different from standard printing, but it feels more like cursive because most of the strokes are one continuous curve; only eight letters require the writer to stop and change direction. I found it very easy to write notes quickly with this script. I think I may have mentioned in the last book how Gretchen was able to read this script, sight unseen, and type up a report for me to complete my undergraduate degree. I did have to explain the Theta and the Phi to her, since she had never studied Greek.

abcdefghij kl mno pqr σ τ uvwxyz
Θ φ

My short script includes all the letters of the Roman alphabet plus the Greek θ for 'th' and φ for 'ph'. Notice that all the letters are one continuous stroke excepting eight (h, k, m, t, v, w, y and z). Even the θ is actually one circular stroke. 'Th' is 4 strokes and is the most commonly used digraph in the English language.

The quarter came to an end, exams were over, but there was no way I would have enough time to return to Washington given the work I needed to complete for Dr. Rappaport, as well as getting started on my graduate thesis work for Dr. Peng. So I conceived the notion of having the boys come down to stay with me in Davis for the summer. The details of how I worked that out are very sketchy in my mind. It is hard to believe that Mzae would have been allowed to bring Jimmy on the train by himself, but James confirmed that they did. Yet I am sure Charity did not come to Davis until the next spring. Mzae was probably 10 years old then. Whatever the case, they did arrive in Davis by train, and they stayed with me in Central Hall, in my one bedroom accommodation, in the middle of Squatters Camp for the duration of the summer. I believe I probably let them have the bed, and I slept on the floor in a sleeping bag which I had asked Charity to send with them from Tenino. It was not a stretch for them, because they were used to sleeping in close quarters. And I had certainly spent many nights sleeping on floors in my 32 years.

I think the boys considered it a kind of adventure; certainly riding on the

train was new. The weather was "warm", and the town was flat so it was easy
to walk anywhere. I think it was amazing to the boys that you could walk
right though a crowded roundabout without being hit by the bicycles, but if
you stopped, everyone would crash. There was the arboretum along Putah
Creek, and they could use my bike when I was not gone off to the campus.
They would go to campus with me at first, but that was boring, because I
would be involved in some work activity. So they startled to travel around on
their own. Nowadays and when my daughter was growing up, I would not
have thought of letting young kids roam around on their own on a college
campus. But I was allowed to roam all over the logging town of McCloud
when I was their age, and it did not cross my mind that there would be any
problem. They had pretty strict instructions where to be at what time, and
I think I only had to look for them once. I can't remember if the Campus
Police brought them to me, or whether they finally wandered back from their
"adventures." As far as I know, they never got in any trouble. James takes
the Fifth Amendment, claiming he does not want to incriminate Mzae and
himself. I think that is bluffing, and I will go to my grave believing the boys
had a "blissful" summer in Davis.

I doubt if we went to the Recreation Pool often, because it was so far off
campus and we only had one bike. I don't remember that we used the Hickey
Gymnasium Pool, because later on, while I was using that gym to shower, I
didn't use that pool at all. I don't know if Jimmy was even able to swim by
that time. Everything we did in Davis, we did on foot. I know we did manage
to take in a movie or two. Tuesday was student night at the Davis Theater; I
believe the admission was only $2. I think the James Bond film, *Live and Let
Die*, was one of the movies, and it was a bit of an eye opener for Mzae. It is
possible that we might have seen Star Wars together because it was released
two years before that summer; and tended to replay every summer. I can't
remember for sure. I remember being very impressed with that film. There
was also a summer movie series put on by the Student Union in the lecture
hall next to Briggs, mostly older, but classic, movies. I remember seeing *Cool
Hand Luke* and *Buffalo Soldiers* there, but I am not sure that the boys were
with me then. I think those movies were only a buck.

As far as the typical activities that most Davis father did with their sons,
I was a total failure. I don't even think I took them to the city library to get
books to read. We didn't play ball, we didn't do outdoor hikes other than
within town and campus. They were not in Little League or soccer. We didn't
even have a TV. I don't remember if the boys went over to stay with my mother

and Father Carl. I know Mzae spent time in Galt one year, but I think that was before the Davis summer and by himself, not with James. I am sure that Mom and Fr. Carl came to visit us in Davis, but I have no direct memory of it.

Finally I resorted to a simpler task than writing complex papers and involved microscopy projects with limited or non-existent funding. I contracted to teach a course in photomicrography at the Student Craft Center. It was paid a whopping $13 per hour, but of course that was only for the class hours. Thankfully, I had done this before, so the preparation was not that difficult. I frankly cannot remember where we held this course, and what equipment we used.

I was watching *60 Minutes* on TV tonight; they were doing a segment on superior autobiographic memory. That is the incredible ability to recall virtually everything that happened in one's life. Since the scientists have recognized this ability, they have discovered only 20 such individuals. These are not savants in the typical sense. They are perfectly normal people except in their propensity to organize, and their ability to recall. I presume such rare people have probably existed throughout history, but in ancient times they might have become the bards, or sages like Homer. I mention this because I am amazed at how little of the details of my life that I can recall. Nevertheless, certain areas of knowledge remain intact, and all I need is a reminder to recover information about techniques and instruments that I have not used in 40 years. Yet the circumstances and the people that were enrolled in this microphotography course were completely buried in my memory.

I am not sure if Jairus took my course in photomicrography; if he did not, he should have. I do remember arguing microscopic theory with him on late evenings after a trip to the "watering hole."[70] Those watering hole trips did not occur when the boys were in Davis, but Jairus and I did do things together with the lads. Can't remember exactly what (movies, I suppose), but Jairus was like a family member by then, since we lived in rooms right next to each other. The microscopy arguments tested our friendship to some extent. Jairus was a very intelligent fellow, and was beginning his research on high-temperature pressure processing of liquid foods for bacterial thermal death time. Of course, to study bacteria, you have to be able to use a high magnification microscope, of 900x or above. At that magnification, how you adjust the condenser and align the objectives (the primary magnifying lenses)

---

[70] The Graduate was a bar and grill with a large dance floor. It was very popular with students, particularly on Tuesday night with a pitcher of Margarita's was $2.

makes a big difference in what you can see. I forgot what the basic dispute was about, but Jairus was not satisfied with my explanations. Of course, the quantity of margarita's consumed (at $2 per pitcher) was an augmenting factor in the heated arguments. This discussion will probably come up again in this book!

I don't remember exactly when the boys came to Davis, but I know they were still there later in the summer. This is because, when Mike Carlson and his family went on vacation, we house-sat for them. That might have been during the break between the first and second summer session. The boys loved it, because the Carlsons had a TV. Mzae would go over to the house with James when I was at the lab, so that he could water the plants and feed the cat. Then I would come and we would sleep at the Carlsons' house on the living room rug… where the TV was. I seem to remember losing quite a bit of sleep during that house sitting session. For the boys it was nirvana, watching movies to the wee hours of the morning. Is that parenting?

Mike Carlson was the same fellow from Weyerhaeuser. The way I found out he was in Davis is that we took a statistics class together that first summer session. Summer courses at Davis could be quite intense, so I was just taking the one class in Multivariate Analysis along with research credits working on my thesis. Mike actually was auditing the course along with his other subjects for his PhD. Mike had two daughters, but I don't think we hung out with his family much, if at all, that summer. I don't know if there was an issue with his wife because she may have thought that I had left Charity. Although, the fact that I had the boys should have dispelled any concern that I was abandoning the family. I don't really know the situation. Maybe they were pressed to keep the girls occupied and didn't want them hanging out with two rather unsupervised boys, albeit younger lads. Of course, Mike had been the instigator of the family outings that we had done together in Washington, and in this environment he was far too busy to be planning family outings. I don't remember how his wife was occupied. In addition to being a mother, I think she was doing some kind of coursework at UCD. I would have liked to have brought my whole family to Davis, but the opportunity had not presented itself yet.

I was also working on my thesis project, so I spent a fair amount of time in the lab. Of course I always felt that I did not have enough time, but the boys were a diversion. I really wish I could remember what we did together. I remember going for breakfast at Sambo's when I had enough money. The breakfast special was 1 egg, hash browns and toast; it cost $1.50. $4.50 was a lot of money on my budget, but I liked to splurge on the boys once in a while. The rest of the time we had cheap things like toast and cheese or pancakes. Ironically, that is about what I eat now in my senescence, only I don't know if I knew about throwing some frozen corn in the pancakes then. I know that Mzae took a photo of Jimmy holding a plate of hot dogs, in color, as a matter of fact. I wish I could find that photo. The reason Mzae was taking pictures was that I had enrolled him in a photography class at the Student Craft Center. I think it was every Saturday morning, fairly early as I remember. Towards the end of the course, Mzae came home one day with a rather sheepish look on his face. When I pressed him, he was embarrassed to admit that they had displayed a nude female model in the class for everyone to photograph. I saw many other pictures that Mzae had shot, developed, and printed, but I never saw any pictures of the nude. Ah well, one must learn the facts of life sometime.

I don't know exactly when the boys took the train back to Washington, but I had started the second summer session by then, and besides research credits and a work-learn internship, I was auditing a calculus class. I can't remember whether I enrolled in it, and then withdrew, but I knew I was in over my head. About all I really remember about that class is that there was one large old fig tree in the courtyard in front of the building where that class was held. I do remember wondering whether the boys would have enjoyed eating the fresh figs as much as I did. So I think they had already left when the figs were ripe. Part of the reason I had to send the boys back to Washington was that my funds were pretty much depleted. The photomicrography class was not a big earner, the contract with Robbin in the almond pollination was over, and the contract with Dr. Rappaport was wrapping up. I wasn't exactly sure how I was going to survive the fall quarter. As it turned out, I did not have enough money to enroll that quarter, so I took a planned educational leave. I continued to work on my thesis project, but without credit or support. I couldn't even keep paying for the room at the Central Hall, so I had to start being creative.

The insect physiology lab on the ground floor of Briggs Hall was not used except for the Dr. Charles Judson's class in the winter quarter. Dr. Peng had arranged for me to occupy a bench in that lab, and since Dr. Judson was on my thesis committee, he was agreeable. The only other person using that lab was Doug Light, but he actually had his electro-physiology recording device set up in an adjoining prep room. He was studying the electrical response of insect antenna to odors blown over them. His device, which he had developed, was housed in a fine-mesh metal cage to dampen stray electrical signals that could mask the extremely weak impulses of the sensory cells on the antenna of the insects. Doug became quite famous for this work, and later he was hired as Electro-physiologist in residence at the USDA Agricultural Research Laboratory in Albany, California. He quickly rose in the ranks to a GS 15 (highest pay scale in the USDA Research Division) on the basis of the many research papers he produced with virtually the same equipment he had designed at Davis. I know that, because my employer in later years worked with Doug to set up his own electro-physiology unit at the Tropical Fruit and Vegetable Lab in Hilo, Hawaii. By the time I was working at the latter lab, Doug had already been moved on to head up the Walnut Husk Fly Suppression Project. You see, the USDA had figured out that Doug had risen so swiftly, with only one technician to assist, primarily because he could concentrate on his science. He had no administrative or management duties to speak of and the USDA decided they were paying him too much to let that continue. While he had a number of peer reviewed publications in the 1990's, I could only find two subsequent papers printed in 2001 and 2005.

Therefore, back at Davis, Doug and I both had plenty of lab space in which to work, I just didn't have anywhere to sleep. So I started doing a lot of my microscopy work at night, and developing film and prints in the Botany darkroom until the wee hours. Then I would slip into the Insect Lab and clear a space on the bench to lay out my sleeping bag. By then my mother had given me the electric deep fryer pot. I could hide that in a cupboard under the lab bench and whip up a pot of stew or curry when I had the money. One thing I always did before I went to sleep was prop up a chair against the lab door. That was because the old technician, who took care of the lab supplies inventory, would arrive about 6 AM every morning and check in the lab. So I would catch a few hours of shut eye and then wake up around 5 AM in order to be up and at it by the time the technician arrived. Only once did I oversleep, and awoke to the sound of the technician trying to get in the lab door, which was blocked by the chair. I presume he probably suspected I was sleeping there, but he never turned me in. There are a lot of people working strange hours at a university, and I was probably not the only student that ever slept in the lab. I might have been the one who did it the longest.

Aside from the inconvenience of having almost no income, it was a productive time for me. I accomplished a lot on my thesis research. I embedded honeybees in methacrylate, and thin sectioned the abdomen for histology of the intestines and I freeze sectioned other bees with my unique technique to display the condition and architecture of the pollen in the bolus of the honeybee intestine. For that, I was able to acquire the use of that cryomicrotome which, although bulky, fit nicely into the insect physiology lab. It is amazing how much you can accomplish when you don't have the money to do anything else but work!

Not that there were not some diversions at Davis that summer and fall. Free lectures were common. I can't put them together chronologically, but I remember listening to Ed Teller in his raspy diabolical voice explain his objectives in proposing the Star Wars program, punctuated with thumping of his cane on the wooden stage. Richard Leakey, son of Louis Leakey, was very impressive in his lecture on the recent discoveries about the origins of man. Desmond Tutu spoke in the quad about the advances of equality being fought in South Africa. That was perhaps the most inspirational speech I ever heard at Davis. There were also free performances in the music department, as I had remembered from my time in UCD in 1972. The great thing about Davis was that I was right there for everything. The campus was where it was all happening.

I believe it was sometime in the fall when Meritt wrote to tell me that he was going to give me some money. I guess he had been communicating with my mother and she probably told him how difficult my situation was. I was remembering that he was distributing assets from his wife Eva's estate, but it was definitely not after she died, and I will explain why. Eva had been suffering from Alzheimer's disease for going on 20 years. I think it may have been when Meritt finally committed her to a nursing home (or hospital), that he began the financial process. The reason I know she had not died yet is this: what I bought with the money he sent. When the money arrived it was $2000.00. Now there are many ways I could have used it, but what I eventually did with the money proved to be very wise. I bought a camper van. It was a 1969 Ford F150 with a pop-top camper, which became my home, When Eva did die that fall, I drove my mother to the funeral in Bend, Oregon, using the van.

That funeral was one of the best wakes I had ever attended. I am sure Eva would **not** have approved. She was long time separated from the Catholic Church, so there was no religious ceremony, although she was buried next to her parents in the Pilot Butte Cemetery. Consequently, the ceremony was the coming together of the family at the home of Eldon Smith. Of course the Smiths were in-laws by the marriage of my Aunt Mary to Vernon Smith. Eldon was paraplegic for many years before that day, but his wife Evelyn was a faithful wife, and they had one daughter, Karen. Eldon's wife was a gracious hostess and Eldon and Vernon's mother was there. That is what made it so interesting, because Grandma Smith, as we called her, was a contemporary of Meritt and they were telling interesting stories of their youth and years in the logging camps. Their children would chime in with stories, and we the grandchildren were fascinated by it all. It had been a long time since my mother and I had been able to sit down with Meritt and enjoy jovial conversation. Not only had Meritt had the difficult job of caring for Eva in the later stages of her disease, but when she was still marginally lucid, she had virtually banned us from Meritt's house and severely limited his opportunities to visit us. Consequently, we had seen very little of Meritt over the years after I graduated from high school. Meritt had come to my graduation with his sister Nina, but not Eva. I think he had only met my African family once, and I had only visited him and Eva on very rare occasions. Consequently, my mother and I remember that day as one of our most pleasant with Meritt, and the rest of the Seely and Smith families. There were surviving Whitlocks there as well; I know that Uncle Vern was there although I think his wife Elma had died by then. I can't remember which of the relatives from Seattle came. My mother and I did not participate in any family reunions after that until Uncle Vern died by his own hand in 1986.

I think that trip was also the longest time that my mother and I had spent together since the time I spent in Galt after I returned from Kenya. Of course, Mom had visit my family in Tenino, but there was not much alone time on those trips. I don't remember most of what we talked about, but I remember the feeling of it being very nostalgic. It is probably where I had heard the bitter story of Eva's first family and the death of little Ellen, whom my mother had loved. I don't know how much of that story I have previously related, but it is a tearjerker. Eva had been a hard woman, and was quite severe with her daughter, who was a sickly child. My mother never explained what Ellen's illness was, but she died before her teen years. Her father was so heartbroken that he also died not long after her death. My mother had always felt that Eva was somehow responsible. Her animosity towards Eva may not have been justified, but after the years of estrangement from Meritt, I could be convinced that perhaps my mother had been right about Eva all along. It is an ominous thought to think that one's death might actually be the cause for rejoicing amongst one's own relatives. I am glad Meritt is not alive to read this, but I think it has to be said. Some people dominate the scene throughout their lives at the expense of others. Eva was one such person.

After I delivered my mother back to Galt, I headed back to Davis, and began to strategize how I could live in my van without violating any laws. I think I did buy a campus parking permit, but that really didn't help much. That was because, beside the fact that there were not a lot of spaces available close to campus during most academic sessions, it was also against campus rules to sleep in the campus parking lots. One campus officer in particular was on the lookout for me, as I found out later. Another campus cop, who befriended students in the Entomology department, explained that the officer who was after me was one of those sticklers for the rules. His joy in life was nabbing students. I finally ended up staying under the Yolo Bypass; it was a multilane overpass that was built along the Sacramento River. Its purpose was to prevent the frequent seasonal floods from shutting down that vital link between Sacramento and San Francisco. The land around and under the bypass was primarily farmland, and it seemed a good place to sleep. That worked for a few weeks, but then one day the local Sheriff came knocking at the van door. I thought I was going to jail, but it turned out that the Sheriff's department was looking for thieves that were raiding the farms for equipment. I gave them my most dire story of my financial plight, and they were very nice about it. But they asked me to move to the levy on the north side of Davis. Apparently there had not been any criminal activity out there, and the levy was county property, so they did not feel the need to prevent me from sleeping there. This was all well and good with me, because the levy was actually closer to the University, and it was a whole lot quieter than under the freeway. So that is where I slept.

A little description of my sleeping quarters is in order so the reader can inhabit the isolation of it all. The van was a standard issue of the Ford motor company, but it had been modified by a northwestern camper trailer company. It was an aluminum pop-up frame with a fiberglass roof. When it was raised, there were sliding windows with window screen along the full length. This was idea for the Central Valley because it gets very hot in the summer. With the windows on the top, and the widows in the rear doors open, there was cooling air exchange. On hot evenings I might open the sliding door on the side as well, so it was really quite pleasant inside. The van also came with a port-a-potty, which I never used; can't remember whether I sold it or just left it somewhere. The previous owner had built a bed across the back of the van, and a cabinet to one side with a sink which was provided with water from a tank under the cupboard. There was also a refrigerator, but that required a 110 volt plug-in to work. I don't think the van had a table when I bought

211

it, but I built a high table at which I could work either sitting on the bed or using a bar stool. It was high enough that I could just stand up at the desk as well. There was a curtain that could be closed between the driver's area and the camping compartment. I explain all of these details because, as I proceed with the story, the reader will wonder how I managed to live out of that vehicle and do all the crazy things that I did with it. It was kind of a fantasy that I had when I was getting ready to leave the seminary… sort of the modern version of St. Francis? Only in this century, traveling light meant having a self-contained little house on wheels. At some point I build a couple of 5 L x 1.5 W x 1 H feet boxes that I could slide under the bed and which would hold all my books, reports, thesis, etc. I was really quite self-contained, and mobile. Of course I had to use the Athletic facilities at the UCD for taking showers and my morning constitutional.

I have not yet mentioned Al Wilder. He lived in one of the houses across from the Central Hall in the squatter's camp. That was odd because he was the engineer for the public television station in Sacramento. He was Scottish, and very frugal, so to him the little 20 x 20 house was ideal. He kept his living room full of electronic equipment, TVs, and guitars… but no computers. Jairus and I had gotten to know him, because he enjoyed playing his guitar on his stoop, and Jairus and he would attempt a little jamming as Jairus was learning to play the mandolin. Al might have helped Jairus find the mandolin -- I am not sure. I longed to play with them but my bass was still in Washington. When I moved into the van, it was Al who sold me a little 9 inch black and white TV. I didn't even know you could have a TV that ran off a car battery, but he found one for me. It did not have a cord adapter plug, so Al showed me how to make one by twisting the stiff connector wires into a corkscrew shape that fit neatly over the male prongs of the AC power socket on the TV. Now I could watch the news at night in the Insect Phys. Lab, and then put myself to sleep watching TV programs in the van. This was before Beta and VHS videos were common.

When the fall quarter rolled around, I did not have the money to pay tuition, so I took a leave of absence. My transcripts called it a "planned educational leave," which makes it sound like I was on some experimental expedition to some far away land; but frankly, I was just broke. So broke that at one point I went 10 days without food. That was before the van, and while I was living in the lab. I was so relieved one day when I found a dollar bill on the sidewalk. You would say now that a dollar would not buy much, but then, it would buy 1 dozen eggs. Smartest food purchase I ever made. Yes, you can live on one egg per day.

Around Thanksgiving, I had received payment on one of the contracts, probably with Veg. Crops. It was enough money to get me to Washington to visit the family, and get certain things that I needed in order to "get by" while living in a van. When I arrived, the family was in a state. They had survived to that point on what little I had sent them and what Charity had been able to earn working for Oti and Charles. Fortunately, I had paid the electric bill, so the freezer full of venison and garden produce, and sustained them, as well as the chickens and other resources that farm folks have that city dwellers do not. But they had no transportation, so laundry had piled up. There were so many garbage bags of clothes that we could barely fit the family and all the clothes into the van to take them to the laundromat. Of course, I was the only one with any cash, most of which was spent on that laundry expedition.

I don't know whether we even had a Thanksgiving meal. If we did, it was much less than memorable. We went to church together for Thanksgiving, but the reaction of the parishioners was extremely ironic. In fact, the mother of one of the boys just laughed at me as I tried to explain what I was trying to do in Davis. Her son was a friend of Mzae and Samba, and he had been in my catechism class, I had the distinct impression that they all thought that I had already abandoned the family. I guess you could say that it looked that way, but it was not true. Maybe those people had a right to be critical; maybe they understood what I was not admitting to myself. Nevertheless, I never had any evidence that any of them helped Charity and the kids in their time of need. I think Mrs. Bardsley and the Soniers might have helped as much as they could, but Charity never said how generous the Catholics had been to her (with the exception of Charles and Oti). And I don't know if Gertrude or Edward were helping Charity, either. Somehow, perhaps falsely, I always had the impression that it was entirely my responsibility to take care of the whole family. After all, I had brought them to America, and now I was singularly responsible.

This was a little hard for me to take. Here I was struggling to send some little money home to pay the bills, and I paid to bring Mzae and Jimmy down to visit, and now my former neighbors and fellow Catholics were looking at me like a dead-beat dad, before the term had ever been coined[71],

---

[71] [65] In <u>United States law</u>, the **Bradley Amendment** 1986, Public law 99-509 <u>42 U.S.C. §</u> <u>666(a)(9)(c)</u>. Requirement of statutorily prescribed procedures to improve effectiveness of

I might add. I guess I had hoped that perhaps I could get some part time work at Weyerhaeuser to tide us over. When that did not materialize, my options were diminishing rapidly. If I stayed in Tenino, my funds would be completely depleted. As it was, I barely had enough to get back to Davis. At least in Davis I had a chance of getting contract work, or, if I enrolled in the Winter Quarter, I might still be eligible for financial aid; and if I could stay until March, I could apply for residency in California and not have to pay the out-of-state tuition. Irrespective of whatever I might have wanted to do, my only sensible alternative was to return to Davis. After all is said and done, failure to have completed my master's degree would have been a huge failure and waste of money on my part. At the same time, it appeared to me to be a gigantic mountain to scale with very little resources to do so. Although I was rapidly losing my faith in people and God and myself, I determined to give it another try.

Before I left the homestead in Tenino, I gathered up the things that I thought would be useful to me in Davis. Some books, various papers from Weyerhaeuser, and a collection of microscopic tools, stains etc. that I had taken from Weyerhaeuser because there certainly wasn't anyone there that was going to use the tool of the trade I had developed. To transport these, I build the boxes that I have previously mentioned. I also determined to take my bass with me to Davis. Who knows? Besides a consolation on the lonely nights on the levy, I thought that the bass might lead to some pleasant hours of music with Jairus and Al.

I may have cut some firewood for that family, I don't remember. All of my tools and equipment were still there at the homestead. Mzae would probably have been old enough to learn to use the chainsaw, but I don't remember teaching him. All of the construction that we had done on the farm, all of the rabbit hutches, all of the storage buildings, etc. were exclusively things that I had built myself. Edward may have helped on some, but the kids had been too young to learn all those useful skills that I had developed, and I would not be back to help them learn. For how long I did not know? They all knew how to work in the garden and take care of animals, and they could help Charity in many ways around the house, but there were things they would need to know, and I was not able to be there to help teach them.

After I left, I returned directly to Davis, because I did not have enough

___

child support enforcement. Bill Bradley requires state courts to prohibit retroactive reduction of child support obligations. https://en.wikipedia.org/wiki/Bradley_Amendment

gas money to get to Galt to visit my mother and Fr. Carl. They probably came over later to hear what I had found out on my trip. My economic situation was not improving, but I managed to hold out for the month of December. There were some positive developments that could lead to employment, and I may have been able to secure financial aid. I am not really sure how I survived.

At the same time, I think it was during this period that the electricity was cut off to the homestead and all of the food in the freezer rotted. No one has ever explained to me exactly what happened then. Apparently things had gotten so bad for Charity that she moved the whole family to Tacoma. I don't know if they moved in with Gertrude who had bought a house with Keith Thurman, her husband. I think Gertrude quickly went to work on trying to get Charity on welfare. I was not aware of the timing of all this, because I was getting no communication from Charity. Apparently, during that time they had sublet the house in Tenino, to be eligible for welfare, of course. Charity had to claim that she had been abandoned by me. No one from the state welfare ever contacted me, so I don't know if they even told the agents that they knew where I was. I am sure under normal circumstances I would have been contacted and probably garnished for child support. Nothing like that ever happened. As far as UC Davis was concerned, I was still trying to support my family, and apparently all the Washington State Welfare office knew was that I had disappeared. It all seems very sketchy to me, although I didn't know any of this at the time.

Meanwhile I was able to reconnect with Dr. Peng, and get some work done on my research. Also I did, somehow, pay the tuition to enroll for the Winter Quarter. The possibilities for work were much better when I was an active student that when I was on leave.

This went on for the duration of the fall quarter and through the December break, and it was not until January that I was hired by Dr. Barbara Webster. Grady Webster, her husband, had recommended me for my microscopy skills, and she had an eye to making me her teaching assistant for the spring course in Plant Morphology. She was also working on a grant to study the tepary bean for a development project in East Africa. Of course, I could not be hired until the quarter began, because I would be hired as a Proctor, also called a Post Graduate Researcher1. This would eventually be a problem, because Barbara indicated that there was a deadline on how quickly I needed to finish my thesis in order to qualify for that post graduate position. Nevertheless, I began working in earnest, for no pay I might add, helping Dr. Webster prepare the grant proposal for the project funding as well as prepare materials for the upcoming plant morphology course that I was to proctor.

My interactions with Barbara were a little strange. I said strange, not strained. At first she was very positive and enthusiastic. Before I go farther, I must say that I just ran across an article about her daughter, Susan Verdi Webster. Like her father, Grady Webster, Susan was just awarded a Guggenheim fellowship in history. She accredits much of her success to her parents, her father for his brilliance, and her mother for her Bostonian persistence. Though Grady died in 1978, Barbara is still alive, and emerita and former associate vice chancellor of research at UCD.[72] I will concede that they were a fine family, but I must say I found Grady much more personable. He was brilliant but humble. Barbara probably had to contend with male chauvinism throughout her career, so I guess it is not surprising that I found her difficult.

Very soon after I went to work for Barbara, she asked me to bring a draft of the proposal to the Webster home in north Davis. I thought nothing of it, and went straight ahead. She greeted me at the door in her bathrobe. I thought it a bit unusual, but I dismissed the thought, thinking I would be leaving directly. Instead she invited me in. Her golden retriever was a bit of a handful, and was all over me with the drooling wet licks. I normally like all dogs, but that dog was making me uncomfortable. I don't remember what we discussed, but I do remember thinking that she seemed not to want me to leave, but I was anxious to depart. Grady was on a trip, and Barbara was apparently alone. I am not suggesting anything, but it was a strange experience.

As I remember it, Barbara was difficult to pin down on things. She was gone often, and when she was around, our dealings were not always clear to me. While we were working on the proposal, she asked me to review it for applicability to the Kenyan farm situation. I made suggestions, which seemed to be accepted. When it drew near the time to submit the proposal, Barbara seemed nervous. I think the idea of directing a research project in Africa was a daunting thought for her. I didn't help her confidence with this next

---

[72] A memorial service for Barbara Webster, 1929-2017, will begin at 11 a.m. Sunday, June 3, at Putah Creek Lodge in the UC Davis Arboretum. Webster was a professor of agronomy at UC Davis from 1979 to 1992, and associate vice chancellor of research from 1989 to 1992. In 2008 she earned the Botanical Society of America's highest honor, distinguished fellow. Her husband, professor Grady Webster, predeceased her in 2005. Daughter Susan Webster holds endowed chair in art history at the College of William and Mary. https://www. davisenterprise.com/obits/death-notice-barbara-webster/

mistake. She asked me to deliver the proposal draft to the typist, and then take the printed version back, make 20 copies of the whole document, and collate them. The typist was working on a Wang word processor. Who knew that a Wang could spew garbage... about 12 pages of complete gibberish? Unfortunately, I assumed that the typist would double check the printed output before she gave it to me, so I assumed the proposal was ready to be copied and collated. That I did without ever even noticing the 12 pages of garbage. To this day, I don't understand how a word processor could do that. But of course, Barbara couldn't believe that I could be so stupid as to collate a document that I didn't even read.

I seem to remember that it was a couple of days before I saw Barbara again and she was fuming. She had needed to take the proposals apart insert the corrected pages and all on the last mailing date. That did not bode well for our working relationship. She wasn't much on forgiving failure. Nevertheless, she kept me as proctor for the morphology course. She had another woman working for her who had been her proctor in previous years. She was now doing Barbara's office work such as publishing the *Journal of Horticultural Science*, etc. As the course proceeded, the proctors job was to give training about various microscopic and tissue preparation techniques, which I did, and then supervise individual student projects. I was more familiar with new techniques like methacrylate and epoxy embedding, and freeze chryotomy, as well as electron microscope techniques. The previous proctor was very familiar with tradition wax embedding and sectioning of plant tissue. As it worked out, she helped the students that wanted to do that traditional technique, and I helped the students that were doing more current techniques like critical point drying and Scanning Electron Microscopy. I don't remember which projects got the better grades from Barbara, but I think I made a mistake to let the other employee help with the traditional technique. I was, after all, also taking a course in environmental horticulture and working on my thesis.

In spite of these "failures" on my part, Barbara was ecstatic when she learned that the tepary bean project had been accepted for funding. I would like to think that some of the practical input that I was able to offer may have helped make that possible. Now Barbara knew that I had the family from Kenya, and I think she assumed that I would be assigned to go back to Kenya, and that I would probably want to take my family. I may have mentioned my intentions in that regard if ever it was possible. So in February when the funding came through, she was anxious to meet Charity.

Finally, I was able to get a response from Charity, and asked her to come to Davis. She did so and brought Sam with her, instead of my own son Jimmy. That did not faze me, because I was excited that finally I had gotten a real job and would be able to get the family back to Kenya. When Charity arrived, we were invited to a celebratory party at the Webster's home. There were a number of professors and staff there, who were all anxious to meet Charity. Barbara seemed to be most cordial to Charity, and I thought that Charity was quite impressed. After the party, I began to explain the details to Charity; that I had gotten this research associate job, and could afford to rent student housing, if she were willing to sign the lease. I fully expected that she was "on board" with the plan to move the family to Davis in the near future, and later that we would all move to Nairobi. Charity did agree to sign the lease, and perhaps she appeared at that moment comfortable with the plan.

Meantime, Barbara herself was making plans for her own trip to Kenya to coordinate the setup of the project. She was very excited about the trip and bought the full safari gear complete with pith helmet and desert tan skirt and jacket. It was very unfortunate that Grady could not go with her to Kenya, because he was a far more seasoned traveler than Barbara. She planned her trip around the finest tourist hotels in Kenya, but even then there are still diseases and pests for which we Westerners have no resistance. Without careful training, she didn't even know what to try to avoid. The net effect was that Barbara got deathly ill during and after her trip. I forget exactly how long it took for her to recover.

I had been left with the assignment to start raising tepary bean in the Botany greenhouses. The project started off well enough, but I had no idea how susceptible tepary bean would be to the greenhouse pests that were ubiquitous in Davis. At that time, the hopeful plans for the future of my family were as tenuous as the survival of those bean plants.

# Chapter 15

# Divided and Conquered

Again I saw that under the sun the race is not to the swift, nor the battle to the strong, nor bread to the wise, nor riches to the intelligent, nor favor to those with knowledge, but time and chance happen to them all. For man does not know his time. Like fish that are taken in an evil net, and like birds that are caught in a snare, so the children of man are snared at an evil time, when it suddenly falls upon them. **English Standard Version (2001) Ecclesiastes 9:11-12.**

Since Charity had not given me any new contact number or address, it is possible that none of my written instructions about her move to Davis ever got to her. To this day, I don't know if she was living in Tenino at this time or in Tacoma. I was not able to get through to her by telephone. I had gone ahead and moved into the married student housing apartment. At first I was quite hopeful that all would be back to normal and that we could enjoy a few months in Davis, and then move back to Kenya. But when Charity did not contact me, or respond to any of the message that I sent, I became despondent.

I have to be honest with myself. Normally, you would think that a husband and father, who could not contact his family, would go back to the place where the family resided to see what had happened. I probably could have done that, because I was finished with my horticulture course, but I was afraid to spend the money, because I knew we would need every cent to move the family. I fully intended to go pick the family up in the van once Charity let me know that they were prepared to move. But as the silence grew deafening, I had the sinking feeling that I was no longer the trusted head of this household. This threw me into a deep depression that was aggravated by a physical injury. Coming out of the post office I fell down a flight of concrete stairs. Obviously, I had been distracted by my concern about the lack of correspondence, written or verbal. Nevertheless the hairline fracture to my elbow added excruciating pain to the ordeal. I will never understand why the doctor at the student medical center just gave me a muslin sling and told me not to move my arm. It was a hairline fracture in a very sensitive area, and any time I even touched my elbow it sent electric shocks of pain through my arm.

So here I was, alone in the apartment, the only furniture being the pads from the bed in the van and my 9 inch TV. I could not ride my bike for the pain, and I could not motivate myself to leave the apartment for the pain in my heart. I don't remember how long I was in a virtually catatonic state, but I think it was a month before I started to leave the apartment. I would lie on the pads and watch the boob tube that Al had sold to me, including Japanese programing without subtitles. I would take hot baths to try to relieve the pain in my arm, and I barely ate the little amount of food I had stocked in the kitchen. When I finally came out of the apartment, the most activity I could muster was to ride my bike (painfully) to the pool and swim. It was a small accomplishment; only a few laps at first, and then doggedly I increased the exercise to a mile. I think it was the swimming that saved me.

I still had not heard from Charity, but I began to regain my composure. It was hard to face the lab and Barbara because I had essentially neglected everything. The tepary bean plants had all but died, after I had been able to apply one application of TEP to kill the leaf minors. I tried to explain to Barbara that I had been ill, but I think she was distraught that she had put her faith in me to carry out the project in Kenya, and now she could not trust me. She asked if I had finished my thesis, and I had to admit that I had not. Consequently, her excuse for firing me was that I was not matriculated. She and I both knew it was because the pipedream of a competent technician with in-country experience, knowledge of the language, and a Kenyan family was just that: a pipedream!

I accepted the dismissal, and quickly moved to see if Robbin Thorp would accept me back on the Almond Project for the spring... which he did. I didn't think I had been treated fairly by Barbara but I certainly didn't want to work for her after that dismissal. I did contact the Dean of the Plant Science department, Dr. Calvin Qualset to see if Barbara had been within her rights to fire me summarily. He listened to my situation, and the matter of the depression, broken elbow etc. Finally I asked if Dr. Webster was within her rights to fire me for not matriculating. He said no! Even leaving aside the health issues, it was not a University rule that I had to have completed my thesis to be hired as a post graduate researcher. As long as I was progressing on my thesis, I was eligible. There was no deadline. He asked me if I wanted to pursue a personnel action, but I declined. Other than listen to Barbara, at the Commencement Ceremonies, murder graduates' names with her Bostonian accent, I never saw Dr. Barbara Webster again.

After that, I ran into Grady Webster from time to time; we never discussed the fact that his wife had summarily fired me. Grady was a good man. Barbara may have also been a good person and a good scientist, but I could not deal with her intolerance. I never inquired as to the success of the tepary bean project, but I see from the internet that the drought tolerant bean is planted in East Africa, so the project must have had impact although I found only one publication on which Barbara was a co-author[73].

There are few things that impact a man like being fired from a job, and particularly when it is for the first time in my life, and by a woman. But strangely, it was actually a kind of relief. The whole premise had been this: I was aiming at the reunification of my family and return to Africa. Barbara knew this when she hired me. Now it was apparent that those dreams were not going to materialize. I didn't know where this would all lead, and I am not sure that I cared any longer. In one sense it was a shame that Barbara and I did not see eye to eye. She was later recognized for her work on the structure of pollen walls; who better to have been a technician for her with all of my advanced microscopy and pollen research skills. I think I would have been good for the tepary bean project as well, but the family situation precluded that.

I immersed myself in the pollination season and the data analyses that Robbin and Dennis wanted from me. Nevertheless, for diversion I started playing music with Jairus and Al; mostly we played for ourselves, but I could see we were getting pretty good. I don't know if I got us a gig at the Blue Moon before I left for the summer, but the ideas were knocking around in my head.

When the quarter was over, I needed a job, and I needed to find out once and for all what was going on in Washington. So I wrote to Bob Megraw to see if he needed a farm manager in Puyallup, which he did. So I accepted the job, and took off for Washington. Also there was the issue of unpaid house

---

[73] Barbara D. Webster and J. Giles Waines. 1985 Tepary bean: a resource for improvement of common beans. *Research Highlights.* Michigan State Univ. Bean/Cowpea CRSP

payments. The Lukenbills had contacted me to find out what was going on. They did not want to foreclose, but they didn't want to be stiffed either. When I arrived in Tenino, imagine my surprise to find that it was not my family that was living in the homestead. Renters, to whom Charity had sublet the house, were living there. When I visited the Lukenbills at their home, they already knew about the sublet, and they were not happy. Nor did they know how to contact Charity. I did not know where to look for her, either, but I paid the Lukenbills all that I could afford (about $700 as I remember), to bring the house payments up to date. I told them that I would try to get Charity to agree to sell the house, if I could find her.

My only contact who might know of Charity's location was Gertrude. Previously I had known where the house that she and Keith had purchased was, so I showed up at her place unannounced. She was surprised to see me, and I was surprised to find out that she and Keith were in divorce proceedings. Gertrude gave me Charity's address in Tacoma, and I went there to confront her. She was actually not at home at the time. She had left the boys alone while she was visiting, in Seattle I think (and Samba may have gone with her). So I spent the night at Charity's apartment, actually sleeping on the floor with the boys. The next day when Charity came home, she was very upset that I had spent the night. Of course, the reason was that she was on welfare and my presence could have jeopardized her welfare checks. I was flabbergasted! Here for eight years I had not even taken food stamps from the government, and had struggled against great odds to keep a house over their heads and food on the table. Now Charity had run off to Tacoma and gone on the dole without even letting me know. So really, it was quite apparent that she had moved on to a whole other life, and I was living in a fantasy world of this big happy family. Apparently Charity was just as happy without me in her new life.

That was disheartening. I went ahead and made contact with Bob, and arranged to stay on the farm in the van and the little trailer that Bob had purchased for the farm. Apparently it was getting more difficult to get pickers and the packing houses had conspired to freeze the prices, so he asked me to find pickers and to see if I could direct-market the berries to get a higher price than the packers were offering. Some of the other farms had joined together in a coop, and had arranged to flash cool their berries and ship them to east coast markets. But Bob didn't trust those growers and wanted to strike out on his own. Of course, he didn't have the time to do it, so it fell on my shoulders.

But the next day when I talked to Charity, she wanted to pick berries along with the kids, but they did not have transportation. So I agree to drive into Tacoma every day to pick them up and deliver them home in the afternoon. Fortunately, a Laotian family came to the farm on the second day of the season. It turned out that they too had no steady transportation, but were willing to work as a group. The Laotians proved to be the best pickers we had all season. Unfortunately, they quit right before the end of the season, so they did not get their bonus. I felt bad about that because they were a truly hard working bunch from the oldest to the youngest. Apparently, the daughter who first contacted me was married to a GI, and they had somehow managed to get her whole family to the US. I don't know if it was any connection to the Vietnam War because I didn't know how long they had been in the country. Most of them spoke very little English, I seem to remember the youngest were the most fluent, and would translate for their elders.

After Bob advertised for pickers in the local paper, applicants started showing up and among them was the neighbor lady who had worked with the previous owner of the berry farm and with me the first year I managed it. I am sorry to say I do not remember her name, because she was a great help to me that year. She was of Scandinavian descent, and her husband had died and left her a home, which was a couple of houses down the road from the berry farm. She had a grandchild whom she cared for during the summer, but he was old enough that she was able to pick berries with him. For lack of her real name, I am going to call her Mrs. Loritson.

The first time I managed the farm, the two daughters of the previous owner were paid to check the punch cards of the pickers as they brought in the hallocks of berries. This year, Bob didn't want that expense, but he wanted me to find markets for the berries. Yet I also had to be at the farm all day to punch cards and supervise. This couldn't work, but Mrs. Loritson was a life saver, because she took on the responsibility to check the berries while I was off the farm. Since she and her grandson were picking, I paid them by giving her extra punches on her card. Generally this worked pretty well, with a few notable exceptions. For example, one day, a family of Samoans arrived to pick. They were pleasant people, all smiling and friendly. The problem was that they didn't follow any of the rules. They would jump from row to row picking only the biggest and easiest to reach berries. This means that someone had to go back to that row and pick after them. I warned them several times, but they pretty much did whatever they wanted to do. I eventually fired them, but it was a scary proposition because the males were huge! They could have stuffed me in a hallock if they had wanted to.

At first I had a difficult time finding other buyers, so I ended up taking some of the harvest to the same packing house we had supplied in 1978. Finally I started finding fruit stands and mom and pop stores that would take a few hallocks of berries at a time. I charged them fifty cents a pound, which came out to about $15 a flat. Finally there was one fruit stand that was so pleased with the berries that he sent a vehicle to pick up the berries at the farm as long as I could guarantee him a set supply. The irony of it all is that by the end of the season the packing houses had hollered "Uncle. Whereas they had said they would pay 32 cents per pound, by the end of the season they paid, 52 cents. So, for all the effort I had made to find market for Bob, he ended earning more for the berries I took to the packing house. Kind of the story of my life, work you butt off to beat the status quo, only to be consumed by it.

Since everyone in the Lao family and my family were dependent on me for transportation, and because I had to get the berries to the packing house at the end of each day, the former had to wait for the latter. I think that is probably why the Laotians finally quit. I tried to compensate them by taking them to the local dairy queen and buying them ice cream. There again, damned if you do and damned if you don't. At least it gave me a little time with the kids, because during the day I was so busy I could hardly spend time together, except perhaps for lunch once in a while. But they were anxious to pick berries because they all wanted the income. Charity did not come every picking day, but when she did, she kept a pretty close tab on the children. Jimmy was still a little too young to work, so he basically played around the farm. Occasionally he would spend the night at the farm with me.

Semi-tractor drawn by **James Kevin** when he was eight. (Photographed by the author with permission of his son James Kevin Klungness Mshoi)

One of the things that James enjoyed the most was the semi-trucker and his wife. They would bring their big rig (semi-trailer truck the power plant of which is called a tractor) to the farm and pick berries. James was so impressed that they were able to live out of their truck; I think it impacted his whole life. He drew a picture of the big black tractor with sleeping quarters, which the wife had shown him. I think they let him sit behind the wheel too. Now James has a big diesel truck to which he is attached as if it were his home! He also has a Class A driver's license and drove truck for Pony Express Co. before it went belly up. The company did not pay his final paycheck while he was visiting me in Hawaii with the future mother of his child. It is ironic how things you did when you were a kid, affects the direction of your life. My folks bought me a microscope when I was just a kid. Now at age 64, I wish I had one. James rode shotgun on the Gimmy when he was growing up, now he is a truck driver... among other things.

So the summer proceeded like this; I drove the kids to and from the farm on picking days, and usually was worn out by the time evening rolled around. I would try to talk to Charity about selling the homestead in Tenino, but she would have none of it. So I tried to keep things together, not losing my sanity or screwing up what visiting arrangements we had been able to work out. I have no idea whether the Washington State Welfare office even knew that I was in the state. I certainly wasn't going to try to find out, because I didn't know what Charity had done to be able to qualify in the first place. I sure would have appreciated knowing about it, but it was becoming increasingly obvious that my part in the family was on a "need to know" basis. This was irritating and it was exasperating. I don't even know if the Welfare office knew that Charity was collecting rent from the family subletting the house in Tenino. Whatever the case, the most frustrating thing of all was that Charity categorically refused to even consider selling the property. The economy was recovering from the oil crisis, but home prices were good and the demand was good. We could have made money on the place, but that was not to be.

Finally, in August Charity went to Olympia with me to meet the Lukenbills at their lawyer's office. They informed us that they were proceeding with foreclosure, and we would be evicted from the property. I don't know if Charity was stunned, or if she thought in her mind that she would somehow beat the law. Of course, she had no chance, and probably would have been in trouble with Welfare if they had found out. So at that point I divorced myself from the whole problem. It was a terrible blow, but in another way it was liberating for me. Who even knows how many of the tools and hours of sweat and tears I left with that homestead, but now I could be free of it.

I had visited Bob Megraw's family a few weeks before and explained that I was trying to work things out with Charity. Jana, his wife was very concerned. I can't remember if Jana had invited Charity and the family to a picnic at Bob's home previous to that, but it seems they did. Because Jana and Bob knew Charity, I now had to explain that, after the visit with the foreclosure lawyer, the problems were becoming insurmountable. I admitted that, although I had never intended to leave the family, it was now clear to me that the prospects for saving the marriage were very marginal at best, and likely not at all.

At some points in the season I had needed to visit Bob at the Weyerhaeuser Laboratory in Federal Way. During those visits I had met his lead microscopist. She was a very interesting lady, who had managed her own restaurant in Stockton California, and was of great help to Bob in maintaining the Microscopy lab. She was obviously of hippie roots, in that she wore loose fitting clothes, Birkenstock shoes and had a huge head of curly hair down to the small of her back. She reminded me of the Whole Earth Festival, and I was curious.

Up to that point, in all that time I was at Davis, I had not so much as winked at another woman. I had strictly maintained my status as married and wore my wedding ring to prove it. But something had snapped in me. This living the celibate life, sleeping on the farm in the van, avoiding all forms of entertainment, work, eat, sleep work, this was not enough! So one day, when I was at the Weyerhaeuser lab, I mustered all the courage I had, and asked the lead microscopist if she would like to go dancing. Me, who had never danced since grade school. To my utter surprise she said, "Yes." We set a date, and I left thinking to myself, "Did that just happen?"

By that time in the summer, the berries production was shutting down, and I was spending my time plowing under the older rows of berries, because Bob wanted to shift to blueberries. This involved cutting the wires that held up the vines, and getting them out of the field. I rigged up a wire reel on the three-point hitch on the tractor and pulled the wire through by rolling it on the reel. Bob had let me hire a high school kid to help, but instead of cutting the wire and then pulling it through, he just went through the rows and cut all the wires. When it came to the hard part of pulling the wires, he quit, leaving the job with me. Live and learn, I guess. Since the berry harvest was all in, I needed to compute the yields and cost. Of course I didn't know anything about what the price was going to be, so Bob and I had to arrive at an estimate, and pay my portion based on our pre-season arrangement. I was getting strapped for cash so I worked very hard on trying to produce the numbers. I did it all on a Texas Instrument 58 programmable calculator. I had purchased a printer cradle for it, so I sat there in the little trailer plugged in by an extension cord to the only outlet on the farm. Very high tech!

When I presented the numbers to Bob, he offered to let me continue the farm management through the winter. He wanted me to do it for 40% of the next years yield, but I didn't think I could do it on that contingency. In the end we could not agree on a number, so I said I would stay until I found something else.

Since Bob had paid me in a lump sum for my expenses and my percentage of the harvest, I figured I would try to earn a little money hauling fruit from Yakima. I contacted Jean Griffith to ask if the family was interested in produce. Jean in turn put out the word to all of the Honeycomb Fellowship, and the orders came in. I had arranged with Charity to have Jimmy for the weekend that I planned to go over the mountain. I thought he would enjoy the trip, and he would learn more about farming in the state of Washington.

The Friday before that weekend, I took the microscopist on a date. We went to a local Tacoma restaurant that had a dance floor... I don't even remember if the band was live. We ate, and then we did dance a bit, but mostly we talked well into the night. She told me of her career after graduating from University of the Pacific. Although the school had a fine reputation, and she had gone on full scholarship, at that time, UP was a progressive school that did not give letter grades. I don't know whether that had been a problem in her job searches after graduating, but it had been tricky getting accepted to a graduate program in Public Administration at Pacific Lutheran College in Tacoma. However, after running the restaurant and coffee shop that she had founded with friends in Stockton, she wanted a change, which had brought her to Weyerhaeuser. Now she was preparing herself for her next move by attending Pacific Lutheran as a part-time student in Public Administration.

In turn, I told her my story. I don't know how I convinced her of my sincerity, but I explained that I was married, how that circumstance had sent me back to school at Davis and the disconnect that had caused with Charity. I explained that the reason I had come to Washington was to see if I could reconcile with Charity and reconnect with the family. I then explained that Charity and I had reached an impasse that had convinced me that reconciliation would not be possible. I don't know why I was so disclosive; although I think she may have already known some of the circumstances from Bob. My intention was innocent enough. I thought we would just have a date or two, and it sure beat spending the evenings alone. I think we had come to the restaurant in separate cars, so when the evening ended, we said good night and went our separate ways.

So the next day, I picked up Jimmy and we were off to Yakima. Highway

410 out of Puyallup leads right over the Cascades into the Chinook Pass and down to the Yakima Valley. At one point the 410 came very close to the base of Mt. Rainier. It is a beautiful drive in the summertime. James was definitely game to travel. Life in the City of Tacoma was so different than where he was raised on the homestead. He liked being out on the farm, and he loved traveling. We had a good trip over the pass, but when we got to Yakima, I had to work. Some farms had produce packed at ready to go, so it was just a question of bartering the price and loading up. On that trip I did not have to sort fruit, so James didn't get too bored between stops. It was hot but we had fresh fruit to eat. Love those fresh peaches and nectarines. I forget where we ate lunch and dinner but I know we ate well. By the end of the afternoon we were ready to head back over the mountain, but it was getting late. We drove as long as I could keep awake, but about the time we got to the base of the Mount Rainer we stopped along the highway. The moon was out so we had a beautiful view of the mountain. I really didn't take a careful lay of the land, but we drifted off to sleep right away. When we awoke in the morning, we were on the edge of a beautiful mountain valley full of blooming lupines and fireweed. There was a heavy mist on the valley and it was quite magical. We were a bit exhilarated by the crisp mountain air as we dismounted to relieve ourselves. So as we hit the road again, I suggested that we should compose a song. James liked the idea, so we worked away at it as we negotiated the mountain pass. I still have a copy:

### Jimmy's Song

Verse 1

Washington's my home, the place where I was born,
I have never seen a land so green, clean, and warm.
From the mountains to the sea, this is the land for me,
And I hope that God will grant that here I'll always be
In Washington.

Chorus 1

Washington, Washington, rising in the morning sun,
God it's good to be in Washington!

Verse 2

Me and my ol' Pa trucked over to Yakima,
Up the steep and windin' pass and down the Naches draw.
Mountains brushed with breeze, streams trickling through the trees,
Never have I been so pleased such lovely sights to see,

228

|            | In Washington. |
|------------|----------------|
| Chorus 2   | Washington, Washington, basking in the noon day sun, |
|            | God it's good to be in Washington! |
| Verse 3    | As we head back on home hauling orchard fruit and corn, |
|            | Through the wind-swept sunbaked hills and up the emerald gorge, |
|            | Mountains misty blue, the sun's last golden hew, |
|            | Fill my heart with happiness to be right here with you, |
|            | In Washington. |
| Chorus 3   | Washington, Washington, land of the setting sun, |
|            | God it's good to be in Washington! |
| Verse 4    | Now I lay me down to the valley's peaceful sound, |
|            | Berry bushes rustlin' as the sprinklers swish around. |
|            | As I sleep I dream of Cascade mountain scenes, |
|            | And I know I will awake to dream these dreams again, |
|            | Washington. |
| Chorus 4   | Washington, Washington, in silver moon-silk spun, |
|            | God it's good to be in Washington! |

As we bunked down for the night in the little travel trailer on the Pine Creek Berry Farm, I knew that James and I had shared a most enjoyable experience.

The next day I had to take James home so I could deliver the produce up to Seattle, where Jean had kindly agreed to let me put everything the Fellowship had purchased in her basement so they could be picked up on Sunday afternoon. Among the customers had been Emily and John Mattson, and other old friends like Roy and Ruth, but I did not have the time to meet them all.

Returning to Tacoma that evening I had an empty feeling, now that James was not with me, and I feared we might not have a lot of time together like the trip to Yakima.

That afternoon I called the microscopist to ask her if she wanted to have dinner... again? Now I can't keep calling her by that technical name, but I am not at liberty to reveal her name. I am in a quandary. I am not even sure if I should reveal the developments between her and me. Yet I have committed myself to honesty, so I can't really avoid such seminal moments in my life. Some people are still alive who might be hurt, others who might object, and others who might lose respect for me, if respect there ever was. Nevertheless, I must be true to myself, or else I am a liar and a fool. Her name was Windy. I can't remember if I took her out, or she made dinner. I will confess; that night she took me in.

To a Friend

Stormy Gale,
Ah! Be Gale; <u>Donum</u> <u>Dei</u>
Aphrodite, Minerva.
Hot, cold, clean, razor sharp,
Earthen dull brown.
Spark, cinder, fire, ember, ash,
Frosty fear.
Warm wisp, winsome.
Waver, wake, walk, run!
Rise! Aphrodite dance!
Deal diligently.
Dare to throw back your wavy willful golden hair.

To be entirely honest, both Windy and I had been living very Spartan lives. It had been a long time since either of us had known intimacy. She was a hippie free spirited soul who had attended Pacific University on a full scholarship, and then went on to open a coffee shop in Stockton with friends. One of those friends, Jonathon, was the son of the actor Burgess Meredith. They had done well at the business, and sold it for a tidy sum. I think she had moved to Washington from there, and taken the job with Bob McGraw at Weyerhaeuser Corporate Headquarters in the Morphology Group. She had apparently been as competent in science as she was in business, because Bob had come to rely on Gail a great deal to manage the lab and employees there in. She had purchased a cute little home near the laboratory and had her long-haired black Labrador to keep her company on the drizzly Northwestern nights. She was both a free spirit and a much disciplined young woman.

Our tryst was, to say the least, liberating!

Printed in the United States
by Baker & Taylor Publisher Services